THE END OF NIGHT

How Cancer Cured Me!

Lawrence Crowder Davis

ISBN: 0692700676
ISBN 13: 9780692700679
Library of Congress Control Number: 2016907162
Larry Davis, Wilmington, NC

Author's note: This is the letter that started the writing of <u>The End of Night.</u> I mailed out this letter to 30 friends who had helped Joanna and me in all of our hours of need. To a person, I was encouraged to write of our cancer fight.

PROLOGUE

Late December, 2013

Over the past three months I have wondered how in the world I was going to be able to thank everyone who has come to Joanna's and my rescue during our fight against cancer. I even went to Hallmark and shopped what seemed like hours for just the right "Thank You" cards, and kept coming up empty. I liken that to shopping for shoes...mpossible. So I've chosen to write this note in hopes that all of you know that as I write, I remember of each and every one of you with love and heartfelt warmth, so happy that you are our friends. Without all of you thinking of us, praying for us, and your hopes for recovery, we simply could not have made it to this point.

Everywhere I went during my treatments I was amazed at the number of patients suffering from a myriad of cancers. Inevitably, my thoughts progressed to their family members and their circle of friends and the many prayers that must have been floating to the heavens. I have known for some time that there are small communities in Raleigh and in Ezel Kentucky which have had me in their prayers on a continuing basis. Many of these people I don't even know. There were times when I felt out-numbered, out-manned, or out-flanked by the long tentacles of cancer as it permeated the lives of those I came to know through both chemo therapy and radiation therapy. Believe me, the word "therapy" took on a whole new meaning.

During the days of the onset of my diagnosis, Joanna and I toured the oncology center and surely we both gasped when entering the "chemo room" and saw all of the lay-z-boy leather chairs in a room which had to cover 1500 square feet. I thought there was no way all of these chairs, possibly 35-40 altogether, could by occupied at one time. I was so wrong. There were days on those 6 consecutive Mondays beginning the first week of October when it was standing room only, and the staging area was packed with those of us waiting for our turn to sit in the chairs for 2-3 hours as our IV dripped poison/curing honey into our veins. From early 20's to late 80's, male or female, black or white, very sick to almost cured, these cancers knew no boundaries. One day about half-way through my treatments a very old lady was wheeled into the chemo room and deposited just opposite me. On each side of her were other middle aged ladies receiving their treatments. Miss Hallie, as I came to know her, was flanked by her two granddaughters, each of the three of them dressed to the 9's in colorful full flowing attire complete with hats and shoes to match. It was as though they were daring cancer to change their outlook on life. I looked down at what I had on and just remarked that "I need to step up my wardrobe!" That brought the house down, and for that brief moment we were all in this fight together, waging that war with each other, and daring cancer to change us in any way. I learned several weeks later that Miss Hallie had passed on, but my memory of her in life, with her girls, will stay with me forever.

On another day, a very kind lady was having some digestive issues with the chemo and began to bring back up some of what she had digested. She obviously was very embarrassed to have those troubles in front of the rest of us, and yet she did not know that we all understood her dilemma, having those issues ourselves, just not at such an inopportune moment as she. The nurses quickly surrounded her to shield her discomfort and stayed there until the storm had passed. The oncologist stepped in, stopped her IV, and mercifully gave her a reprieve for that day. Fortunately those types of days for me were witnessed only by my beloved Joanna who never flinched in the clean up while always ministering love and a big smile, knowing that no one felt worse about the situation than I did. Oh, she may have had a dig or two later on, but only after she knew we could laugh about it.

Speaking of the oncology nurses, let me tell you, they are a unique bunch. From Nurse Betty to young and beautiful Brittany, to Good Golly Miss Molly, to Hard as crystal Crystal there was never anything but hope, serenity, laughter, humor, hugs, prayers, professionalism, empathy, futuristic thoughts, positive motivation, and words of encouragement...in other words, everything you would expect from an angel. Nurse Betty, at 5 foot tall and 160 pounds would hug me numerous times from the start to the finish of my treatment. Brittany, who was 26 and a tall slender and pretty nurse, had no ring on her finger, so I asked "what is wrong with all those guys out there? " She laughed, put her hands on her hips and declared, "I have been wondering about that myself!" Good Golly Miss Molly was consistent in her portrayal of milk shakes being the cure-all for anything digestive. And then there was Crystal. Very standoffish from the beginning, she was not my attending nurse until my last treatment, and at that point all I wanted was that 2-1/2 hours to get behind me. We got to talking about marriages. Lord have mercy what had I gotten myself into?! But then, anything to pass the time was OK by me. By the end of the discussion Crystal was my buddy. It was almost as if I wanted to come back one more time, just to laugh with her and see her true nature once again. All of those nurses, each in her own right, were precious to me and provided some of the most fond memories that I have, making a horrible situation not only bearable, but at times, delightful.

At the same time, radiation was going on 5 days a week for 35 days. To be sure, the nurses were wonderful in their own way; however, the true heroes of radiation were the techs who administered the "death rays". I met memorable characters in the waiting room, all with various cancers from breast cancer to brain cancer to lung cancer to prostate cancer. The three I remember most were: Tom, who was taking treatment for prostate cancer. As he described what his treatment entailed, which was sitting in a sling-type apparatus, it seemed to be such an easy way to cure his disease and indeed he said it was. Then when he asked me what "mine" was and I told him, his face was etched with empathy. It was impossible for him, when they called him to go back to the treatment rooms prior to me, to not stop half way back, look at me and ask if he could get a hug. We hugged then, and many other times until his treatment was finished and I still had two weeks to go. Twice during my final two weeks, Tom showed up at 7:30 in the morning, just to see me and give me encouragement. It was such a kind gesture and again an experience I will never forget. Deep in my soul I told God that if such an opportunity ever presented itself to me, I wanted Him to remind me of another angel named Tom to prompt me to pay it forward. I relish the thought of being presented with that opportunity.

Then there was a guy I nicknamed "Roy Lee" because he reminded me of a customer that I loved, all 5'7" and 140 pounds of him. Roy Lee was ahead of me by four weeks and so he was able, and more than accommodating, to show me the ropes and give me a perspective of what to expect. Roy Lee pulled no punches and told me without sugar coating what was going to happen to me. He raised his shirt right there in the waiting room and showed me his feeding tube and how it worked. Mine was going to be installed the very next day. He had made it into his 6th week without pain medication, as it was adverse to his way of living, and believe me it showed in his face how much hurting he was experiencing. He made it all the way to week 7 before succumbing to the oxycodone and then his demeanor changed into a much milder and more comfortable outward sign of relief. Roy Lee exclaimed, "Don't wait as long as I did". Indeed, I was already taking pain medicine and was glad of it. I saw him on his last day, and we gave each other a huge hug. I knew what to expect, and that was his gift to me.

Gene had inoperable brain cancer, so his only option was radiation. Gene was 6 foot tall and 220 pounds at 60 years old. He had the type of physique that told you that he was someone who could have been a lumberjack or a bridge builder or drove a big ole Mack truck. In fact he was the Mack truck himself! He described his feelings when 2 years earlier he had gotten the news that his brain cancer was inoperable and that he needed to get his affairs in order. And here he was still fighting the war. When I asked Gene how he coped with everything, his answer was always the same, "The Lord gave me the cancer, but at the same time He gave me the will to fight it. I am thankful for the two years I have had, and look forward to the next two, the good Lord willing." As I walked out on the 35th day, Gene was sitting in his customary chair in the waiting room, and gave me a big ole bear hug on the way out, genuinely happy for me...and for himself. It was those times that were like getting your batteries recharged.

Pete was my lead radiology tech. Spiked hair, 30, engaged, and someone who "understood" everything I was going through. From the first time he put my mask onto my head to the last time, he knew everything that was going through my head before I did. And, by the way, there was a cubby type area on one wall in the radiation room and by the time I got through the fourth week, mine was the only mask in the room. I was then the only one going through this terrible cure. The mask was made of hard plastic and had a waffle like consistency which was soaked in saline water and then molded to my face complete with nose, lips, and ears areas which allowed it to fit snuggly onto my face as I lay on the slab-like table. Then they would bolt it to the table thus producing the waffle indentations on my lips and nose. The feeling was one of unbelievable claustrophobia. I came to hate that apparatus with a passion. (I had no way of knowing that mask would be involved in saving my life in my 7th week.) Pete was also in charge of what music I liked to hear for those 8-12 minutes that I was strapped down and getting the treatments. I never knew I liked Blondie and Fats Domino so much! The first 18 days I was radiated on both sides of my neck, the last 17 days only on the left side which was the area of the cancer. At first it was 7 separate blasts and then only 5. Chronologically, if it had been the other way around, I don't know if I could have made it. By the 5th week and progressively worse each week after that the mucous secretions were so prolific that it became nearly impossible to breathe normally with the mask on. Only once, the first day of week 7, did I have to raise my hands and have them stop the machine and regroup. I felt as though I was being water boarded with my head bolted down and my lips under siege. Through it all, Pete made me want to be there, and encouraged me as one guy to another. He called me "L-Dog" out into the waiting room, in the treatment room, and on my way out. He made me feel as though I was being treated by my son, and I came to know him as such. I knew about his love life in a most loving way and not degrading or demeaning to his fiancé'. He told me about wanting children and how he loved his niece, attending her dance recitals and how she was the light of his life. My most memorable Pete moment was just after I had a run-in with one of the stand-in docs when my face and lips swelled and he told me to just continue my treatments. Pete took me aside the next time I came in, after my 3-day stint in the hospital, and told me I did the right thing and that he would have stood right with me if I needed him to do it. He was that kind of guy…the kind you wanted pulling those 5 or 7 triggers 35 times.

My kids, Steve and Tayleigh were unbelievably attentive throughout the whole ordeal. Tayleigh drove down from Richmond on several occasions even though she was traumatized by changing jobs. Tayleigh's specific job was to give me as much crap as she could, making sure my "mind was right". As most of you know, that is the type of humor I live for. Steve flew in from Denver with 20-month old Lincoln for five days over the Thanksgiving holiday to help Joanna with the feast and to give me a boost with his humor, support, and love. He knew Lincoln would be great therapy and my, how he was. My close buddies, Big Dog and John Musser, Paul, Rich, Jason, Jimmy, Reiner, Bill Lyon, Tom Douglas, Jim Rode, Slade, Bill Hatcher and Greg Brown, Lonnie Robert and Wyatt from St. Louis, Maunie from Seattle and Rick from Spokane, all came to my rescue on numerous occasions. My mentors, Tom Haas in Florida and Jay Brinkley here in Wilmington provided insight into neck cancer that only survivors could paint. It was invaluable.

Way back in the early dark hours after diagnosis, before anyone knew anything, Dan Scherrer in Kansas City took me on his broad shoulders and carried me through those awful days of fear of the unknown. His humor and dedicated concern for those 2-3 weeks was so genuine that it became a mantra with me that I could not let him down by being a wuss. He simply would not let me do that. When I told him that it was he that I picked to be my guide, Dan didn't skip a beat. He called me shithead and asshole just like he always did and all my fears melted away knowing that I was still the same person he had known for over a decade.

Serious illness can bring out the best and the worst, I've discovered. It can cause a reconnect when you least expect it, or a disconnect out of nowhere, and even a continued absence when you would expect a reconnection. My brother and sister, Jeff and Madalyn, live in Ohio and our relationships, though sometimes as distant as the miles between us, have endured differences much like maybe you have with your own siblings. Madalyn, having fought through her daughter's leukemia 20 years ago and then her son's testicular cancer 10 years ago, has the envied batting average of 1000 as both of those kids are now stars in their own professions. To say that she has beaten the odds is an understatement of the tallest order. Jeff has battled heart disease and two quadruple bypass surgeries as well as a chronic and debilitating almost 20-year and still truly undiagnosed illness with his daughter. Here they have been for Joanna and me as stalwarts of strength and advice. Not unexpected, but certainly not expected to the degree that they have come to our aid. My oldest daughter, absent from our lives for over a year, continues to keep her distance to this day. You tend to ask yourself, "If not now, when?"

Though each type of cancer has its own set of side maladies, neck cancer is looked upon as one of the most curable and yet one of the most invasive into your lifestyle. It's like the old commercial, "Pay me now or Pay me later..." Until it is taken away, we have no idea what it means to have your mouth, throat, and digestive system in a state of total shut down. I had no idea that I would not be able to eat normally. I thought early on that I could circumvent that malady. Uhh, no. A person is bombarded by TV commercials about food and drink, everyone around you is eating numerous times a day, conversations abound about restaurants, cookouts, and parties, and the smells, sights, and hubbub aligned with food are at times too much to endure. Trying to eat normally with a mouthful of nasty gunk and a throat that is burned to a crisp is impossible; and yet, all I want to do is try to do it. Some days you can't talk and make conversation, some days you regurgitate something that burns the crap out of your throat, some days you spit seemingly a thousand times, and some days your system is run down by a night's sleep interrupted 8-10 times just to spit. Trust me, you don't want neck cancer of any kind.

The docs, Ken Kotz my oncologist, Charles Neal my radiologist, George Brinson my ENT specialist, James Harris my general surgeon who lost his wife to breast cancer and who is raising 2 young boys by himself, and Jim Wortman my internist, made up my team of docs who have no peers. I was told in the beginning that they actually wrote cancer protocol for Duke and Chapel Hill. Their expertise right here in Wilmington should give us all tremendous peace if the need ever invades your lives. Each in their own right is brilliant at what they do. I felt totally confident that I would be cured of my cancer right from the start. To this very day, I still do.

In the midst of my final days of radiation, my face ballooned up to the point where my lips were the size of small bananas and began to split. Breathing became forced and my temperature was pushing 102. I finally made the decision to drive myself to the emergency room. Eventually, some two hours later I was taken to an examining room and seen by the third of what eventually were 6 doctors in an attempt to see just exactly what caused this sudden life- threatening condition. He too had no idea. And then three miracles in a 24-hour period happened. As Joanna got up to leave the hospital to go home to recharge her batteries, in walked Rich Vena, my golfing buddy and great friend. Rich took one look at me and his face contorted as if he had eaten an entire lemon. My appearance was so awful looking, Rich simply could not bear to look at me. The first miracle was that he ended up staying almost 2 hours, appearing to be in as much pain as I was! As I pleaded with him to go home, the second miracle happened.

Just as he was leaving, in walked Bill Hatcher and Greg Brown. I could not talk at this point as the radiation had rendered my vocal cords non-existent...Bill didn't have his smart phone so I could not even test or email him...Greg didn't have his glasses and couldn't see a lick. Yet, we were able to communicate for almost 2 hours by text from me to Greg and then Greg would show Bill, who mercifully had his glasses, and we three old fogies were able to carry on a conversation for another two hours. I will never forget those four hours of fellowship at a time when I honestly did not know if I would be alive the next day. I was sick…but with what?

Admitted to the hospital late that night, I was awakened at 6:30 by Dr. Thomas Beckett, the hospitalist physician. As we discussed my condition, I immediately felt at ease. Dr. Beckett, now the 4th physician to see me, did not have the answer. But he told me he would return with a diagnosis. I knew he had dozens of patients to see, and thought, "we'll see". Not an hour later, Dr. Beckett returned: Acute Angio Edema. The cause: a reaction of my blood pressure medicine and my loss of almost 30 pounds. The dosage was incompatible. Here was a novel idea: Dr. Beckett actually spent time researching the symptoms! I was out of the hospital in 48 hours. One note: if you look for the negative effects of ace inhibitors, in order of severity, Angio Edema was #2 on the list. "Sometimes fatal" was in the comments section…

And then there is Joanna. Most everyone who will receive this note knows Joanna in some way shape or form. 24 years ago she and Tayleigh came to me as a gift from God and my life has been enriched beyond any dreams I may have had. I have put Joanna through the wringer with my lifestyle, both professional and personal, and she has been by my side every step of the way. But nothing like this…I mean nothing could even compare to this. Joanna knew when to be there close and when to be there from afar. She knew how to sooth my ills and make them seem small. She understood that I needed to share more information than probably I should have about what was going on inside me; and by doing so, she never once shied away from the details in horror or disgust. Joanna has lived this cancer odyssey with me from the beginning moment of diagnosis to the minute I sit writing this to you. She still apologizes when she eats real food, but knows it doesn't bother me. She waits for me to bring back some of the old Larry even though there are many times she needs for me to be there for her and I simply cannot be there. She takes on all her daily tasks and does all of mine when I cannot. She professes her love and devotion for me each day multiple times. She understands that there are days I cannot even kiss her and delights in those that I can. She gets angry at anything that hurts me and cries tears of joy about stuff that makes my life easier and manageable. It's just plain and simple: she loves me. And though I truly have never questioned that in all the 24 years, I know that until I take my last breath, Joanna's heart is beating in synch with mine, and will forever.

With all my comments you have read above, that last sentence means the most. It is for that reason that I decided that cancer would not beat me no matter how hard it tried. No one can foresee what the future tests will show in 1 or 2 or 5 years hence. But I know that my future with Joanna is what I want to concentrate on. I want to be able to give back to her a life free of as much trauma as we can avoid. I want her to know each day that I love her more than the previous one.

And, when the dust settles, if that's what cancer has wrought, I'm all in. Thank you one and all.

L-Dog

FOREWARD

There are times in each person's life when opposite emotions occur simultaneously. That combination of fear and love, whether in real life or perhaps in a cinematic projection, triggers emotions exhibited by the same well of tears. Tears of sadness and tears of joy appear on your cheeks, one the same as the other. Here is the story of one man's journey down a trail littered with breakdowns resulting from horrific and terrifying news yet bordered by floral gardens created by love and hope.

Cancer is a love affair of epic proportions. No matter what type of cancer, it loves your body and in most cases more than you do. It's no different than sitting down to a steak dinner with all the trimmings, complete with a great bottle of wine, and chocolate for dessert. Cancer is there to eat. And your body provides everything it needs to fulfill its appetite. That's why cancer loves you. It can travel wherever it wants to go into the depths of your largest muscle and further into the smallest of cavities in any remote area of you. Red blood cells, full of nutrients abound by the millions, and each day they are regenerated, fresh, clean, and with no cooking necessary. Cancer loves those cells to be 98.7 degrees warm. Cancer doesn't even have to chase those delicious morsels as they flow freely about your veins and arteries, first biting down on a few, then dining on enough for a full meal, and ultimately realizing that there is an endless supply of cells to devour.

After perpetuating this endless smorgasbord of tiny cells for days and weeks on end, cancer's appetite ramps up for the tissues surrounding the body part which it has decided provides the weakest defense against the ever-increasing quest for fulfillment. A lung, the kidneys, a lymph node, bones, skin, the brain, pancreas, ovaries, testicles, prostate gland, colon, throat, tongue, and just anywhere it wants to go. Cancer is stealing this food from you. You don't even know that it is doing so, and in some cases, you don't find out until it is too late. Cancer is an insidious marching army, collecting casualties, hiding its itinerary, and taking what you need without any notice or fanfare. What you need to live becomes what it needs to live, and the stalking happens when you least expect it. Cancer is so cunning your body doesn't realize it is under siege until a few nebulous ticks show up on your radar. By that time it has outflanked your defenses and out maneuvered your will. You become complacent, putting off examining and researching those blips on your radar. Cancer is adept at laughing when it is eating, even to the point where the laughter becomes a constant; all the while you are looking the other way from valuable signs of trouble. You dismiss these hints of something ominous because your body has been so forgiving all these years. Or you fear just a little those nagging telltale signs. Are they getting worse? Have I given it enough time for the blinking light to stop? From clearing your throat to bathroom issues, lack of stamina, low sex drive, headache, pain, blurred vision, bleeding, skin lesions, hearing loss, hair falling out, numbness to every feeling except fear, signs abound. Then, ignoring even the most telltale signs graduates to looking over your shoulder for "what just happened" when the hints become real questions in your mind.

These questions in my mind were emblazoned to remind me forever that I should have acted sooner:

"Did I feel that?"
"Will this go away tomorrow?"
"Wow, is this getting larger?"
"Was that blood I just saw?"

Make no mistake. Cancer is also war. It is as much a war as any battle of arms and artillery and very much like the war in Viet Nam in 1967 where many of our enemies were unseen thus unknown. Memories from Viet Nam had now morphed into my war with cancer, and they traveled over 48 years later, where fear had a new name. Each physician's office wanted to know if I was a smoker or if I had smoked. While in Viet Nam in 1967-68, I smoked all the cigarettes I could get my hands on and in the early 80's, 35 to 50 years ago.

Cancer draws from its armory of bullets, bombs, and other ordinance. It has lymph nodes, and bone marrow, and red blood cells to conquer and does so with alarming speed and efficiency. Make no mistake...have no doubt...realize early on...cancer is a cunning enemy, hungry with an affinity for collection. Cancer wants you dead as much as any other adversary; and, just like any other, it has a head start knowing that it has begun its march toward supremacy over your body with a silent urgency of which you are unaware. Your life, once physically and psychologically normal, becomes a nightmarish and endless list of add-on sicknesses so quickly because of your ineffective way to deal with the consequences of cancer's march. In the very beginning you are at a tremendous disadvantage to what is already ravaging your blood, heretofore progressing without your knowledge and awareness. In Viet Nam, it was the Viet Cong, stealthy, yet an ever-present adversary that knew no boundaries and had the ability to strike right in front of you without warning. Cancer can give no signals, no blood test notice, or no pain. And yet, it's right there within you. You ask yourself questions galore, but only one remains throughout your war with cancer: can I beat it?

Once that ultimate question is etched in your mind, and make no mistake, it is there forever...forever as in "the rest of your life"..., the next one is "how do I beat it"? For me, the answers lie within these pages. Oh...they may not be all the answers, but these are the ones you need to know.

Though these pages embrace a story of one man's not uncommon life, this book became an extension of therapy I received during my bout with neck cancer. Early on during the fight, I was encouraged to keep a journal, but that wasn't my case. Each minute detail embedded in my mind and the thought of writing those immediate moments down on paper would have taken a lifetime. But what I came to realize, as I hope you do as you turn these pages, was that the clichés of all the derivatives of "only having one life to live" morph into plans of action for you all.

Memorable people, figures shrouded in mystery and intrigue, loves won and lost, friendships come and gone, and instances where you have tasted the bitterness of tragedy and the sweetness of victories with those around you, are central to life which yearns for love. With cancer, the quest becomes, "Will I be able to turn everything inside my skin into an offensive force rather than the defensive front that this insidious disease laughs at in there?" And then, "Do I have what it takes to challenge cancer?" And then, "I can't give up." Then, "I don't care anymore." Then, "I don't want to fight anymore." If there ever were a time in a person's life where a love of family, love of friends, and love of God meant so much to survival, I cannot imagine what it would be.

This is not to minimize the miracle medical cures, without which curing your cancer is not possible. Once again, those who supervise and administer chemotherapy and radiation, and those who surgically remove and repair damaged tissue, and certainly those whose relentless research ultimately intervenes between life and death, become part of your short term family and friendships. The physicians and nurses are as unique a bunch of human beings as you will ever see. The pathos, forthrightness, wisdom, kindness, and emotional support derived from these angels are part of the psychological nutrients needed to fight cancer. And then there's the finality that only your doctors can provide; because finality is what both you and your cancer desire. Live or die?

The day I was told that I had cancer. That was the darkest day of my life, and one that still gives me the chilled feeling as I sit here today. What followed that day was a series of life changing experiences, some very short and others continuing on even to this day. The long weeks of chemo therapy and radiation treatments as well as the recovery period are a series of stories about the spirit which resides in all of us, its frailties and its strengths. Big Dog and Paul, Steve and Lincoln, Tayleigh, Hatcher and G-Man, Rich, Jason, Slade, FBI Tom, Orlando Tom, Jay, Jeff, Madalyn, Nancy and Joe, Jenny, John Musser, Pete, Ken Kotz, Charles Neal, George Brinson, James Harris, Jim Wortman, Betty, Bridgette, Molly, Crystal, Dan, Lonnie, Wyatt, Bill Lyon…and so many more.

…and Joanna.

There were so many heroes, only one villain. There are stories of the horrors of cancer. Mostly though, this is a story of love, faith, hope, and friendship and how real people conquered the most feared of all maladies and how the darkest days of this man's life placed me on the planet Octron, a land I never want to see again. The word cancer makes people shiver. Most of the time it's whispered, especially in mixed company. Cancer is associated with death, sometimes quick death. The treatments are ghastly, lengthy, and personal. Cancer makes close conversation difficult, between even the closest of friends, amidst a shared feeling of pre- occupation with both hope and despair. It tears apart marriages and families, sometimes over years and years of suffering. Or, it can make them stronger. It can make a person's will instantly shatter into shards of glass on the inside, deep down and dark as night into the depths of your soul. Or it can lose the war of wills and send you out into a much brighter light of life.

Cancer can also mutate from an explosive mood of despair, to something intrinsic defying reality.

There were bad times, awful times. And yet, there was always someone to lift me up trying to make sure I never lost hope. These people are the reason I am alive today. They for the most part are just like anyone you hang with. Normal ordinary people whose extraordinary deeds made it happen. And so it begins, into the darkness of night...

The fight against cancer is a fight not only for living but also about what you are living for. The stories spawned from my cancer experience embody the human spirit at its finest portrait. So many rescues took place, some from people I hardly knew, some from people I had never known. But the most amazing acts of friendship and love came from those closest to me. Cancer changed me, oh yes it did. If you were to ask any of the people who you will read about in the pages that follow, what I have told them about My Cancer, they will tell you that I say it was the best thing to ever happen to me. I don't know if other survivors feel as I do. But I do know this:

You will begin think differently about the rest of your life, where you have been and where you want to go, what you would do differently, and for sure, how to deal with the continuous diligence of cancer to pull the dark hood over your eyes, should you ever hear those 3 words that I heard From Dr. Jim Wortman.

"You have cancer."

CHAPTER 1

BUDDY'S

It was the second time within ten days in 2013 that the series of bright lights passed quickly, like gigantic fireflies above my head. The ride was relatively smooth, no clickity-clack of bricks or stones crackling to a rhythm that might spur some other thoughts, perhaps musical, to replace what I had going on between my ears. It seemed as though everyone involved was in a hurry. Sort of like wait, hold on, wait, hold on, and then move as close to the speed of light as you can. It was as if the geometric area requiring a 90-degree turn was progressively smaller the farther along we traveled. The only words were advance warnings for impending collisions with walls and doors. All the while, even though there were numerous accompanying guides to my ultimate destination, I was alone with my thoughts and fears of the unknown. I was headed into surgery again. Moments before I was sequestered in the minute staging area, with silly clothes on, stockings on my feet, a tube sticking out of my arms. I was the star of the show until Dr. George Brinson came and stole it away as only he could. He launched onto a hilarious excuse for running late at 5:30 on that morning.

Fifteen hours earlier at his office, in the shank of a Thursday afternoon, George Brinson met with me for a final consultation. I was under his weekly care for four weeks in August and September of 2013, trying to figure out a diagnosis and scheduling tests. I had grown to admire his ability to be forthright as well as clinical simultaneously, and all the while with a grin on his young, handsome face, his curly blond locks of hair flopping around as he nodded or shook his head when answering my million questions. Now in early September, barely a week after I went under anesthetic to remove the beckoning lymph gland, we were about to return to the O.R. at New Hanover Regional Medical Center in Wilmington, North Carolina.

"5:30 tomorrow morning is only about 12 hours away," I exclaimed with fake admonishment. "You need to go home right now and get some sleep!"

"Well, see there's a problem with that," Brinson replied. "Thursday night is the bar- hopping night with my buddies. In fact, that's where we most likely will end up, at Buddy's on Wrightsville Beach. You know the place?"

"Not only do I know it, but we also have a rental condo right next door to it just west of Johnnie Mercer's Pier. How about I give you the key, and you skip Buddy's and get some sleep?"

"Nope. Thursday nights at Buddy's is live music and $2 drafts. And the best part is they stay open later than usual," Dr. Brinson said with his signature grin. "However, I suggest that you get to bed early and make sure you are there at 5:00 a.m. so they can get you all calmed down and ready."

Suddenly serious, I wanted to know, "How long will the procedure take once we are in the operating room?"

"We should know within 20 minutes what the results are. 10 minutes to do the biopsy and another 10 minutes for pathology to get the results back to me. We will keep you under anesthetic in case we need to do any further reconnaissance."

The next morning, here we were again, this time in the staging area before being taken to surgery. It was a small room, only furnished with a hospital bed on wheels, some testing equipment for blood pressure and pulse monitoring, and a laptop to record answers to the vital records questions of a name, birth date, and social security number. On the left side of the bed were two chairs, one for Joanna to sit with me and the other holding the plastic shopping bag containing my regular clothing. Just after the nurse left the room, Dr. Brinson arrived with a blue mask dangling from his shoulders and fresh scrubs looking like a near-sighted tailor fitted them. My first reaction was to stare him down making sure he looked alert and devoid of blood shot eyeballs.

"It appears to me that you did it a short bar-hopping night last night," I said.

"Yeah, my husband told me you were going to end up at Buddy's at the end of a long night last night," Joanna questioned, playing along with the story. It was the first time the Doc had met Joanna, and I noticed how totally disarmed he became with her radiant smile and apparent attempt to carry on the façade.

"Actually, we never made it to Buddy's," Brinson said, having quickly recovered from his moment of delight seeing Joanna's beauty so early that morning. "We decided it was too hot outside, so we had poker night instead."

"Did you win anything?" I asked.

"They're still playing," he said. "I just left the table a little bit ago."

As I look back on that banter these months later, it became apparent to me that Dr.

George Brinson was caught off guard that first time he met Joanna. Oh, but it was a good thing. In my fight with cancer, I had my own person army, and Joanna was the 5-star general. That day in the wee hours of the morning, George Brinson was going into that operating room with a renewed resolve to come out with good news. My beautiful Joanna had that effect on everyone, no matter what the circumstance.

The sublime serenity of the ride on a hospital gurney has a dichotomy of inverse relativity to good and bad thoughts as the seconds tick on. Everyone involved knows where you are going. Everyone knows why. Do I think the worst or do I think positive thoughts while riding this magic carpet to a place no one wants to go? That's it isn't it? The good part is, that all these people know what they are doing, or at least, pose that they know; the bad part is, knowing that there will be an answer to the question which had been researched, dissected, and pondered over these hideously long weeks, and there would be no grey area as to the validity and the certainty of that answer. It either was, or it wasn't, period.

My personal research during the weeks preceding the biopsy yielded the knowledge of a myriad of diagnoses and prognoses, but the only one that mattered at this point had to do with finding a primary cell of cancer. It was the one you did not want that left me shaking. Within just the title, the quest to know my disease had so much mystery. *Occult primary.* Putting those two words together not only spelled mystery, but it also became a foreboding phrase of dark dominance at its pinnacle. There was a menacing and space-deep tone to that first word, one that depicted a black hood over your face and instead of blood, ice running through your veins. And in the second, that doom was accelerated to the zenith of your current life at that very second.

You simply cannot put anything in front of the most primary discovery, the one which would determine your destiny. *Occult primary.* Can we find the primary cell of cancer, the one that caused the golf ball sized lymph node on the left side of my neck or will we find nothing, making it another of cancer's villains?

During that week of waiting, I had researched what the primary cell had to do with the fact that I was diagnosed with Squamous Cell Carcinoma of the neck. Cancers are named based on its

primary site. If you find the primary site, treatment becomes localized, and a higher rate of cure to certain diseases becomes part of
your overall prognosis. Conversely, if a location of a primary cell
cannot be found (15% of cases), well then, your cancer changes
from immediately beginning localized treatment to launching a
total body treatment while continuously hunting down that primary cell. *Occult primary.* I shiver now just mouthing the phrase
under my breath.

I hated it because it made me fear what would become of me
along the way to the rest of my life. It sounded so insidious to have
to go through weeks and months without knowing what was working against me in all the other areas of my body. Would it control
my fate, or would it become just one more distant discarded facet
of this long road filled with countless hazards?

Would I be one of the 15%?

And why was I not hoping and praying for my 66-year old body
to be in the 85% category? After all, maybe the second diagnosis
was false just like the first one was in early August of 2012, the result of a needle biopsy.

On this day, the whole lot of us, the nurses, the doctor, Joanna,
daughter Tayleigh, son Steve, my buddies, general surgeon Dr.
James Harris (who had been leading this same gurney journey a
couple of weeks before), and me, were all looking for the same
answer. It was another fork in the road, a confirmation of what
Dr. Brinson had seen with his microscope, not on a cell or a blood
panel, but on a picture taken by a CATscan. How did he know
to look at something that others had missed? How come he was
truly the only one to know, even before this gurney ride, what the
answer was going to be? And how did it come down to rooting
for "it" to be cancer? This launched the beginning of one of the
central themes in my fight against cancer: most cancer physicians
are smart. Everything they tell you is smart. To hear them tell it,
it's all nuts and bolts. They say everything they know for sure, and

you can take it to the bank. It's what they don't tell you that will drive you crazy with questions. But they're smart after all, and if they don't know it as an absolute truth, they are not going to answer your question. Anything based on statistics bears an affinity for the truth. Except for Dr. George Brinson, you're not going to get a reply from most cancer docs which may lay to rest any and all doubt as to its validity. Cancer doctors deal in truths. Therefore, their reaction to questions which have no definite answer is one of generality with time borders measured in months if not years. But I had Dr. George Brinson on my case. Not necessarily an exception to the rule so much as his ability, in my particular diagnosis, to be truthful because he knows even elusive answers. Dr. Brinson was the one who thought he saw my primary cell, and he did it the old fashioned way. He looked at printed results of a CATscan, which had been deemed "inconclusive" by at least two other docs, including the unknown radiologist who was the original reader. And here we were, rolling along, based solely on his diagnosis that something showed up on that scan that just did not look right under a microscope with a trained eye.

As it turned out, I got two wins during my battle with fate that day, a fight which had challenged as to what its result would be and had lain in the balance less than an hour before. The primary cell was located exactly where it should have been; and, I had George Brinson by my side in the trenches of battle. These were the wins of the highest magnitude as they initiated the course of treatment to beat my cancer and allowed me to look forward with the hope which had been patiently waiting for some good news. That day in the latter part of August of 2013 was at that moment, the most important day of my life. He found it. No occult primary for the L-Dog. Mission accomplished. An extraordinary sense of relief.

"We have found the primary cell and now know how to treat L-Dog's cancer," Dr. Brinson told a weeping Joanna. She said a few days later that she truly could not ever root for it to be cancer until the moment itself arrived. Joanna, ever the realist (except this time), wanted it all to be nothing and to go back to normalcy. She found it impossible to think the ridiculous.

After all, there had been one false alarm, why couldn't there be another? I remember distinctly coming out of the 20-minute anesthetic, seeing her beautiful face and feeling her hand in mine, and saying, "They found it didn't they? That was the primary cell???"

She nodded, "Dr. Brinson told me right away that it was what we have been looking for, and that our future was brighter for the discovery."

The following day I drove across town to his office for a follow-up, and even his nurse had a huge smile on her face. But it paled in comparison to the one George had as he sailed into the examining room. Hugs all around, a couple of jokes about what other revisions he had made to my anatomy while I was under anesthetic, and then it was on to the business of his telling me what my life would look like for the next few years. I heard only bits and pieces of his prognosis because I was still reeling in the obvious delight they I had just seen on George's face. It was a distinctly happy point in my cancer saga that my fears of the unknown were temporarily abated, and my personal anticipation of the future began an upward climb. The sickening knockdowns that bruised each day's attempts to beat the evil that is cancer, all of which began four weeks later, were the new unknown. Knockdowns that were so sinister, thoughts of their abilities to slam me with such force so many times on the canvass, and with such vengeance, impaired my abilities to fight back and get back up. In the beginning, it never entered my mind that there would be other maladies invading my body and arresting my journey to a cure. A life which eventually would become one of the 24-hour nights, the darkness of which was intermittently and blessedly interrupted by those who fought to pull me through, never occurred to me for those four weeks I was awaiting the start of my treatment in September 2013. As far as I was concerned, I was going to make it through unscathed because as all the doc's said, "You are going into treatment in great shape. You will get through it just fine." Honestly, they all said that. Surgeon, ENT, oncologist, and radiology oncologist, to a man, told me that. They just didn't say what could happen along the way. The beginning of perpetual nightfall was September 30, 2013. The light of day began to dim. Everything I had prepared for in anticipation of the onslaught of chemicals and radiation hammering into every crevice of my body vaporized simply into complete darkness, illuminated only intermittently by Joanna and the friends who's faces lit up the room when I saw them.

And, from September 30, 2012, until New Year's Day 2013, I prayed every day for The End of Night.

CHAPTER 2
THE LUMP

I noticed the thing on the left side of my neck in late January of 2013.

This lump in my neck was just another weird protrusion from my body that I didn't believe was anything to worry about. Back in the 50's I would get these lumps all over my neck, and my mom just called them "swollen glands". And they just went away in a week or so. My youngest daughter, Tayleigh, had recently been diagnosed with mono and surely my swollen neck was akin to hers. I had an appointment Dr. Jim Wortman in mid-April and had a test done for mono. Negative. As far as I can remember, a pea-sized bump appeared in mid-January, right at the time of the mono diagnosis for Tayleigh. Not much happened in the way of recognition until I first showed it to Dr. Jim, my internist. Though significant, we decided to take the course of a second reading 60 days hence, which of course I dismissed for about 90 days. But the lump was there in plain sight, and we were going to "watch it".

In early June 2013, Joanna, Tayleigh, and I traveled to Brighton, CO to see son Steve, and Kristi our daughter-in-law, little granddaughter Brynn, and newborn grandson, Lincoln. Almost as I debarked from the plane, the mile high altitude began to wreak havoc on my friend, the lump. Swelling and pain ensued, but I was determined that the next three days were not going to revolve around me. Ibuprofen, in copious quantities, was my friend. More prayer began to creep into my dailies, and yes there was that touch of fear way in the back of my mind. I was just like anyone else. I think everyone would have wondered in worry by this time after three months. Tayleigh was conversing with a new male friend, and Joanna was enjoying our 27-year old's fledging relationship. By each day's end, all I wanted was sleep and to be rid of that plaguing feeling in my neck. But by the time we left Colorado, the marble resembled a golf ball. An appointment with Jim Wortman was made for the first day back in NC.

There is no record that I can find for Robert E. Thieman since I last saw him in 1971. Having searched all the social media sites for clues, obituary columns on line, service resources, and even post office records (his father was the postmaster in Huron South Dakota back then), I still cannot find any reference to the friend I called "Tanks". Tanks embodies down to his DNA the lessons I learned from my experience fighting cancer at the base of my tongue which began in January of 2013 and continues to this day, some months later. Here is the letter I would write to Bob Thieman if only I could find him:

Dear Tanks,

I have searched all over the place and now I finally have located you right here in the back of my mind. All the way back to 1969. There you are underneath some poor soul's 1962 Chevy trying to figure out why it sounds like a blender from second shifting into third gear.

Did they have third gear back then?
You've got your usual grease spotted tan shirt and mainly disgustingly dirty work overalls on and I know you are enjoying every minute of grease. I'd pull up a bucket and sit down and give you a

load of crap about something that we would iron out back at the Grosse Isle, Michigan Marine barracks at some late hour with a cold one. Man, I wish we could do that now.

Every time someone would obey an order from Sgt. Thieman, they would get a "tanks" for their effort. Even that ridiculous captain we had would get a "tanks" from you under your breath as you would obey one of his idiotic orders. There was a reason he was there in the first place at this shithole of a base just south of Detroit. He was just as much as a shitbird as you and I were. Every weekend the reservists would come in to test their skills at flying and fixing the C-119 Flying Boxcars that we had; and, every weekday we would fix what they "fixed".

It was April of 1967 when we first met as I stepped off the CH-43 helicopter on the pad at Quang Tri Marine Corps Air Station in the Republic of South Viet Nam. You may not remember, but it was you who introduced me into the fine art of procuring almost anything for nothing. Under your tutelage I ended up with an air mattress for my bunk, a helmet that didn't have a hole in it just in case I ever needed to carry water in it, and a 25" Philco TV so I could check in on the latest news. I'll never forget the day before you left "country" and you gave me the rights to the TV. You never told me where you got that worthless appliance since there were no television broadcasts for probably thousands of miles from where we were. I want you to know that, when I left for the states, I willed it to the next poor soul and told him some stupid story just like you told me. He bought it just like I did when you left it to me in the fall of 1967 when you rolled stateside and I thought, for sure I had seen the last of my best friend in the whole world.

I made it through the Tet offensive of 1968 by the grace of God and then the Marine Corps in one of their finest hours decided it was time I had my flight physical, 6 months after I had agreed to fly as assistant crew chief on the Huey's. An electrician by proxy, my MOS was actually electronics technician, I was summarily relegated to the M-60 machine gun. You had to be a mechanic or a hydraulics MOS (Military Occupational Specialty) to fly as the crew chief.

The theory was that the bird could not fly without mechanics or hydraulics but could limp home with no electricity. But then, I was only an E-4 corporal. What could I possibly have known about such things? Besides, I was an electrician because the CO only gave me two choices when I got there: fly or walk guard duty. When I showed him my true colors and told him "guard duty" he took me down to the cages to see the guard dogs that would accompany me while walking perimeter guard duty. Then I showed him my new true colors and said "I'll fly". No mean-ass Dobermans for me.

As you may know, the Marine Corps lumbers along slowly with protocol, so 4 months later and countless combat flights later, off I went to DaNang for my flight physical after ten months of flying. You gotta love the Corps don't you?! Failed the eye test with the physical. They did not even let me go back to Quang Tri. Off to Yokosuka Japan I was that next night with a ditty bag full of toiletries and the clothing on my back. I stayed there three weeks, saw two or three different ophthalmologists (can't believe I can spell that) and they all concurred that I should not have ever been accepted into the service. That's right...never into the Marine Corps. This is now going on three years into my enlistment. So what do they do? They ship me and my ditty bag and a few threads of clothing off to Great Lakes Naval Base in North Chicago Illinois. I saw a new doc there and he uttered the sweetest words that I ever heard, "I concur" in his diagnosis. He was going to recommend full discharge from service entirely.

That evening the Doc received word that his mom had passed away and he took leave to go to his hometown and the funeral. I was assigned to a Dr. Berg who was a newly "recruited" ophthalmologist from Brooklyn, New York. To say that he was pissed to be yanked out of private business and stationed in North Chicago was an understatement. Of course, he said ALL of the previous 4-5 docs didn't know their asses from holes in the ground and reversed everything. With 70 days left in my full Viet Nam tour, he was sending me back to Quang Tri, his report claiming I was a malingerer and a fraud. Let's see: whose idea was this flight physical in the beginning of this odyssey?

The next day I made an appointment with the Adjutant General (AG), the chief legal officer of the base. He told me there was nothing he could do since Dr. Berg had the last say. So I called the person who was my last resort, my father, Dr. Ernie Davis, for advice. At that time my dad and I were not, should we say, close.

In this instance, three weeks later my dad did what dads do and called his lawyer, Jack Connaghton, who at that time was on some small craft cruise in the Caribbean. The old man went ship-to-shore to get hold of Jack, who was born and raised in the suburbs of Chicago. His son, Dan, later played on the Loyola of Chicago basketball team which defeated University of Cincinnati and Oscar Robertson for the NCAA national championship. Well, guess who Jack Connaughton knew? Yep, the Adjutant General of the US Naval Hospital in North Chicago.

It was late Friday after our return from Denver. Dr. Jim had his ruler out measuring the diameter of the lump. In whatever parlance he spoke, the end result was that the lump was BIG. He said, "we need to get that taken out. I don't like lumps anywhere." He made a call to general surgeon Dr. James Harris' office just down the street and off I went. Knowing that Dr. Harris did not see patients on Friday afternoon, I thought nothing would be done that day. My first big mistake was assuming the lump on the left side of my neck would recede and go away. And my second was that I let it go on for three months. This Friday afternoon, I was wrong for the third time.

For reasons I would learn weeks later during a subsequent examination, and after an initial interview, Dr. Harris decided to ask his staff to stay later that day and help him get a handle on what was going on with his new patient that intervened in the afternoon off for him and his technicians. While laying on my side with the shining bulge protruding from the left side of my neck, an ultrasound ensued, and a fun-filled needle biopsy was performed there in the office. In fact, it was so much fun, Dr. Harris stuck the needle in twice. Pretty serious pain, I'll tell you. He said the results would be back by Wednesday the following week.

It was during this Naval Hospital debacle in 1968, that I met my first wife, Catherine, through a high school friend, Dave Shimp and his girlfriend. Cathy was the great-great- granddaughter of the man who invented and built the Pullman train cars. She was the great-granddaughter of the former governor of Illinois, Frank Louden. Her step father, Sam Culbertson, a self-made man, and was the founder and CEO of The Murine Company, which at that time was going through the ritual of merging with Abbott Laboratories. I remember your digs about how this country boy fell into what you called "the upper crust".

So the AG passed on his intentions of keeping me in the states. Now the Jarheads don't think too kindly of swabbies meddling into their affairs, so the Marine Corps contingent at the hospital put their heads together and decided where they were going to ship Sgt Davis; and hold onto your grease gun, Tanks, it was to that relic of a Naval Air Base south of Detroit, Grosse Isle Michigan.

Cathy was still a student at Northwestern, so I left for Grosse Isle in her maroon colored '68 Mustang hatchback thinking I was king of the road. And true to any Marine worth his salt, I timed my arrival with about 30 minutes to spare at about 11:30 p.m. one evening in February.

Of course, I had to check in with the Officer in Charge (OIC) so that he knew I was back on base and on time. There on the desk was the board displaying the name of both the duty OIC as well as the Non-Commissioned Officer (NCO). The NCO on duty was Sgt. Robert E. Thieman..Holy shit, it was you!

For the second time in my life I was faced with waiting a week to ten days to get the results of lab work. The first was in 2002 when our youngest daughter, Tayleigh, a cross country and track runner in high school and at East Carolina University, passed out for the 3rd or 4th time while running cross country races. Bone tests, blood tests, and leukemia whispering ensued. Joanna and I were forced to listen to the oncologist say, "we'll have the results in a week to 10 days." On about the seventh day, Joanna and I sat down to have lunch at home, and during the prayer I decided enough was enough and called the oncologist's office. After all, it was our kid and nothing compares to the utter helplessness when you find out your child is sick. We had started at urgent care a month or so prior to this episode. There, after drawing all sorts of blood, they gave her instructions to ramp up her iron intake and hydrate more. Several weeks later we took Tayleigh to see a hematologist that was recommended by the urgent care physician. There they took her blood twice during a three week period. Extremely low red blood cell count and extremely high white cell count. Confirmed. With Tayleigh out of the room, his advice was for us to get her to the Zimmer Cancer Center immediately. He would make the phone call.

Joanna and Tayleigh drove the next day to Zimmer and met with an oncologist. As Joanna would tell me later that night, Tayleigh even at 15 years old, was very calm about what was about to take place. They were called back to the exam room and passing the nurse's station Joanna saw a very pretty middle-aged nurse with a big smile on her face, almost as if they knew each other, but, of course, they did not. While waiting for the doctor in the small room, the door opened and in walked this same nurse. Her name plate said "Monica". She said to Joanna and Tayleigh, "Your daughter is an angel."

To which Joanna replied, "Yes, we certainly think so!"

"No, I mean your daughter is an angel. She will be fine. There are great doctors here." And then she walked out the door. Before long the doctor entered, ordered the perfunctory blood tests and then left.

Seven days later, as the three of us drove across town to get the news about the blood samples taken at the Zimmer Center, Joanna and I were both remembering how lethargic Tayleigh had been after school lately and how utterly drained she would be after cross country practice. This was very unusual. Usually an active 15-year old, she simply did not have the stamina to get through the day. I remembered back in 1984 or so when my niece had myelogenous leukemia and the five months it took to get her miraculously cured. What I especially remembered was that she was the only one out of 20 kids in her unit that lived. I was scared.

When Tayleigh arrived home from school and practice that day, she seemed different. It was as if her strength had returned. The color in her face was radiant, and her smile was wider than I had witnessed in weeks. And here we were now, sitting in the examining room as the oncologist walked in. He was a handsome middle-eastern gentleman with such a kind disposition. In his right hand, he held a group of papers On his face I read a puzzle. He sat on his stool and wheeled over to Tayleigh and laid his hand on hers.

"When I read the reports from urgent care and the hematologist I was alarmed at the severity of the regression of the cell counts as the went from bad to worse," he said. "As a consequence, when we received the recent report on this recent blood test I questioned it immediately and sent the rest of the blood samples off to another lab. I wanted to make sure I had no doubt about what I am about to tell you. "

And, with that, he held up his hand with the papers and said, "Every result is normal.

Your blood counts are perfectly in line with what they should be."

The three of us embraced each other with tears streaming down our cheeks. How could this be, we wondered.

Joanna looked at the doctor and said, "it was just like your nurse, Monica, had said. She told us Tayleigh was going to be all right and that you were a great doctor."

"Who told you that? Which nurse?" "Her name tag said Monica."

"Strange. We don't have anyone on our staff with that name"...

Those of us who know how close Tayleigh is to God were certain that God Himself did indeed intervene that day. No question about it. That clinched it for me. A couple of years later I became the first to be baptized at our new Port City Community Church, and I was the oldest ever. That still stands to this day. That day in 2002 changed the way I lived my life, loving Jesus Christ and knowing for sure that He loved me.

And, now, here in Dr. Harris' office, on this late Friday afternoon, I commenced waiting for a blood test to see if I could also beat the odds. I called the next day, not wanting to wait another minute. The needle biopsy was negative. Antibiotics were prescribed for ten days and the lump diminished back to the marble. Stayed that way too, for about a month.

CHAPTER 3

GOOD FELLAS

I asked the duty clerk where to find Staff Sergeant Thieman and he gave me directions to your hooch. You actually had your own little place on the grounds, which of course was nothing new for you. I don't recall the story, but I do remember you kissed some-one's ass to get the billet. Alas, all I found in that small room was your mongrel of a dog, Bro. I checked into the barracks and was told that Sgt. Thieman would most likely be at a bar in the small downtown area of Grosse Isle. I was so excited to be reunited with my best friend. Through all the trappings of the Marine Corps, Viet Nam, eye doctors, my dad, his lawyer and ship-to-shore radio, the first love of my life and her Ford Mustang coupe, I was on the precipice of seeing your ugly face once again.

It was late, now after midnight, a weekday, and in a part of a neighborhood where everyone was asleep. Everyone except Bob Thieman. One barstool was occupied. Smoke trailed up from the person hunched over his scotch. I knew it was you the second I walked into the joint. As I slid in next to you quietly, all I could think to say was, "I couldn't bring the f'ing TV with me." You gave me the same look that Richard Dreyfus got from Roy Schieder in Jaws when he emerged from under the water after Quint met his end with the shark: Calm and ecstatic disbelief. Of course, you remember, you made me buy until that bar closed in the wee hours of the morning. I remember that as a man, our friendship was the first that I thought could last a lifetime. It meant a great deal to me because I knew it meant a lot to you too.

The next day you took me out for a ride in your '68 Pontiac Bonneville 2+2, 428 hemi and it made me gasp for air in first AND second gear. It made my sports car look like a roller skate. But then as I am today, cars mean only transportation to me and I was happy that I had been able to convince Sam to get Cathy a different vehicle and let me take her car to use to burn up I-94 on my way to Winnetka Illinois every Monday and Tuesday so that we could be together. Reserve bases you may recall had duty 3 out of every four weekends. After a few months of that, Cathy and I began to talk about a wedding and, sure enough, we planned for December 28, 1968 at the Glenview Country Club, north of Chicago. There were to be 600 guests at this gala affair, and yes, I was going to get to wear my dress blues.

One night, about a week before the wedding in late December, I was coming across the bridge leading to Grosse Isle and our mutual friend Danny was driving away from the base in a big hurry. I know we both remember what happened. The head on collision was caused when Danny came across the center line because the bridge was icy. All of us were glad that his horrific injuries mended and he was good as new in a few months. But Cathy's beloved Mustang was history. You took one look at it and told me, "no one can fix that". And our wedding was less than one week off. How was I going to get there?

In mid-August, three weeks after the needle biopsy, the bump on the neck had become a full-fledged raging golf ball. I called my internist, Dr. Wortman, and his office made an appointment with Dr. James Harris for the next day. As the surgeon entered the exam room, I sensed he was carrying what seemed to be a heavy heart. It was as if there was some burden from a previous surgery procedure, or maybe he lost one of his patients…something heavy like that. I remembered back a month earlier his urgency in having the needle biopsy on that Friday afternoon. Just as I had that day, now I saw concern, albeit a more heightened look of concern, on his ruggedly handsome face.

He remarked, "Sometimes needle biopsies simply do not tell the whole story. Although we went into the lymph node twice, there was only so far into the tissue that we could safely go without compromising other areas. The only way we are going to know for sure is to take it out."

"How big of a task is that?" I asked. "And when you say take it out, what exactly does that mean you are looking for?"

"We won't know until we get into the surgery what we may find. But, something in that area is causing trauma to your lymph node. It may be an infection that was in its infancy when we put the needle in and simply did not draw fluid from the exact area. And now, perhaps the infection has spread," he replied with an obvious degree of mystery.

Having been raised in a medical family, I knew that a physician is usually cautious when answering questions about what "it could be," so I truly did not press for more information.

Besides, it sounded plausible to me.

The lumpectomy surgery in early August was over in 20 minutes. Joanna remarked how Dr. Harris had visited with her very briefly after the surgery and then left her with the opinion that he was uncaring. I couldn't understand that because I liked the guy as a person, let alone as a physician. As it turned out, he knew before the pathology ever came back that there was cancer in the lymph node. He simply could not bear to look Joanna in her eyes and thus chose to be aloof until the true diagnosis, and the real proof came back from pathology. That's the way it is, isn't it? If you care about someone, it is tough to give them bad news. I don't know about anyone else, but I put bad news off as long as possible hoping something changes, and that news becomes old news. Dr. Jim Wortman called me the next day and broke the news to us. I am certain he had shed a few tears before the call. I didn't know what to say or think. I was just uncertain and subdued right from the start. And, at that point, it was normal because I certainly did not know what was in store for me. As it developed, I became aware that God was going to test me to the limits of my core, always with the promise that His plan for me was to get through any ordeal, in the same way that it had been my whole life.

As you remember well, it was snowing Christmas Eve in Detroit in 1968, and snowing pretty hard. I was a few hours away from catching my bus to Chicago when you sat down on my bunk. You told me that you were not going anywhere for the holidays. It was just too awful outside to think of driving to Huron South Dakota, your hometown. You dangled your keys in front of you and said, "Take my car. I won't need it." I was stunned that you would trust me with your most prized, well really your only possession. You would not take "No" for an answer. And so, early the next day, I left for Winnetka Illinois and watched in my rearview mirror as you faded away. I wasn't allowed to tell anyone but Cathy about your kindness because that's just what you did for your friend. I knew Sam would make a big deal out of it, but that just was not you, so you made me swear to secrecy. I was filled with joy and love for you as my friend all the way until I hit the Dan Ryan Expressway in Chicago.

The wedding reception list included Senator Charles Percy, who was fighting some racketeering charge at the time. The legendary shortstop for the Chicago Cubs, Ernie Banks, was there. Cream performed on the stage. Even my mother stopped yelling at me. And there Cathy and I were, shaking hands with every one of those 600+ guests. About number 450, out of the corner of my left eye, I caught a quick glimpse of the owner of that 1968 Pontiac 428 muscle car.

There you were all dressed up in a slightly wrinkled suit that looked like it had spent the night in a suitcase. You had a scotch in one hand and bourbon in the other. You proceeded to spill about seven years of both of them on my dress blues. I didn't care. For that brief moment, everything stopped. There was no music, no glasses clinking, no laughing, no small talk, no worry about blowing some protocol of wedding etiquette. The rest of the 150 people stood in amazement as the tears streamed down my face with such love for you, my most gracious friend. I will carry that feeling to the end of my days as one of the most meaningful embraces a man could ever have. Your friendship knew no boundaries.

Later you told me that as soon as I left Grosse Isle, you proceeded to hitchhike in a blinding snowstorm to Huron South Dakota to be with your family for Christmas. You arrived one day late. They had postponed their holiday celebration until their son and brother had arrived. The next day you hitched back to the Chicago area, got a ride with a trucker all the way, and even HE knew what type of guy you were because he took you 50 miles out of his way to get you to a motel near the reception just in time. And there you were. I am still stunned to this day, almost 45 years later, at this act of kindness, friendship, love, and genuine thoughtfulness for your fellow man. I was getting married. All you were doing was hitch hiking a total of about 4000 miles in blizzard conditions to take care of your buddy. All I can say is "Tanks."

Bob's life crossed with mine three times after his magnanimous gift in the winter of 1968. The last occasion was on Memorial Day, 2015, when I received a call on my cell phone labeled "Portland OR" which of course I did not recognize and, therefore, did not answer. I thought it was just another phone solicitor. Several hours later, I listened to the message and heard a sweet voice say, "Larry Crowder Davis, this is Joy Thieman. I have been searching for you all these years, and I think I may have found you. You have to be the only Larry Davis with "Crowder" in the middle. Please call me and let me know if you are the former Marine, who knew my husband, Robert Thieman."

After their early courtship in 1969, Bob and Joy had a couple of periods of time where they did not hear from each other, Bob from a standpoint of living a different life and Joy from a posture of not knowing where he was or what he was doing and moving on with her life. In the summer of 1970, while I was on vacation in Vero Beach, Florida with Cathy's family, I called Embry Riddle Aeronautical Institute to see if a Robert Thieman was enrolled there learning how to fly, his lifelong ambition. Sure enough, he was, we connected, and I spent one afternoon on the back of his Triumph motor cycle seeing death flash before my eyes several times. What a maniac he was on that bike. At one time we blew past a cactus bush, brushed it slightly on my right leg, and it proceeded to swell up to the size of a football the next day. That was the first time I had seen him since his discharge from the Corps in late 1969.

In 1970, halfway through his first year, Tanks was hit by a stop light-running drunk driver and fractured 17 bones south of his right knee. He was rushed to Halifax County Hospital where emergency surgery was performed to mend somehow those 17 fractures. A couple of days later, Bob wrote to Joy telling her of his ordeal. Soon after that, he was transferred back to his hometown, Huron, South Dakota. Many trips to the Mayo Clinic in Minnesota ensued to have further surgeries on his injured leg. He battled gangrene with complete success, although the result was in doubt for months. After several more months of no communication, Joy moved to St. Louis to attend Washington University, working at a dry cleaning store to earn money to pay for her education.

During the many months of the healing process, Bob attended Huron Community College. Unable to drive a car, he rescued an old discarded bicycle to ride across town to and from school. To accomplish this, Tanks had to devise a platform on the right side of his bike to rest his casted leg on. He would then use only his left leg to propel the bike into motion.

Through rain or snow, hot or cold, for an entire year, that's how he got to classes. When Tanks eventually healed, he attempted to find Joy by calling her mother. Of course, just as he always did, Bob surprised by showing up at the cleaners and asking Joy to attend the annual local Marine Corps Ball with him, showing off his slightly limping but agile dancing ability. At that point, Bob was working for a cosmetics company, KOSCOT.

After KOSCOT, a pyramid type organization, folded under intense scrutiny, Bob made his way back to St. Louis and surprised (again) Joy by attending her graduation from college. She used her degree to hire on at the highly regarded Barnes Hospital in St. Louis, and Bob looked for work, eventually finding employment at Lambert Field, which is still the international airport in St. Louis, still harboring the desire to become a commercial pilot. He used his earnings as a mechanic and flight trainer to take flight lessons, eventually finishing multi-engine training and becoming licensed. During that time, in 1972, Joy and Bob were married. His first real flying job was piloting second-seat on a DC-9 twin-engine prop plane, flying from St. Louis to Omaha, to Kansas City, and then home to deliver Wall Street Journal newspapers on a daily basis. They would leave at one o'clock in the morning and return just before dawn each weekday.

Bob and Joy took their honeymoon in Colorado and upon returning to St. Louis made the decision that they wanted to live near the mountains. So, in the winter of 1973, renting a U-haul truck, towing their car behind them and with about $200 in their pockets, they started their move to Portland, Oregon. With little money, they decided to drive straight through, taking 6-hours shifts, and stopping only for gas and food. Joy was driving one night in the wee hours of the morning and was going through the mountains in a driving snow storm. She stopped for gas after driving for a couple of hours with a sleeping Tanks next to her in the cab. Joy was at the point where she hated to wake her husband but knew she could not safely drive one move mile in that rig. As she rolled down her window for the attendant, she remarked how cold it was. He replied, "Well I guess so! It's 32 below zero!" Joy thought, "No wonder I have been so cold even with the heater on full blast..."

Once in Portland, Joy got a job with Kaiser, pulling double shifts while Bob used the GI Bill to finish earning his commercial pilot's license with his Designated Instrument Instructor's Rating. Bob's first job was flying a twin-engine Aztec for a paint company while also moonlighting as an instructor for Flight Craft out of Portland's PBX international airport.

In 1978, after five years of marriage, Tobin Robert Thieman was born on June 12. Three years later, in 1981, Bob was approached by an aerial photography group to fly them to Napa Valley for two days of work. Bob asked for permission to use his company's Aztec to participate in the adventure. In an act of complete trust, his company granted his request. They flew to Chico, California, landing at noon, and decided to rest up and start photographing early the next morning. Bob called Joy that evening before going to sleep, remarking that the others were "on the prowl" and that he did not care for them. He spoke to Tobin and then signed off with his "I love you".

Sometime mid-morning the next day, while spanning the beautiful sights of the Napa Valley, a down draft from the Santa Rosa Mountains hit their plane as Bob was attempting to keep the starboard wing up so that they could photograph out of the port side of the plane. Their plane nosedived and disappeared from radar. It was Father's Day weekend, three days before his son's third birthday.

Bob Thieman personified the true meaning of friendship in every way. Nothing in the next 45 years of my life ever came close to the feelings of friendship I had for this generous, full- of-heart man who showed me at an early age what mano-a-mano meant. As those years passed, and my life moved into its sixth decade, Bob Thieman's friendship had become a memory recalled only every so often. The phone call from his widow reminded me, that his legacy to me was that if you are going to be there for a friend, then you have to be there every time. He not only rescued me that wintery few days in 1968, but once again, now late in my post-cancer life, his memory once again set the tone for how I was to handle friendships for the rest of my days.

And why do I tell the story of Bob Thieman? His gift to me may very well have been the cornerstone of my fight against cancer and the ensuing friendships before, during, and after, to this day. For all these 45 years I had never met anyone who came close to Bob as a friend...until September of 2013.

One final note about this kind soul: The name of the bar in Grosse Isle where we reconnected in 1968? Good Fellas.

CHAPTER 4

TRUE LOVE FOUND

S he sat impatiently in the waiting room of New Hanover Regional Hospital's visitor's area of the outpatient surgical wing. Her buddy, her best friend, her lover, her husband, the L- Dog, had been back in the operating room for longer than she had hoped, given the information she had from the surgeon. Her thoughts vacilated from family to friends, his, hers and theirs together, and from the darkest of hopes to the hopes of the eternal.

Three weeks before, James Harris MD, the general surgeon, had performed an impromptu needle biopsy on a late Friday afternoon upon request from James Wortman MD, L- Dog's internist of 20 years. L-Dog spoke of these men as if they were HIS buddies. So much respect and so much laughter, what a great combination of circumstances. The needle biopsy was "negative", no dead tissue in the left lymph node which pooched out of L-Dog's neck like a golf ball. Prescriptions were given for the antibiotics and office he went to Costco.

An antibiotic many times is a real cure. Things you get simply go away. The older you get, the less effective they may be. L-Dog was 66. Not a great age to be taking an antibiotic for anything. In this case, however, the golf ball shrunk to a ping pong ball, then to peach pit-size over the next three weeks. Now, in the shank of August, it was back. And it was angry.

Snow was falling in mid-March in Middletown Ohio in 1989. Looking out on the magnificent magnolia tree which was in full bloom, I was anxious. Julie had slow played it, as it turned out, so I was still in my three-piece suit just home from a supplier meeting in St. Louis.

Three times divorced by 43, marriage was not a commitment I wanted to consider, and yet deep inside of me I yearned for someone to truly love. I wanted the type of love whose endless boundaries were made of rice paper, you know, the type easily shredded by the beating of a truly loved heart. Previously enthralled by three others, extraordinary women in their own right, my inner soul simply had remained dormant. There had to be a catalyst which, when cooked up, could pull it out of me, shred by shred. But today, a mutual friend was going to introduce Joanna Long to me with the promise that she would not just find that place in my heart, she would take hold of it and never let it go. I think it's called stealing...and take my heart she did.

I made sure the martinis were double the strength during that first hour with Joanna because I needed all the help I could muster from every pocket of pixie dust and the unlimited cache of good fortune God had blessed me. She had a vibrant smile, long flowing blond hair, and her outfit would befit a princess though Joanna was far removed from that royal hierarchy. No cutesy manner with this woman - just enough common sense and a heart seemingly filled with gold. The conversation was so easy it was as if we had known each other for a long, long time. Joanna was an "old soul" at 31, just mature enough for me to relate easily to the 11 years' age difference, but still displaying her youthful demeanor. She was in my living room at the owner's table, sipping on a martini, and thinking about how she could list and sell my home, which of course was the ruse used to cause her to drive the 30 minutes from

Dayton to Middletown, Ohio. She was a real estate broker with Coldwell Banker, so the "plan" was to have her come down and see about the listing. It was the only instance in the 26 years we have been together that I lied to her.

Remembering the scene from three weeks ago, Joanna's thoughts zeroed in on her fears about the length of time it was taking for the actual removal of the golf ball. Back to its original size and menacing, the protrusion had prompted James Harris to suggest, "We will only know for sure if we take it out." Nothing more, nothing less. It was, she thought, silently understood between the two of them what they would "know" one way or the other. And Joanna's thoughts turned once again to prayer, asking specifically for God to intervene on the side of "negative" again. She knew that God liked specific prayers.

Dr. Harris made his way to the waiting area. His eyes caught the TV high up on the wall, just after he caught a glimpse of his patient's wife. L-Dog had told him he would recognize her. "She was the most beautiful person in the room"…every time. To hostesses at restaurants, to bartenders, from business meetings to conventions…Those were the words I said for sure. They were the words I always said about Joanna. James Harris' eyes flickered back and forth from the TV to Joanna as he sought the words to say. All he could conjure up was, "We won't know for sure until the pathology finishes in a couple of days." Later that day, Joanna was to say it wasn't what he said that took her farther into the dark place. It was how he conveyed that innocuous news of the delay. Joanna had looked in his eyes to find the truth, but those sad eyes trained on the TV high above.

She knew what he knew, now. L-Dog had something bad going on with him.

She began to think about the future, now. How she was going to handle whatever would come along. She knew her husband of 23 years would not be happy with the news that they had to wait a "couple of days" to get the results. After all, the first biopsy had been negative, and the antibiotics worked. We just maybe needed to take another, stronger dose of those. Still she thought. "Why couldn't Dr. Harris look at me when he talked with me?"

We talked briefly about the home in Middletown itself during that hour in 1969. I'm not real sure when Joanna figured it out that she had been hoodwinked. Kids, jobs and the history of our lives dominated the conversation. But Joanna was wary of me, later to describe her thought that I was a "little too L.A." for her. She knew I was seeing my ex-wife at the time and inquired why in the world I would do that. I quickly changed the subject. When Joanna walked into my home, the last thing that was on my mind was talking about previous marriages, and I certainly was not thinking about another attempt down the aisle.

The hour went by quickly, and since the snow was still freezing my magnolia blossoms, it was time for Julie and Joanna to leave for dinner. As I helped her with her long black wool coat, I experienced for the first time the electricity which spiked through my veins, hastened by the exquisite smell of her hair, a hint of perfume, and a body temperature that bordered on fever. I vividly remember that I had to catch my breath without being so obvious that she would turn around, not knowing whether I could handle her beauty so close, face-to-face. I trailed behind Joanna all the way to the front door, reached past her, and swung open the door to let first Julie and then Joanna pass by me onto the front porch. As I held the door open for Joanna, I lingered long enough to see her make her way through the falling snow to her car. She left small footprints in the gathering snow, her black coat and blond hair casting a stunning contrast to the dark green leaves and snow white blossoms of the tree just outside the porch. I followed her every move to the end of the walk and then, as I stood there still trying to breathe normally, she hesitated. I will never forget that next moment...about halfway down the walk, she turned around and smiled. Then a few more steps. Still resting on the open door, I wondered why Joanna was coming back. It was if she had forgotten something, but I was sure that she hadn't. I was wrong and never had I thanked God for being so wrong as I did that instant. Sure-footed and quickly walking on the slippery sidewalk, Joanna came back. She stood on her tip toes, grabbed my tie, and looked at me with her stunning green eyes and pulled my quivering lips to hers. And then she was gone. As it turned out, she had forgotten something.

I am confident that Dr. Jim had shed a few tears before the call. When the number showed up on my cell phone, a phone number I recognized after having seen it for 20 years, I thought it was Candace or Donna calling to remind me of an appointment with Dr. Jim Wortman. Right number, wrong person. It was Dr. Jim himself.

"Hey, guy," he said in his usual voice. Instantly I felt at ease, and I knew he was calling to give me the good news. In a whisper, he said…

"You have cancer. I can't believe it."

I didn't know what to say or think. I was just uncertain and subdued right from the start. There had already been plenty of hurdles in my life, just like the next guy has. Car wrecks and near-miss car wrecks cross your mind when your doc says you have cancer. Almost losing a son in a jet-ski accident 25 years ago came spirited back to mind. And then there were miracles.

Way more miracles… and maybe we got some room for just one more.

Dr. Jim told me of my appointment for the next morning with James Harris, who became the lead surgeon of my illustrious cancer team. All stars, every one of them as it turned out.

You hear the phrase "He's a good doctor"; these people you will read about were above stupendous. These guys and their operations are not flashy. They don't have huge, finely decorated office complexes. It's way better than that. The instant you walk through that front door of Coastal Radiation and Oncology, or Wilmington Ear Nose and Throat, or Cape Fear Cancer Specialists you are in the family. You're not just "family", you are IN the family.

And smart. Here's how smart they are: even if I needed open heart surgery or maybe a double hip replacement, or if something critical happened to Joanna, I would want any or all of these guys in there with us. No matter that their specialties weren't cardiology or orthopedics; this team would still be my team. They work miracles.

Dr. Jim tried to console me, asked me if he wanted me to stop over and talk to Joanna. Respecting him so much I thanked him for his call but told him "no" and that I would handle it. Joanna and I have forever been most at ease simply being in each other's company, alone just the two of us. Without hesitation, I knew this event in our lives should be no different.

That evening we sat at the kitchen table in our modest villa home in Wilmington, holding hands and reading each other's faces, seeing something that had never left in the 24 years that we had been together: honest to goodness true love. Joanna came through the news ready to begin to fight. Throughout all those years of the trials of parenthood, the move to a strange city where we knew not a soul, to the trauma of our son Steve's life-threatening accident, to the kidnapping of our youngest daughter Tayleigh, to all the trivial and not-so-trivial ordeals that healthy couples endure, Joanna and I never lost our searing love for one another. And now we were faced with the real possibility that the demon cancer would shatter that storybook romance.

Joanna's reaction was one of sadness, yet also one of hope. Immediately after our sobbing embrace, we bowed our heads and prayed for guidance and grace. And in less than 5 minutes, we were standing tall ready to get on with it. As the day became night, we had both retired to our normal routines, except for countless moments of frightful bouts with emotion, and an ocean of tears, hidden from each other.

The next day, back to Dr. Harris's office I went this time with a sense of fear of the unknown. My usual laidback self was rescuing me as I entered yet another exam room. Soon Dr. Harris entered, this time with what seemed to be resignation. Perhaps it was because he was the one who had to find "it".

"I suppose Dr. Wortman called you and told you the news."

"Yes, it was not easy for him to call me. We have been friends for a long time. I have lived a long and fruitful life, Doc. I don't know what more I could have done to fulfill my dreams."

"Well, let's not get ahead of ourselves here. I have you lined up with three people to see, and they will become your team," he said. "Now, you can call Chapel Hill or Duke, but they will tell you the same thing I am going to say to you, and that is this team writes protocol for your type of cancer FOR Chapel Hill and Duke. You can't do any better than that."

"So what's the prognosis, Dr. Harris?" I asked. "I have no idea whether to just be worried or to get my things in order... ". I broke down for the first time, not able to hold it in any longer. All I could think of was what Joanna was doing and thinking while I was gone. She had offered to go with me to my appointment, but this, I told her, was something I had to do alone for now. I was still trying to get my brain around this cancer thing.

Dr. Harris, looking a bit melancholy and speaking in almost a whisper, said, "I, unfortunately, have some history with cancer. My wife died six years ago from breast cancer. I have two young sons that I am raising," he told me, his voice cracking, his eyes closed. "I will say this, though; you are in good shape and are going into this thing with a body that can withstand whatever they throw at you. Your blood work shows strength in their numbers. You are neither overweight nor thin. You don't smoke or use any tobacco.

That more than makes up for your age. All things considered, I like your chances."

This from the surgeon who excised my cancerous lymph node. *I like your chances* from the guy who had seen the cancerous area. And he knew what cancer "looked like" after battling it with his wife. He had to balance his professional life knowing that his primary responsibility was raising two once infant boys to manhood… all by himself. Talking with me, someone he apparently cared for, became testy for him, obviously reliving the nightmares he and the mother of his children had endured. It was so different from that day in the waiting room at the hospital talking with Joanna. Today he was looking straight at me across the room with eyes that told a story of sadness in his life and now a new chapter for Joanna and me. It was all out in the open now, and all that remained were memories of a failed protocol for his wife and the hope for his patient to write the opposite outcome.

Suddenly my dim plight became secondary to me. I had to bail this man out. All I could think of at that moment was to walk over and hug him. And so I did. For the first time since hearing the word "cancer," I felt the darkness lift a bit, looked into his sad eyes and said, "If there was ever a Dad, who could raise two boys, you are the guy."

That was the first of a mile-long list of shared moments, with a multitude of people that can be described only as: "what cancer did for me". The black shroud hanging over me lifted slightly at that instant. Oh, it wasn't nearly completely gone, just a little shrug that showed me that its dominance perhaps wasn't permanent. Dr. Harris had given me a massive dose of hope that the result for me would be different than what had taken his wife from him, and mom from the boys We became two men, not just physician and patient, sharing the sorrows of life and the determination that both his boys and I would live to fulfill our dreams for the rest of our lives.

On the way home, my thoughts drifted back 24 years…

In 1989, I traveled almost 400,000 miles a year to customers and vendors for my business, Wordata Inc. We manufactured computer printer ribbons and had for ten years at that point. I lived and breathed that little company with 50 employees including my older sister, Madalyn, and my younger brother, Jeff. I was returning from a three-day trip out West, just a few days removed from my first encounter with Joanna. The taste of her kiss on my lips still lingered, and I longed to see her. The flight took forever with delays everywhere it seemed.

Upon getting into my car at the airport, I dialed up her number on my car phone, but got her voice mail, just as I had several times before leaving on my trip. No return call had been forthcoming before, and neither would it this time. I decided not to give it another thought and made it almost two weeks before calling her one last time. Excitement roared through me when you answered. It was almost a relief hearing that she had been down with the flu and had taken no calls from anyone, especially someone so "LA". After we had spoken briefly, I sat down at my desk and handwrote Joanna a letter, letting her know that even though I had been married three times before, I was not as "L.A." as she thought I was. After all, this was Middletown, Ohio...not Los Angeles.

As it turned out, this letter sealed my fate with Joanna for the rest of my life:

Dear Joanna,

I arrived back home tonight with memories and new projects from a fruitful trip to Los Angeles and Seattle, but to tell you the truth my mind was pretty much on you the whole time I was gone. All the times I had called I hadn't received a call back. Here I was bummed because you won't give me a clue about going out with me, and now I know you had the flu. Funny, I feel better now that I am aware you are sick. And of course, the way you said it gave me hope that we will see each other again. I'm pretty good when it comes to making home-made chicken noodle soup. Maybe a piece of toast with peanut butter. But I wouldn't stop there just with nourishment; I would make sure you wanted for nothing, waiting on you, running errands for you, whatever you needed, I would do for you.

Maybe what I should do is come up to your condo and make sure Tayleigh is doing OK. I'm positive she and I would hit it off. Having raised another daughter I have cataloged all the things I did wrong and I remember the few things I did right so I would start out treading lightly and maybe keeping her company watching a video or playing whatever games your 3-year old plays these days. Coming back from the trip to a mute home is not as fun as being with a family. That old saying is that "absence makes the heart grow stronger", but it's making for an unyielding heart for me because I'm not there with you making things easier for you while you get well.

I am off this entire weekend starting tomorrow. I can be up to the condo in time to make breakfast for you and Tayleigh. Breakfast is one of my favorite times of the day. I like my hash browns crispy and my eggs over easy, but I know that everyone likes their eggs the way THEY like them, so anything you want I can do. We can start off the day together. I respect that you will not feel up to par and may need to cut the day short. Joanna, I just want to see you, and I will take all the time you'll give me. If it goes well all day, then I will sleep on the couch, and we can do it all over again on Saturday. You'll pretty much know me by then, and we can go from there.

Naturally you are suspicious of someone who had been married three times, and, of course, divorced three times. I would be too if it were the other way around. But right now, I'm not talking about marriage. I am suggesting a 24-30 hour relationship built around giving you a rest and some serious TLC and making sure Tayleigh is content and safe. If that happens, I will be a happy man. Please let me show you that I care.

Larry

P.S. The ball is in your court.

That ball came back into my court the next day when I heard her sweet voice tell me we had a date. Joanna likes her hash browns crispy too...

CHAPTER 5

THE MAN I WILL NEVER FORGET

Mentoring has always been something that I thought I should do, and up until now, never did. I was sure I could offer some bits of so-what information to someone who was floundering in life, but just never followed through with that type of plan. Sitting here today, I find that was one of my more glaring frailties, knowing I possibly could help someone and then neglecting to push myself to do it. Mentoring male or female, black or white, child or adult, elderly or disabled, or maybe just someone normal who was floundering...those who need guidance to get back on track and finding that there are not enough kind human beings there to help them is a noble cause which I had neglected. The irony of all that is the story of Tom Haas coming to my rescue this late in my life and filling that same void that I could have experienced in reverse and affected someone else's life along the way of my life. Also, most men have this inherent aversion to taking advice from their wives. I have always tried to accommodate Joanna by at least listening to, if not always following through, on her advice.

In September of 2013, she gently pressed me, actually insisting for the entire three weeks between diagnosis and implementation of treatment, to contact Deonna Riley in Dayton, Ohio.

Deonna knew a business associate with Woolpert, who had recently suffered the same type of cancer, having completed his protocol with chemotherapy and radiation. Here I was on the precipice of beginning both of these treatments without any first-hand knowledge of what to expect. As the day of the inaugural treatment drew nearer, Joanna's gentle insistence became more relevant to me as my independent thoughts of *this is MY cancer* gave way to wanting to know what was going to happen to me over the next few months. Did I want to share my fears with someone I did not even know? Well, yeah. Better to share with an unknown person who I will never see than to bare my feelings to someone I would be around on a daily basis. At least, that was my thinking during the build up to treatment.

What an idiot I was. When would I learn that Joanna knew best?

For most of my buddies, I have a nickname. It reminds me of the internet joke that tells of a group of four women who go out for lunch. Their names are Joyce, Barbara, Susan, and Jennifer. At the same time, their four husbands are eating lunch elsewhere. Their names are Darkboy, Ace, Big Dog, and Turk. I guess we guys think that we can say "I love you" by pinning these monikers onto our close friends and then we don't have to say really "it." Not so with Mr. Tom Haas, the man who became my mentor through the darkest hours of my life. To say Tom is a big shot is a vast understatement. He has all the trappings of a success in his business and a personal life - with a beautiful home, beautiful wife, family extending down to grandkids, a boat in the garage (where it has been stationary for 10 years or so), 400,000 frequent flier miles, a plethora of white shirts and ties to go with his suits, and a pair of well-worn but shiny Florsheim's. Tom's brain is large as Montana, and his heart is as big as Texas. When in early September Joanna's oldest and dearest friend, Deonna Riley, pretty much demanded that I call Tom Haas soon after I was diagnosed with squamous cell carcinoma, I of course wanted nothing of the sort. I was too busy building a massive addition to the walls that had already been erected around me and MY cancer, and certainly did not want anyone tearing them down and climbing into my world of fear and loathing. The guy was in Orlando for God's sake. So I resisted. And Joanna persisted.

Deonna is Joanna's friend of almost 50 years. A diminutive figure, always well-tanned, Deonna weighs 90 pounds on the days she wears her fat jeans. To say that she is outspoken is an understatement and most will say she is that way just to make up for her lack of height and bulk when she is trying to force her will on someone. She's the prototypical feisty, tough little chick with a heart of gold. Though Deonna was eager to help her long time buddy get through the tough times as a spouse of a cancer victim, I felt from the beginning that her priority was to get me on the right track. Ironic as it turned out because Deonna had worked for me in the late 80's in the office of our ribbon printer factory and I had to let her go at a time when she needed the stability of a steady job and income. It came at a time when we were downsizing the business which we ultimately closed a couple of years later, so it was no surprise. The irony of the situation was that Deonna was not happy with me then and carried a sort of silent grudge for a few years, and rightfully so. As time went by, Deonna's conversations with Joanna intermittently included a "how is Larry" question or two. And here she was coming to my rescue two decades later.

Cancer sometimes has a way of bridging all sorts of gaps in peoples' lives. To my thinking, it's because of the slow and persistent chronology of the disease, no matter what type of cancer someone may have. First, there is a sign or signal, immediately and for far too long, the denial, then the discovery, then the diagnosis, then the planning stage of treatment, then the treatment itself, and then the recovery. And oh yes, then there is the worry for the rest of your life, no matter how many months or years or perhaps only days it takes to pass on to the hereafter. Deonna knows all about that because she has lived around cancer since she was a freshman in high school. That was the year her mother died of breast cancer back in the dark ages of treatment for that disease. Then she had to relive those nightmares and watch as her older sister died of melanoma some years later. And as fate would have it, Deonna would have to endure uterine cancer in her own all too recent past....and survived. She knew all too well what I was facing and what someone the likes of Tom Haas would bring to my stable of rescuers. This turning point in my life, the relationship that was forged between my mentor, Tom Haas, and me, was another early brick in the foundation of the positive and enriching outlook that came with my cancer fight.

As September 30th, 2013, the date of my first chemo treatment and a few days before Day One of radiation "therapy" approached, I found myself grasping for anything to hold onto internally. Outwardly I was okay. It was inside down into my gut where the turmoil had erupted. To those who will experience cancer, as a patient, or a caregiver, or just as a friend to someone afflicted, this story of the nuts and bolts of my battle with my cancer peering through the lens of the friendships that developed, over those tortuous weeks and months, revolved around the core relationships between me, Joanna, and Tom Haas. You will get a glimpse deep into the souls of three people and our quest to wage these hideous crawl-through-broken-glass battles that left scars both psychologically and physically that will always be with us. There will be stories and conversations that you may not believe could ever happen. But you will learn to trust what you think could not ever happen to a person's body because Tom Haas said it was so. I know of no better way to tell this story than with the help of my friend whose

41

diligence and faithfulness were not to be denied. His pedestal is erected right next to Bob Theiman's in my own personal Hall of Fame. There is no finer man on the face of this earth, as you will discover. And so, on September 27th, 2013 I wrote an email to Tom Haas, a man I had never met…a man I will never forget.

Friday, September 27
Mornin' Tom. It seems as though my dear wife, Joanna, and your bud-
dy, Deonna, have cooked up this scheme to get you and me talking about
Squamous Cell Carcinoma. I am scheduled for first treatments (both Chemo
and Radiation) this coming Monday. Since I'm the one busting in on your
day, when you get a couple of minutes, just give me a call. I know Deonna
Riley has mentioned my plight to you, and I totally understand why you
have not reached out to me. I have a hunch you know exactly where I have
been for the past few weeks. If you are so inclined to get in touch with me,
I'll look forward to speaking with you. L-Dog

To simply imply that the above email was another turning point in my life isn't entirely true. It was THE turning point in my life, even after 67 years, Marine Corps, Viet Nam, several jobs working for the man, four marriages, and owning and running three companies. This man, at age 64 and all 265 pounds of him, had suffered through Stage 4 tongue cancer, multiple surgeries to remove dead areas in his throat, 10 brutal weeks of chemotherapy and radiation (a full three weeks more of chemo and FIFTEEN EXTRA RADIATION PROCEDURES than I would have), and, who, in the beginning of his ordeal had no idea really what the future had in store for him and his cancer. Stage 4 carcinoma is one breath away from the dreaded phrase, "you need to get your affairs in order".

In most cases, by the time the condition had reached stage 4 it was for one of two reasons: either the disease had been so dastardly as to hide while it raged through your body; or more than likely, it was that you had ignored the signals and lead yourself to believe that it was nothing to worry about because "it" (whatever "it" was) would go away of its own accord. The latter reason caused Tom's ordeal. Oh, he worried like crazy about it. Too busy to let it interfere with his work habits or too scary to bother his wife, Linda, about it; or, maybe he was too confident that his body could overcome whatever it was, Tom simply did not heed any of the warning signs. If I had known about that denial beforehand, I'm not sure I would have fired off the first word to him, wondering what kind of advice I could trust a person who neglected to recognize the signals and answer the call of distress his own body was sending him. Ultimately, I realized it was I who benefitted from Tom running right through those red lights and turning a deaf ear to all the sirens.

He was always, at least one step ahead of me.

Tom was one year and three months removed from his last day of treatment, so by my way of thinking, he was well on his way to normalcy. I thought looking from his perspective would be all positive input and sugar coated advice amidst an air of invincibility toward a happy ending. And so at first, my mind failed to grasp the gravity of what his experience would add to my attitude toward treatment and an ultimate end, whatever that may have turned out to be. Add to that, all of this advice about my cancer was news to me at the beginning stages of our friendship. Doctors had given me hope, but not advice, since that information was not based on fact for the most part. And my docs dealt strictly in facts, not wanting to let individual cases and personalities interfere with their job at hand. Tom also dealt in cold, hard facts. And that made Tom Haas another part of my team of experts.

As it turned out, he became the expert who I relied upon most of all.

CHAPTER 6

THE MASK

The second week of September, two weeks before my 67th birthday, I visited Coastal Carolina Radiation Oncology for the first time. It would become the building I would enter every weekday for seven weeks starting October 6th, 2013. I had not even surfed the internet to research the mask because I just never gave it a thought. The mask was destined to become the most unwelcome addition to my various treatments. I can't tell you how much it sucked having to wear that mask.

In reality, it wasn't even a mask. When you have the type and location of cancer (in my case on the far left side of the very end of my tongue) in the head and neck area, the massive doses of precisely aimed radiation are shielded from the rest of that vital area. The mask deflects or absorbs anything that is even minutely off target due to the person under the mask moving, or in most cases, just breathing. The radiation that is supposed to find its precise mark is in direct correlation to the tiny grids in the mask, how they are lined up on the table where you lay your head, and in what the exact position is that your mask pins your head down on that table. I would describe it as a full face vise made of a hard plastic-like substance fashioned in the shape of your face including nose, ears, and most definitely your lips. An immediate reaction was for me to think the texture was like a tightly knit waffle.

The mask started out looking like a rigid plastic flat sheet about 16-18 inches square. The size varied according to the size of your face from scalp to Adam's apple and from behind each ear. The consistency at that point caused me to think of it as a fencing mask, with what looked like a thousand small oval holes throughout the sheet. The technicians measured and called out numbers as I lay there on the stainless steel X-Ray table, "A-6," "C-7," "94" and then they were gone for a few seconds. When the three 40-something techs returned each of them had hold of the plastic sheet, and it was dripping wet with what turned out to be water. As transparently as possible, they positioned the sheet of what now looked like they had cut out a big square from an expensive rattan rocking chair with a lighter shade of flesh-colored bamboo. In an instant, all three techs pushed down gently, hitting my nose first and then plunging all the way until the sheet became a mask. Immediately, everything associated with my head and neck became restricted. I found breathing to be somewhat constricted, and movement in that area was impossible. I felt like I was being buried alive. A strangulation was in progress.

In the final analysis, my guess was that someone who had the exact shape of my face had stumbled, launching themselves face first, slamming into the back of that rattan chair. The techs took that profile and added a flat sky blue horseshoe around its outer edges consisting of very hard plastic which came in two identical pieces. The edges of the mask slid in between the two horseshoes like a sliver of cheese on a ham and cheese sandwich. Pressed together, the blue edging became the basis of the mask, not allowing for any expansion or contraction, shifting from right to left or up and down, or any possible deviation from where it was and where it would always be.

The numbers they had yelled out written on the face of the horseshoe, along with my name, birthdate, and the word "mouthpiece" (to remind them to give me my mouthpiece before each session of radiation). I didn't think a whole lot about it being a big deal for me to handle, even after seeing the finished product staring right back at me. HA! The mask was a colossal deal...the next day I invited Dr. Steve Edgerton onto the team. Aside from being nationally recognized for his advancement in the country's dental community, Steve Edgerton was a happy guy. And so, then, were you in that chair in his office in Wilmington, North Carolina. You could give him a load of crap, and he would laugh and give it right back. I had liked him instantly. The office was adorned with all the latest machines, gadgets, tools, and lights all of which was ultimately pieced together with, as my dad used to say, "smoke and mirrors," to enable Dr. Steve to work his magic.

Of all the parts of my body that were going to be ravaged by chemicals and radiation, the most vulnerable of my facial area during the radiation period was my teeth. Warnings from all the docs about the softening of enamel and the general decline of the foundation of my teeth in the back of the mouth were voiced each time I had an office appointment. It seemed so far off in the distance, early on I paid little attention to the precautionary announcements by non-dentists. And yet, I came to think of it as a rallying point, just one more thought that they expected me to survive, at least long enough until my teeth fell out! The mask was designed to preclude any radiation from entering the teeth and so, as an extra cautionary measure, the "mouthpiece" was cast.

The result was a standard mouthpiece, upper and lower, set inside a metal frame, all which eventually slipped over the top and bottom rows of my teeth each time I laid down on the radiation table. It seemed like a good idea to me. This process took three trips to Dr. Steve's office, all for about an hour. He and his techs had made this device with all the newest of technology, knowing my teeth needed all the protection we could muster. I went to check out, and I heard, "No charge, Larry," Mary said, "You just take care". Some months later, my very first restaurant meal was with Steve, his wife Martha, and Joanna at Blue Water Grill at Wrightsville Beach.

To cancer survivors, phrases like "my first restaurant meal" depict post-treatment moments in time which are based on the next day after the last day of all treatments of the various therapies. That date becomes the "after" while the day at the time of diagnosis stands as the "before". Life as I know it ended when Dr. Jim Wortman whispered, "you have cancer".

Life began anew the day I received my diploma for reaching the end of radiation. As far as I was concerned I was cured. Didn't matter that I did not know anything of the sort because my life had started over and I was so unbelievably relieved to be where I was. I was alive.

The mask and the mouthpiece, as innocuous as they sound, became the single most hated pieces of apparatus that I had to endure. Looking at both of them separately you wouldn't think they could wreak such havoc. Together, they posed significant problems for me every day for seven weeks. There was. However, a foreboding feeling creeping into my soul at that point and I know it was hastened every time I looked at that mask. I sensed that my radiation/dental team was gearing up for an onslaught on my body from the neck up. I never let it show as anything more than a worry; but inside, I became haunted by the mask. It was a huge contributor to the darkness slowly enveloping me. I was a creepy-looking L-Dog staring right back at me in a mirror. Early on, a twinge of doubt streaked through my veins and vanished as quickly as it came. Then the doubt began to show up weekly, daily, then minute-by-minute with each trip to radiation oncology and the ensuing 8-10 minutes listening to the hovering equipment pour radiation into and around those areas on my neck and face. Though for the most part, I could not feel the radiation being applied, sometime in the second week of treatment I for sure knew what damage it was doing to the tissue, muscle, tendons, bones, and organs. The pain, once just a nuisance, became unbearable, calmed only by doses of oxycodone and Tylenol. Each day brought more radiation and more pain. I would look in the mirror and see my face becoming more hallowed out and my skin color turning pale, except for the crusty dark brown skin on the left side of my neck - evidence of the excruciating pain rendering it impossible for even the most menial tasks of swallowing mucous and what little saliva I had left. I took solace in the hope that the metal upper and lower mouth guards were state-of-the-art, thereby shielding my teeth from the same death rays that were permeating the soft tissue areas of my mouth and throat. The fear of wondering whether the mask truly was the answer to deflecting any radiation from my eyes, nose, ears, and even my brain was unrelenting as I lay there listening to blaring hard rock music seemingly in tune with what sounded like thick glass edges rubbing against metal. I came to rely on my pills to get me through those rounds of fears, too. Numbing the pain became a secondary reason to pop a pill or two, as time slowly moved on and brought me into a nether-land of carefree consciousness. But behind that nirvana, a storm was brewing of epic proportions, the likes of which never crossed my mind until it was too late. The mask provided cover for radiation, and yet the sheer bizarre and heinous look of the apparatus merely added to the macabre' feeling of darkness and horror.

In Viet Nam, I had my helmet. Now I only had rigid plastic mesh. And of course, I had my drugs adding to the insulation from the reality that parts of my body were being destroyed not only by massive doses of radiation but also the poison of the chemicals administered each Monday morning at chemotherapy. On those Mondays that I would forget to take my pills before the eight a.m. radiation therapy and enter the world of chemical oncology an hour later, I would beg for a shot of morphine just to keep the wolves of biting pain at bay. The nurses would inject the juice directly into the port in my upper left arm, and I could feel and taste the rush of painkiller over my teeth, instantly absorbing and bringing what had become normalcy in my life right back where I needed it to be. The pain would build over time...relief was instant.

All I could think was how lucky I was to have those drugs.

CHAPTER 7
OUR DAUGHTER TAYLEIGH

I have started to write about Tayleigh a number of times and simply failed to capture the relationship I have with my daughter. I hope I get it right this time...

You will learn in chapter 10 about the kidnapping of our little girl during our honeymoon.

To this day I see nothing on Tayleigh's face nor anything in her heart that reminds me of that incident. That goes to her inner strength anchored by her relationship with God, and her innocence which displays acceptance into her world.

When we moved to Wilmington in 1993, Tay was a second grader. What she wanted more than anything was to be accepted as a southern girl. Her splendid teacher, Mrs. Morris Jackson, was a charter member of the Tarheel fan club and many of her musings outside book learnin' were of Tarheel lore. Tayleigh loved Mrs. Jackson. Joanna's mother was the victim of a drunk driver when Tayleigh was 6 months old, and shortly thereafter she lost her other mamau to divorce. Enter Mrs. Jackson...she did just fine. "Mommy. I wanna be a Tarheel!" burst out of her little voice just after school one day. After a brief silence, "Mommy, what's a Tarheel?"

Tay was a killer tennis player and travelled all over North and South Carolina on the junior circuit. Of course I got thrown out of several tournaments for going crazy over line calls going the other way. She was a lefty and it gave her an edge in doubles. During one match, her opponent was obviously cheating on line calls. The whole gallery was pissed about it. Tayleigh had just about as much as she could stand and approached the net, down 5-1. She bounced her racquet on the net cord and looked Jessica right in the eye and told her to stop cheating. "I'm not going to take it anymore", she said. She walked back to the baseline and proceeded to reel off 6 straight games, to the delight of everyone in the stands. It wasn't so much as the win. To Tayleigh it was always about being fair. And to win, of course.

We were in the old St. Mary's gym one Saturday morning watching 14-16 year old girls play basketball. As the tallest member of the team, a great team I might add, she was always in the middle...of everything. She begged the coach to allow her to bring the ball up and over the hlf court line. She ran the court like a gazelle gliding over the flatboards. This particular morning the crowd in the stands was raucous and it was a great game. The ref blew a whistle and completely missed a call. It was as if God himself, right there in the St. Mary's gym, silenced the crowd...

...just as I shouted out, "Ref, you suck!"

The small boy two rows down turned around and totally shamed me with his gasp. But it was too late; the ref knew it was me and banished me to the stairway on the side of the building.

Not sure what I taught Tayleigh that Saturday morning in the St. Mary's gym, but I remember it being a relatively big deal around our house for a few days. I remember staying out of the line of fire.

I received a call from my daughter on May 28, 2004 inviting me to lunch, an invitation I gladly accepted. For her to call me, her stepfather, on her birthday, melted my heart. As we were guided to our table, I noticed a large white envelope held closely in her hand. And just like her mama, she couldn't wait to divulge the contents of the envelope. I mean, our sweet tea hadn't even been ordered yet! Tayleigh produced the envelope and ceremoniously slid it slowly over to my side of the table. I noticed a very professional manner about her during all of this, but all that faded away when I opened the envelope, saw a very official declaration sealed by the NC Secretary of State and read the proclamation that Tayleigh Ashton Long was now Tayleigh Ashton Davis. On her first day as an adult in the State of North Carolina, she thought of me. A stepfather no more...I was officially her dad. Once again one of my children had presented me with another of the sweetest moments of my life.

Later that evening Joanna relayed the story about how Tayleigh and she had met with an attorney 3 months earlier to start the process. The part I like best about that story was how Joanna described Tayleigh opening her checkbook and paying the $350.00 fee, holding onto that check with reluctance to let it escape her grasp.

Though Tayleigh was accepted at most of the schools she wanted to attend, Chapel Hill was not among them. So her allegiance to the Tarheels switched to the Pirates of East Carolina University in Greenville NC. She received a partial scholarship to run track and cross country, having excelled in long distance racing at Hoggard High School in Wilmington. Through our daughter, we became members of Pirate Nation, became close friends with the legendary basketball coach of Ralph Sampson, Coach Terry Holland, who at this time was the Athletic Director at ECU, and were privileged to blend into Division One athletics all over the eastern part of the US.

Tayleigh majored in Communications to train her for a lifelong dream of becoming a television news anchor. She minored in International Studies and spent nine months studying at the University of Wroclaw, Poland. When asked why she chose Poland for her role in the college exchange program, Tayleigh said that kids from Poland never got a chance to study in the US because no one ever wanted to go to that part of Europe. Once again, that was her idea of giving back. Though Joanna was sick with uncertainty, she knew Tayleigh would not be denied, and so early in her junior year, Tayleigh made the trip. That decision broadened her horizons and taught her how fortunate she was to live where we do. While she was in Poland, and during our only visit to her in Europe, we all travelled to Warsaw where Tayleigh set up her camera in the lobby of our hotel and interviewed the U.S. Ambassador to Poland, the Honorable Victor H. Ashe, the former roommate of George W. Bush at Yale.

After graduating with honors from ECU, Tayleigh landed her first TV reporter position at WMBF in Myrtle Beach SC. People starting out in the news business are hired by contract for two years. From there she landed the lead reporter and weekend anchor position at WALB in Albany GA. In October, 2012, Tayleigh was hired by her first "Top 50" station, NBC12 in Richmond VA, where she currently resides. Burned out by the long hours, weekend shifts, and countless violent reports, Tayleigh now is an account executive with Allergan Pharmacueticals.

My love for her mother has been enhanced by my relationship with this beautiful person who became my daughter at the young age of seven, and then again at eighteen. At her mother's insistence, I became a true father, active and entrenched in the life of one of God's greatest gifts to me. Tayleigh helped me become a better father to her brother, Steve, by embracing my quest to make my last foray into parenthood a segment of my life that is beyond happiness. Whatever frailties plagued me as a parent prior to 1989 when Tayleigh entered my life are long since forgotten.

CHAPTER 8

INNAUGURATION

J oanna had allowed herself a small celebration when I finally called Tom Haas. She had been nearing the end of her already frayed rope trying to get me to realize how much Tom could mean to both of us individually and collectively. All of my other close friends were at this point keeping their distance, mainly out of respect for our privacy, but also because of the uncertainty of our situation. She heard, "How's he feeling?" so many times from those who meant well, but the question began to weigh on her because she truthfully did not know the answer. So to get me on board with Tom Haas was truly, she thought, a blessing from above. She was so kind to me those weeks in September trying to balance her feelings of despair caused by the unknown and her search for outlets of sheer fear. Deonna's preaching about her buddy Tom in Orlando gave her hope that someone other than she would hear the questions we both would have about our plight, and this guy would have the answers she could not possibly have.

After the real estate boom in the mid-2000's, she was totally burned out. She had toiled relentlessly for over 250 straight days and nights without so much as one day's break. The onslaught of real estate sales, new homes being built, supervising our new construction and move in, deals won and lost, and the never ending psychological counseling of clients took its toll to the point where she finally gave into the pressure and took a sabbatical in 2009. Along the way, for a chunk of 19 hectic months, Joanna had become the top new agent for the top company in the region with over $31 million in sales. The three years following this triumphant return to real estate since her days in Dayton Ohio with Coldwell Banker, she had built her physical and mental state back up to the point where once again she could qualify to run in the Boston Marathon, her second trip to those hallowed 26.2 miles of torture. Ultimately, her 15 marathons and countless half-marathons became a rallying point for her self-esteem as an athlete equal to her professional career.

Our youngest daughter, Tayleigh had matriculated through East Carolina University from 2004 through 2008, with an 8-month stint as an exchange student at the University of Wroclaw in southwestern Poland. If there ever was a mother/daughter relationship so close as this one throughout the years, I have yet to find one. So to say that Joanna was an intense and fiercely competitive woman is vastly understating the zeal with which she attacked every challenge.

Tayleigh's moves to Myrtle Beach, Richmond, and Albany, Georgia to chase her professional dream of becoming a television news reporter necessitated many long drives to help facilitate geographical moves and to gather hugs along the road to her successes. Joanna demonstrated through those years a non-stop quest for excellence while giving me the fruits of a love affair that were both innocent and exciting.

Now, after a couple of years of being able to sleep for a little later and have breakfast with her work-at-home husband, have a gym membership to work out with her buddies, and practice her lifelong love for landscaping, she once again found herself at the beginning of possibly a horrible new chapter in her life with me.

Though her insistence that I contact Tom Haas in Orlando was never mean-spirited or heavy handed, I could tell how much it would mean to her for me to call him, at least once. And when I told her that I did send an email to him asking for him to call me, she realized that help had arrived.

Friday, September 27, 2012
Mornin' Tom. It seems as though my dear wife, Joanna, and your buddy, Deonna Riley, have cooked up this scheme to get you and me talking about Squamous Cell Carcinoma. I am scheduled for first treatment (both Chemo and Radiation) this coming Monday. Since I'm the one busting in on your day, when you get a couple of minutes, just give me a call. 910-xxx-xxxx
*   Larry Davis, Wilmington NC (L-Dog)*

Tom Haas returned my call the evening of September 29th, and I liked him instantly. A new team had been formed; and, the dynamics created by this wonderful man would carry all of us out of an abyss and into an arena filled with startling reality, shocking photos of his plight, warnings and admonishments, and also shining a light and abundant hope. Suffice it to say, Tom pulled no punches whether the news was positive or negative. He knew that was what we needed from him, and his portrayal of our mentor was as important and any doctor, nurse, or caregiver.

By the end of my protocol in November, I loved Tom Haas as if he were my blood brother. He was a mentor, a motivator, a guardian angel, a prognosticator, a coach, a cheerleader, a pastor, and above all a friend like no other I had known since Bob Thieman. He massaged me, yelled at me, consoled me, chewed me out, warned me, gave me solace, beat on me, applauded, cried, cussed, and prayed for months, all the while he was fighting his demons, a mere 15 months' out from his battle. Through me, Tom would re-live all the excruciating moments of treatment that he had endured. Through him, I became his alter-ego, from confidence in my own strengths to a realization that I wasn't nearly as tough as I thought I was, to desperation when there was nowhere else to turn. As time went on my transformation from believer of miracles to non-believer to a believer again was just one of the battles I would fight.

Tom made sure that I knew he was a fighter and above all, a realist. In the end, in so many ways, I became Tom Haas…and what a blessing it was.

Monday, September 30ᵗʰ Innauguration
At 9 o'clock a.m. I walked into the Chemo Therapy Lounge, Kindle in hand, complete with earphones and reading glasses, nervous but confident. After all, I had turned 67 five days before that. I guess when you reach that age you certainly should know your own limitations of fear and joy. I had my port on the inside of my left arm, so I figured there would be no other needles sticking into me today. I had been advised to get the port, a device which had a pad on the end of it with a small tube protruding out about an inch or so. Needles could be inserted into the port to administer any liquid needed such as chemotherapy poison, saline for fluids, or morphine for pain.

As I scanned over the 30 or so brown leather recliners spaced out in six rows of 5, I saw no faces of apprehension or fear. Of the dozen blanketed patients, their ages ran from mid-teens to mid-eighties, male and female; and, etched on their faces were their own private reactions to the chemicals. Each person seemed to be dealing with their treatment in their own unique ways. The young woman furthest from me was sleeping on her side, either at peace or upon resignation, something I never figured out during any of my 20 hours of chemotherapy over the next seven weeks. It was so difficult to tell what stage in treatment they were, of course what cancer they had, what their prognosis was, or even how they were feeling, once the drip began flowing poison into their veins, the drops of liquid hanging in mid-air for what seemed like an eternity before they would fall into the reservoir. For those minutes and hours, their eyes were affixed intermittently on those clear plastic hanging bags as they marched on, emptying themselves into veins and bodies wanting the cure but not the damage each drop would concurrently wreak. At that time, we were all equal, and it did not matter where we were in life. Imaginary walls surrounded our recliners as thoughts of doubt and hopes of recovery passed over us.

Three people were waiting for me as I arrived. The first was the receptionist, Judy, who celebrated her last day of work on the same day as when I walked out of the chemo room for the last time, some six weeks later. The hematology nurse would collect me from the waiting area and take me back to the examining room. And Dr. Ken Kotz, my oncologist, would sit down at his computer with me each Monday morning.

I had spent about 10 minutes in the waiting area of Cape Fear Cancer Specialists before being summoned by the phlebotomist for the weekly drawing of blood. There was a chill in the air as summer had faded into fall on the coast. I had been warned that the chemo room was cool, bordering on cold so I had worn a long sleeved shirt and a jacket each which had to come off so that she could draw the four tubes of blood. These tests became an insistent barometer for how my body was handling the chemotherapy; "normal numbers" became a moving target as the weeks went on. Blood counts became important first as a weekly guideline and, ultimately near the end of chemo, burning flares of warning as the levels of chemicals increased week-by-week. As blood counts diminished into dangerous territory, the risk of infection became greater, and the normal defensive effort by a once strong body evolved into a distressed call for help. Even a flu bug could spell disaster. I spent another 15 minutes in the waiting room until a nurse came to take me back to the examining room, where I would come face-to-face for the first time with Dr. Ken Kotz. A handsome, 40-something, stocky 6-footer, Dr. Kotz wore his standard short sleeved blue or yellow-starched shirt with an understated yet perfectly suited tie as he entered the room. My immediate reaction to his handshake and verbal greeting was that this man was all business and no bullshit. I could tell after just a few words that Ken Kotz was cerebral, focused, and tuned into my plight already even though we had just met. At that point, the only thing he did not know about me was the results of my blood counts as this was the first day. We hit the ground running.

As Dr. Kotz scanned the information on the screen of the ever-present laptop, the room was eerily quiet for a few moments. I couldn't decide whether I was comfortable with him or not. That is until he turned to me and spoke in detail what was going on, what was about to go on, and oh just one other thing:

"I've looked at everything that has taken place so far. I agree with the results of your biopsies as diagnosed by Dr. Brinson". And then with perhaps the kindest eyes I have ever seen, Ken Kotz looked at me and said, "We can cure this." Remember, this from a man who did not go for BS when describing anything clinical. For having known this man for only a few minutes, I was not skeptical, just guarded, of his statement to me because I had not yet experienced anything but an hour-long run through on what maladies to expect from chemotherapy and what remedies they would have for whatever chemotherapy wrought on my body. But to hear those words spoken directly and succinctly to me simply blew up any misconceptions I had about physicians and their reluctance to verbalize a prediction. It wasn't "we will" but "we can". No guarantee of success. I understood that no doctor can guarantee. And it was so early in the whole protocol that I realized immediately that this was an opinion based on facts as he knew them right then. It was a statement which relied on statistics. Earned run average...yards gained per game...tee to green in regulation...

And yet there it was for the first time: "We can cure this." I knew I was in the right place. Praise God!

"I want you to understand that our goal here is to kill every cancer cell you have, but in doing so, we will kill many good cells along the way. That is why it is important for you to understand and be very cognizant of your blood counts as they will indicate how well your body is fighting back", Dr. Kotz explained.

Of course, I heard not much of that explanation because I had just realized that I had come from *You have cancer* to *We can cure this*. It made me wanting to fight whatever cancer was doing inside me, and never letting up no matter what the chemicals would do to me. Those four words profoundly affected how I viewed the horrifying side effects that cisplatin, my poison chemical mixture would extract from my body and ravage it like nothing I had ever experienced.

Ken Kotz became my buddy. The bond created by this great man who had a cornerstone of wisdom, an adhesive realm of calmness, and a sense of humor that allowed me to mess with him to the point where he would laugh as if the weight of the world was lifted off his shoulders even if just for that instant. I felt the excitement in his demeanor each time he would see me, which became every Monday for six weeks beginning that day. The way he tackled my illness made me believe his prognosis was spot on. When we had our sessions, I sensed Dr. Ken honestly thought we could cure my cancer. It seemed as though the heavy hand on many of his patients weighed a little less on me...someone who he could help... someone he could cure.

Weekly chemotherapy would begin at 9 o'clock and end a little after noon and would include a discussion with Dr. Kotz regarding my weekly blood readings and the disclosure and remedies for whatever new maladies ensued from the barrage of chemicals that would be running through my veins. Constipation, diarrhea, waves of nausea so powerful you would do anything to mitigate them, rashes, headaches, total loss of libido, loss of taste except for a metallic residue that never went away, a sense of smell that would turn hot apple pie aroma into a steaming landfill, you name it... if it was awful, you got it. The loss of a desire for sex was troubling in the beginning, mostly because I was married to the most beautiful woman I had ever seen, and for the first time in almost 25 years, I forgot what it was like to be intimate with Joanna. I say desire in the beginning because in about two weeks hence, it wouldn't have been physically possible, let alone psychologically.

Through the eyes of Dr. Kotz, I came to realize that kindness happens at the speed of lightening yet with a truly calming cool breeze in your face. Kindness is so soft that you don't feel it land on you. Your skin is involuntarily previous to it. Cancer nurses are moms and sisters who feel your anguish to their core, and then you start feeling their touch, their whisper. They personify kindness with their eyes and their touch. The sound of their voices is a persuading melody asking you to follow them down whatever road they travel. I never thought in those six weeks that I was anywhere but a wonderful place to kick cancer's ass. It's as they move around about 2-3 inches off the ground. Total respect for your privacy, even though most of the therapies were not private times. But they made you feel like it was private. So many kind miracle workers... an experience I likely won't see again in my lifetime. Cancer nurses understand how truly scared you are, somehow sensing your dependency on them at a time when fear of what is happening is surpassed only by fear of the unknown.

As a precaution, and to get the lab cooking the formula of chemicals prescribed just for me and my cancer, I checked in again just as I walked into the chemo lounge. I was ushered over to the chair of my choice and calmly sat down to await the nurse who would administer my first cocktail. That's when I met Good Golly Miss Molly. In her mid-40's, short brown hair, undoubtedly a sunscreen candidate, and with a face that immediately made me feel I was in the presence of an angel, Nurse Molly was all business, knowing that this was my first foray into the chemo lounge. She made sure the one-to-ten items on her list were carried out in the same order, with the same precision, after double and triple checking the entire protocol. It became apparent that she was in charge of about a half dozen of us, all in various time frames, each with our own specific protocol of treatment.

I had brought my Kindle with me along with glasses to read and an ear piece to listen to whatever I got into with the Kindle. Though I know I made it through several movies, to this day, I could not tell you any of the films I watched on my Kindle at any time during chemotherapy. Though I loved reading authors such as Lee Child (Jack Reacher), Vince Flynn (Iron Man Mitch Rapp), and David Baldacci (Oliver Stone), I found it increasingly difficult to deal with fiction as time went on. Everything and everyone in the chemo room was so incredibly real that Reacher, Rapp, and Stone became meaningless figments of my imagination. True stories of bravery, fear, excitement, pain, sadness, tragedy, and triumph, unfolded every Monday morning right before our eyes.

"Good morning, Mr. Davis, could I have your date of birth please?"

Molly was pushing around a Craftsman rolling tool chest, all silver and red, with labels on all of the drawers which contained the various and sundry items we would need to clean/then insert needles, and finally begin using the port for the first time. Of course, I had no idea what feelings I would have at that point, but I heard the glorious words, "Well, the port works just fine, and we are flowing." I had read online that about a third of ports either did not work as they were supposed to or simply stopped working at some time during the weekly sessions of chemotherapy. By the grace of God, I had started out on a positive note. Dr. James Harris, my general surgeon, had inserted the port a couple of weeks earlier. Having performed the needle biopsies and the removal of my lymph gland back in August, Dr. Harris had offered to get things started and insert the port. In the sterile room environment of his office, there was a sting of local anesthetic, the foreign feeling of a scalpel slicing into my skin, and then the pressure of something being pushed under that slit in my skin. It was not until the port was removed in mid- December that he showed me what had been installed. I thought it was the docking point for the chemo needles and was about the size of a half dollar. And indeed, it was. But that was at the end of a plastic tube which he ran all the way up my arm into my shoulder area, across my upper chest, and down into my chest cavity. Shuddering then as I saw how long the tube was, I was still feeling good that the port worked as advertised. For now, the port was my friend.

Then worry set in. It was one of seemingly an endless list of concerns that would not end for months.

There are a plethora of stories about chemotherapy and its side effects. I, myself, had heard many over the years. I guess what worried me the most was nausea that supposedly came with the chemical infusion. In retrospect, it seemed odd that my thoughts were more on throwing up than they were on the cure the chemicals would bring. Dr. Kotz had stressed both things: nausea and treatment. And yet I was inevitably more focused on what was going to happen tomorrow than I was with the rest of my life while experiencing chemo. If there is one thing I learned while going through my treatments, it was the adage made famous by Ray Croc at McDonalds, "duplication". Everything is administered in order, each step built on the previous one, and above all, take one day at a time. It would seem that I was already within the realm of a chemo veteran by the time the first 5 minutes of my inaugural chemotherapy session had ticked off.

There would be four bags of chemicals dumped into by body each time during the process of almost 2 and a half hours One large bag of saline solution would provide fluids which would help dehydration over the next few days. There were two smaller bags of glorious anti- nausea liquid, Zofran, that had been specifically discovered and produced at just these times in a person's life. And then there was the semi-trailer sized bag of Cisplatin, the cancer killer. I gazed at all these bags hanging there on the rolling coat hanger and postulated that the scale of the bags should have been reversed and that the anti-nausea drugs didn't stand a chance if I were basing my calculations on sheer volume. It looked as though the amber liquid in the chemo bag could fill up the underground gas tanks at Costco. Just to look at the color made me think of weed killer. Suffice it to say it was not a pretty sight.

Molly expressed her happiness with the operation of the port as she inserted the first needle, the one with Zofran. And the first drop of liquid followed an instant after I heard the plastic clip release of clamp on the tube. At that moment, I realized this was no fairy tale. I had cancer, and today, right then, my life was in the balance. My first thought after that leaped to Joanna and how much I missed her by my side where she had been for 24 years, just as I had been for her. And that was it, wasn't it? Would I be there for her for years to come?

It was as if Molly had read my mind. She said, "You're going to be just fine. Don't worry about anything."

And for some strange reason, my anxiety ceased. I turned to my Kindle, downloaded a movie, and became lost in a protocol that I would come to despise and then count as a great blessing. The Chemo Lounge was now a regular part of my life, and I truly felt a sense of calmness now that everything I had waited for with hesitant anticipation for six weeks had finally come full circle. I was in cancer treatment, and I was under the expert care of Good Golly Miss Molly.

As the weeks dragged on, I came to view this time at the cancer center as a quiet time. One of reflection on days passed as well as a somewhat foggy look forward. My Kindle was great for the first couple of weeks, but soon I realized that I wanted to get all I could out of the rest of my life, starting right then and there. Though I never came to know any other patient's name, some of their stories became known to me through conversation they openly discussed with the nurses and their visitors. I studied the new patients and smiled as proclamations came forth when a patient was finally through their entire chemotherapy ordeal. Several times over those seven weeks I noticed a visitor or two arrive and stay only a few moments amidst a broad collective smile from all the nurses and receptionists. These were survivors, returning to the hugs and good wishes of the angels who had once guided them through the endless hours of dripping bags. I think it lifted the spirits of everyone in the room and is a process I prayed that God would afford me the opportunities to give back.

"I'm good"' I replied to Molly. And then I lied, "I'm not worried".

The protocol which guided me through my cancer experience was a well-coordinated effort by the Chemo Lounge facility and the Death Ray Chamber, AKA Coastal Radiation Oncology. Since both facilities were in the same general proximity of the city, the two offices set up my treatment schedules so that I would not have to return home between appointments. On this day, however, there would be no radiation treatment as they were still setting up their strategic radiation locations. I gave Nurse Molly a huge hug, thanked her for everything, and drove the 15 minutes across town to home.

Tuesday, October 1st

As I sat on the edge of my bed this morning, I realized there didn't seem to be anything different with me physically. And mentally I was in control of my emotions. I experienced no side effects with the possible exception of a light feeling of euphoria. Much later in the protocol, I came to understand that a bag of fluids, at any time, is going to elicit a "thank you" from my body. My body loved the consumption of fluids in any capacity and by any means.

Concurrently, it also enjoyed riding the foreign chemicals from the nooks and crannies where they were summarily destroying cells, both bad ones and good. I noticed bathroom breaks were on the rise. I had counted on the anti-nausea drug, Zofran, to work as advertised and forestall any stomach issues. Meals that day consisted of standard food for me and my time was as normal as it could be. There was no doubt in my mind that the first chemo treatment was not going to affect me.

At that point I was still working a full day at Perfect Network, the company started by Joanna and me when we closed our ribbon printer factory In Middletown. Though working from my home office accounted for about 90% of my work routine, I still at that point made regular visits to Orangeburg SC, Warsaw NC, and Davidson County NC where the finest customers in the world were located. Though the accounts in these areas had been part of Perfect Network for more than two decades, you would expect a fairly significant turnover in personnel. And yet, in the case of my customers, the vast majority of people continued to exist in my professional life.

I had made a decision early on not to say anything about my cancer to them, and to conduct business as usual as far as they were concerned. In the beginning, the reason for this secrecy was to make sure they did not worry about the fulfillment of their needs for laser toner, the point of sale ribbons, and other office consumables. However, after so many visits over the years, these wonderful customers had become trusted friends. As time went on and my strength and resolve had waned, I came to tell them the truth about the situation. But not before I had proved to myself that I could take care of their needs as I always had. That resolve was just another rallying point of normalcy that I relied upon to keep my sanity. In the end, and as you will read, the character of their friendship validated everything I already knew about them. They gave me hope, prayers, and laughter, just as they always had done. I was good.

Wednesday, October 2nd

As usual, I was up around 7, collecting the cats, cleaning litter boxes, filling little cat food bowls, and opening Perfect Network for business. I was actually looking forward to getting my radiation treatments started, especially after the first chemo treatment went so well. I took a different route across town just to see what traffic was like at 7:30 AM on weekdays, because I wanted to discover the most expedient ways to and from the hospital area just in case there was ever an emergency. This was Day One of radiation hell.

"Lawrence Davis?" was the call from the opened door. After a brief stay in the staging area, where patients of many different cancers sat waiting for treatment, I was ushered back to the treatment room, past the second-story glassed area which housed the controls of the multi- tenacled radiation machine. A stainless steel table resembling one used for CATscan or MRI purposes was situated underneath. Lying there and looking up at the machine I mused that it looked like something out of Star Wars, but much scarier. I wondered how such a massive machine could possibly target a tiny area as my neck in its efforts to eliminate cancerous cells.

Pete was the lead tech and one of the best men I ever met. A youngish looking 30- something he never showed me anything but respect and friendship, as well as a resolve to help me beat my cancer. His first time instructions were explicit by kind, and occurred just an instant ahead of the questions running through my brain.

Suffocation and claustrophobia slapped me almost immediately after the mask snapped into place. The pressure on my lips was so severe that I felt as though there had to be small cuts running along the ridges. The teeth guards pressed up on the inside of my lips to the point of numbness almost immediately. My nose was enveloped inside the rigid mesh mask to the point where it became almost impossible to breathe through my nostrils. The sides of the mask pressed my ears hard into my head. Forget bobbing my Adam's apple if I dared swallow.

It was all too clear. For the next 8-10 minutes I was effectively going to remain motionless. Pete had told me that this procedure was painless and that I would never actually feel the radiation entering my body. This first time went smoothly, punctuated by the music of Blondie mixing with the metal on glass movements of the radiation machine. Radiation therapy had been performed on both sides of my neck. The first 18 sessions would be bilateral and the final 17 would be left side only directly on the primary cell. Within second the techs descended on my head, quickly unsnapping the mask and raising me up to a sitting position. Pete inquired, "How do you feel, Mr. Davis?"

"It's L-Dog, Pete. My friends call me L-Dog.

After a normal morning, I went to lunch with Joanna. Sometimes we look around the restaurant and see couples who, without a hint of communication going on between them, reminded us of what a blessing it was to have each other. Most times it is because one or both of them are on their phones, visiting Facebook or texting replies to incoming messages. Then there those couples who obviously don't have a lot to discuss with one another. Not so with Joanna and me. Today, of course, the conversation skirted around "how do you feel" and concentrated on our normal issues and plans. It was as if neither one of us wanted to fan the flames of uncertainty. Maybe we both were waiting hour by hour to see which one would win the battle, Cisplatin or Zofran. I had momentarily forgotten the powerful destructor that Cisplatin was and all the warnings about its aftereffects. Joanna had that effect on everyone who knew her.

Around mid-afternoon, on this the second day after the chemo treatment, I felt tired and decided to take a nap. Afternoon naps became another savior as time progressed. My favorite napping spot was the master bedroom, king sized, sleep number bed. I'm pretty sure that I realized early on that this place where so much love had been made, as George Strait said in Give It Away, would soon be off limits for me. From my chats with fellow radiation sponges, Ole Roy Lee in particular since he was five weeks ahead of me with the same cancer as mine was, I came to learn that the treatments would take a pretty severe toll on everything. There were two new homes under construction just outside my bedroom window. Just after eight every morning Monday through Saturday and sometimes on Sunday, hammers would smash against wood either by hand or by gun. Sawing commenced powered by a generator, and cement mixers had to be cleaned out by a significant noise and vigor. There in the afternoon, the sun would creep through the window, a cat or two would be resting silently on some part of the bed or somewhere close, and my worries and hurts would go away for 90 glorious minutes. The blanket coupled with the sunlight added to the promise of raising my body temperature which would serve as catalysts for instantly falling asleep. Those sounds eventually were the symphony which drew me to lie at 90 degrees on the bed with the window open and the sunbeam radiating warmth across a sleeping L-Dog. It brought me peace. I loved it.

91 minutes later was a different story...

CHAPTER 9

MENTORING

Dizzying. That's the only way to describe the nausea which consumed me just after setting my feet down on the floor after napping. In retrospect, it wasn't even close to REAL nausea which roared into my life one week later, but just then the feeling of helplessness was heaped upon me quite rudely. If you think about it, that's what nausea is. It renders you stunned as it naturally takes center stage and trumps every other activity you want to do. I thought, "what did it take, two and a half days?" I went from a conviction of whipping its ass to utter doubt that I would make it to supper time. My next thought was, "it's a good thing Paul and Big Dog took me out the past two weeks to fatten me up!" My normal weight was about 160 and those feasts of wings, ribs, burgers, barbeque, potatoes, donuts (only Krispy Kreme, of course), and ice cream and cake put about 6 extra pounds on my frame going into the protocol. I never in my life have known two men who could put away such enormous quantities of food, protesting all throughout that they were "as full as a tick" and yet continuing as if there were a conveyor belt of food on non-stop mode. They were my "food mentors, each with a Phd in consumption.

I felt light headed and had trouble putting one foot in front of the other for the first few seconds of being vertical. After throwing down a glass of Alka Seltzer, which seemed to put that worst at bay and allowed me to return to some sense of normalcy, my thought was that it wasn't as bad as I once believed. This was, as they say, a harbinger of things to come. That Wednesday afternoon in early October signaled to me that I wasn't going to be immune to nausea. Even so, I vowed to not ever throw up.

As was cancer's penchant for surprise, a creepy bloated feeling developed slowly into my stomach area. Wait a minute! Always searching answers for why I was not feeling normal, I realized that I hadn't had a "sit down" yet. That had to be the reason for the pain in my lower tract. Soon, I developed an uncharacteristic diminishing amount of saliva with an accompanying dull headache. This was indeed constipation but it was obviously much more than that. For the first time the panic of the list of things I had been warned about appeared and once again the worry crept into my thinking. And this was a big one. It was the beginning stages of a 24-hour freefall into what became full-fledged, knock you to your knees nausea.

During the orientation meeting at Dr. Kotz's oncology center a couple of weeks before, one of the first mantras was to "EAT". I should have known of course that eating would become an issue due to the nausea and the way it was described was exactly how I was feeling in the early hours of this day. Though not completely void of an appetite, I found the smells and tastes of breakfast to be of a foreign origin. I did manage to throw down some toast with butter and jelly, but the traditional breakfast of bacon, sausage, eggs, etc. was out of the question. There was no doubt that I was way more nauseous today than yesterday. During my first visit to Dr.

Neal's office at Coastal Carolina Radiation Oncology, the nurses had indicated that the majority of neck and throat cancer patients they treated had opted to install a feeding tube in their stomach. They however were telling me this from a totally different perspective, that of reluctance to eat solid food due to the soreness of the mouth and throat area caused by the massive doses of radiology, now scheduled to continue the following Monday and to continue each weekday for 7 straight weeks.

So my new hurdle was how to handle the absence of eating solid normal food in my new future. What with the mounting nausea causing my desire for food to diminish, I now had to factor in the "possibility" of not even being able to process food normally due to soreness caused by irritation as well as swelling of the tissue in my mouth and throat. The reality of what lie ahead for both Joanna and me began to swell with something more than just a *possibility* of a body numbing nausea coupled with a lack of solid food. Cancer was winning the war of attrition in my body and instead of the ability to fight back I was going in the opposite direction with no contribution of nutrients and a rejection of even the thought of food. It was a partnership of penalties cancer donated to my body and became another one of the huge life-changing experiences of my protocol. As the chemo flowed through my veins, my cancer, formerly on cruise control, was ramped up as if it were turbo charged.

Defining it correctly: going forward, my ability to consume food became the second most important component of the process of rousting the cancer from my body.

This was the continuation of constant chatter between Tom Haas in Orlando and me. In the beginning we were able to talk with each other which was so important. I could hear how is voice inflections portrayed the seriousness of certain situations, or how his emotions would get the best of him when memories got too vivid. Tom is a man of high integrity so when he spoke of what was to come I knew what to be on the lookout for. His mentoring of my cancer experience became almost a religious experience with his specific instructions on what to do if this or that were to happen. It became not too farfetched for me to believe that what was happening was akin to God talking to Moses. I'm not trying to be evangelical here. I want you to know that your mind will go to any lengths to legitimize any facet of assistance as if it were the gold bullion of advice.

At this point in the protocol, days and nights slowly became indistinguishable with the pain, the physiological changes as well as the psychological realignment becoming a constantly moving target. I had no idea what was in store for me other than it was not going to be anything good. What a great blessing it was to have those few actual conversations in the early stages of radiation because soon it would become impossible me to speak even the most simple of words. Neither Tom nor my docs ever warned me about my voice patterns. They did not know of course, because every person's cancer is different. Tom's was close, but not the same. He was way braver than I was. But I didn't need to be brave for too long.

My friend, oxycodone, was just around the corner.

Thursday, October 3, 2013
11:34 AM
Good morning, Tom. Evidently my first email must have gone into your junk mail back on the 27th. Just let me know you received this note and then I'll write further.

11:41 AM
This one worked. It looks like the first email was missing one of the "o's" in Woolpert! I have a board meeting that starts at noon today...but would be happy to give you a call this evening if that works. Just let me know.

6:16 PM
Hey Tom, I'm going out for a walk for about a half hour. Between 7:30 and 8:30 should work. It would be a pleasure to talk with you and pick

your brain. Finish the first of my 8 week saga tomorrow. I say 8 weeks because I didn't start my radiation therapy until yesterday. So far my only real hurdle is my lower digestive tract. My second round of chemo locked me up until yesterday. The first one was experimenting with the pain killers which are notoriously bad for constipation. They gave me a supply of 75 oxycodone pills. I have not discovered what works when yet on that front and fortunately I don't really need them for pain right now. Throat is beginning to thicken but so far has not posed a problem except I am starting to question the whole food thing. Nausea is one thing, but a raw throat is another. I know you know about all that. If tonight does not work, then tomorrow or the weekend is fine. I appreciate your help, Tom. L-Dog

Friday, October 4, 2013
8:18 AM
Sorry about last night. I had shut the ringer off on my phone during an all afternoon board meeting at work and forgot to turn it back on. Didn't realize I had incoming emails until I got to work this morning. I too suffered through the constipation saga for most of the first part of the treatment. I took an over the counter pill…I forgot the brand…but their ad was "it works gently overnight as you sleep". As the radiation burn started kicking in, my ability to eat diminished, so there wasn't too much to digest. Did you end up with the feeding tube?

Fortunately, I had 50 lbs of excess fat that had built up from sitting at the desk too much and not exercising. So my silver lining was getting rid of that fat over the course of my ordeal. I am 160 pounds soaking wet now, so not much to draw on there. Just starting taking the anti-nausea pill this morning (Compazine) and I do feel better now after an hour. So suggestion #1 is eat while you can and build up your strength and reserves as much as possible. Taking the walks is an excellent idea. I did the same thing for as long as I could.

Do you know what they are giving you for chemo? Cisplatin? Is your head strapped down in one of those plastic masks during radiation? I'm looking forward to talking today. Let me know some good times today. I'm just catching up on some paperwork and can take a break any time this morning, this afternoon or this evening.

Tom

Friday, October 4, 2013
9:22 AM
Anytime this morning, Tom. This afternoon will be radiation and then my normal Friday afternoon bar hopping...uhhhh, not really. Just starting taking the anti-nausea pill this morning (Compazine) and I do feel better now after an hour. The drug also used to treat schizophrenia which is a little unnerving.

Tom Haas and I talked at length that morning. We chatted about such scintillating subjects as constipation, swallowing everything from pills to steak with a swollen throat, various and sundry drugs, using marijuana in baked goods to combat nausea, prayer, and combinations various foods and beverages that he used to combat all sorts of digestive maladies. The mention of a feeding tube came up, and Tom told me that he never had one inserted into his stomach. He just refused to do it. As a result, ALL that man "ate" for months and months was chocolate milk and melted vanilla ice cream. Sometimes he would jazz his meals up and mix the two of them together.

Tom spoke of Linda, his wife of 35+ years, in terms which I could only describe as a powerful yearning to make up for things said while under extreme duress. I gleaned evidence that his struggle, in part due to ignoring early signs that something was wrong, in part due to his lack of use of pain killing drugs, but mostly due to cancer's hideous power grab over everything once sacred, was now fair game. Linda, he said, was an angel of such strength that she and she alone never let the love subside.

He reminisced about looking forward to the weekends even though the nausea was really at its peak on Friday mornings. He also eschewed as much pain medication as he could during those months because he needed to work through the entire ordeal. His job pretty much demanded it. His boss, who was the head guy told Tom that he could take as much time off as he needed, but for this man of such conviction, he simply gutted it out.

I asked Tom why he felt it was necessary to carry on with work. His answer created the most poignant thread within our relationship thus becoming the most common measure of character that I have used as a rallying point since that very day:

"My boss is a wonderful man, smart and dedicated to all of his employees. The only thing he lacks is the ability to organize and prioritize so that things get done in an orderly and timely fashion. We discovered early on that those were the attributes that I brought to the table, so it was a natural match for both of us. But that's only on the surface," Tom said. "The dedication to his employees and also to our clients is so unbelievably strong; it was imperative in my mind to do everything I could to match that quality myself. What he lacked in organization skills was more than eclipsed by his integrity. And, to me, that is the most important trait any human being could have. Through each other we became better men."

And as fate would have it, here Tom Haas was, passing that legacy on to me. It became another rallying point for me in defeating the enemy. I knew that if I never caved into the traps my cancer laid at my feet, I would be victorious. I knew that I had to be diligent in sustaining my relationship with Joanna so that if there were scars that developed, the integrity of our marriage would win out over my snippets of indecency toward her. That, of course, became easier said than done.

Friday, October 4, 2013
4:15 PM
Enjoy your weekend. 2 days with no trip to the radiation room was always a break that I looked forward to in later weeks. The nausea stuff they gave me was called Prochlorperazine.

That didn't work well, so they changed me to Ondansetron. That thing help'ed, but I still had the bad stomach feelings. I never did try the "special" cookies/brownies, but understand that it can help. I am going to check and see what else each of those meds used for commonly. Maybe they treated schizo too.

We sent the word out to the Haas family to get you on everyone's prayer line. It all helps to have as many folks pulling for you as possible.

Friday, October 4, 2013
7:46 PM
Yes, indeed it will be good not to get strapped in for a couple of days. I'm going to ask about Ondansetron tomorrow. The porch...really is not working much. I have two surrogate sons locally here who are 39 and 37 respectively. Both are professionals. One of them has some "vaporizer" that when filled with liquid THC lights up like a cigarette smoker's quitting tool and there is no smoke. I am talking to my oncologist Monday morning about that. Thanks so much, Tom. Like it or not, you have become my "go to" guy. I have a new friend in our neighborhood, ex-FBI, who had lymphoma (twice) but did not have radiation, so that is great to have someone close by, too. And the prayers are wonderful. The outpouring of affection and support has been way more than I ever imagined. It makes me want to fight through all of this BS. Hearing from you, Tom, is like music to my ears. Truth and the whole truth.

I sent Deonna a text yesterday thanking her for the intro. I sincerely hope that after this ordeal is over, you have made a friend for life. I think you're worth it, and that's what I live for.

Friendship and trust.

L-Dog

If you think about it, the entire human digestive system begins with the tongue and ends all the way at the other end. Simply because my cancer was at the base of my throat didn't preclude my lips, teeth, gums, throat, esophagus, stomach, small and large intestines, and rectum from damage. There was a point in my protocol that I went 13 straight days without a sit-down. Eventually after trying everything from poop pills to enemas I had success in that realm on the 14th day. Then 11 more days without another. Try that trick on for size.

Of course, the culprit in all of this was the pain medicine. At the end of the first week, I had run through half of the allotted 75 oxycodone pills. They, together with Tylenol, were my defense against an already raw mouth and throat. The narcotics not only kept the pain at bay, I found that they also provided welcome psychological relief. I did not dwell as much on what may come down the road and was able to live in the moment with a sort of refuge from the unknown. At first, I was concerned about the lack of regularity, but then I just figured that was just one event per day. The pain was an all-day constant. That outweighed any reason to limit the number of pain killers and after the first week I was up to about 8 pills a day.

My visit to the oncologist midway through the second week included his suggestion that I have my gastroenterologist, Dr. Joe Kittenger, install a feeding tube in my stomach. I knew about the apparatus and had earlier been shown one by Ole Roy Lee, a man I met in the waiting room who was about five weeks ahead of me enduring the same protocol. He lifted his shirt to show me his tube which dangled about 18 inches out of a small hole the size of a dime just north of his belly button. Roy Lee described in detail how it worked and why he chose to use it during his treatment. Having seen the tube which I can only describe as bizarre and scary looking, I decided right then and there that I was going to forego that little ditty. I was eating real food and certainly intended on continuing that. The radiation oncologist, Dr. Charles Neal, who was a soft-spoken and kindly gentleman about ten years younger than I, gave me a stern look and a warning just as stern about thinking twice before deciding not to install the tube.

Dr. Charles Neal was just like I hoped he would be. Slightly younger than I, soft hands with which to probe my neck, a kindness in his eyes which conveyed calming and hope, and the white coat with its signature crispness. His forcefulness on some issues conveyed a path toward a cure and this acknowledgement of each patient's special plight took no time at all to convince me that he was on my side. Me determination which was pointed at avoiding the feeding tube slowly dissolved into a questionable decision on my part. But I was still of the mindset to eschew the tube and run my own food show. As our visits continued throughout the weeks and months beyond inauguration day, I came to realize the tremendous toll radiation therapy would extract from my body. Concurrently I discovered the same hideous pounding Dr. Neal's psyche must have taken as he wended his way through a myriad of cancers on dozens of his patients. If my weekly time with Dr. Neal were mornings he would display the gleam in his eyes that told the story of a few hours of rest and evening time with his family and friends. During afternoon sessions I could plainly see the concern and utter resignation he had after visiting with patients in various stages of their treatments. People who began as normal human beings morphed into shadows of themselves as the therapy wore them down after weeks of radiation.

"I won't be needing a feeding tube," I triumphantly touted.

With that aforementioned foreboding stare, he said, "Oh yes you will". We left it at that and moved on.

"How are you doing with pain management so far?" Dr. Neal asked. I showed him the bottle which contained 30-some pills.

As the nurse showed me out of the examining room, she handed me a sheet of paper with another prescription for oxycodone. This time, it was for 100. It stopped me in my tracks. And I told myself, "They know something I don't know."

CHAPTER 10
CHEMO AND RADIATION

We live in a community of 86 villa homes about a mile from the Atlantic Ocean guarded by one of the most pristine beaches in North America, Wrightsville Beach. Joanna and I moved to Wilmington in the spring of 1993 having made one trip down from Cincinnati in 1992 and purchased a home under construction in another neighborhood which fed an excellent school system. Our daughter, Tayleigh, was in the second grade, so schools were certainly important. As is the case many times, Joanna and I made friends with the attorney who had closed our deal and filed the deed. But the vast majority of our early friends were parents of kids Tayleigh went to school with. We spent every dime we had on the house including an in-ground pool in the backyard which proved to be a catalyst for friendships for all three of us. Our other two children, Olivia and Steve, were in the third year of college at Ohio University and a senior in high school respectively. They had lived with us while we were in Ohio so living with only Tayleigh and Joanna was difficult for me at first. Better as time went on. So Tayleigh was indeed our main conduit into adult friendships.

About three weeks into the school year, I received a call about 10:30 one evening from Neal Musser, who came to be known as

"Big Dog". To this day these 22 years later I am the only person who calls him that, but it's so fitting. Big Dog played football for the Wolfpack at NC State and went on to play linebacker for the Atlanta Falcons in the early 80's. Eleven years my junior, Big picked me up in his truck and off we went to a spot he knew where we could see the Intracoastal Waterway flow by as we sipped a cold one. Big was a slow talkin' but assertive southern boy who had reached the pinnacle in the NFL only to fall prey to a career-ending knee injury. It was through Big Dog that I met his friend Paul Squires.

The first time I saw Paul was a weekday late night in 1993 when he had just come off "graveyard" shift at DuPont and according to Big Dog would be snoozing in his recliner watching TV through his eyelids. The sliding door on the porch was where Big and I stood and knocked on the door hoping to get Paul to wake up and play some gin rummy. Knocked as we would, there was no answer. So Big Dog, in all his eloquence turned to me and said, "He must be upstairs getting' him some. Let's go get us a donut and come back". I have laughed at those thousands of times. As it turned out, those two statements began my shift from being a Yankee to a southerner. I figured Big Dog's way was just to come out with it and not mince words.

We still go out a couple of times a month, Big, Paul, and me. We drink sissy drinks like Singapore Slings and Sex on the Beach, and every once in a while a Frozen Strawberry Daiquiri. Paul was taller than Big Dog, so I figured I was safe having those pink concoctions on the table. No one was going to mess with me with these two guys sitting with me. We went through every plateau of school, elementary, middle, high school, and even college with our three girls in the same grades. Most of the time that we went out it involved copious amounts of food and alcohol. I usually drove because they both had trucks and quite frankly I was the short ball hitter of the three. Even so, there were times I drove home when clearly I should not have. Early on, one of our nights out we decided to partake in a movie. It was Drop Zone with Wesley Snipes before he ran aground with the IRS. Entering the theater, I noticed that there truly was not another soul seated anywhere. So Paul went up the stairs. First, I was second and Big Dog third. When we got to the row that suited Paul, he slid over to the middle and sat down, and I sat next to him. Big continued to stand. Paul immediately moved one more seat over. So I move one seat over too. Big continued to stand. Paul got up and moved one over again and looked at me and said, "I ain't your wife so you don't have to sit so close." With that large dose of homophobia, Big Dog sat down one seat removed from me. When I told Joanna about that incident, we laughed so hard it hurt. These were men born and raised in the deep south. Another lesson learned for this Yankee.

Friendships of over 20 years are not uncommon; yet, close friendships are earned through years of respect for each other. They don't get close unless you have the trust. Big Dog and Paul became my trusted friends faster than anyone before them. I knew if I ever needed help in any way, they would come to my rescue and never ask why. Somehow, someway if I needed something, they would find a way to get it done. But sickness, real serious illnesses, are individually sacrosanct to southern men. When I learned of my cancer and told them that I needed to put some weight on because I was going to lose a lot of it, they jumped at the chance to fulfill that need. Sure, it was fun to go out. But this was entirely different. Paul and Big knew that once I began the fight, they would not see me for a long time. They didn't say that, but I had learned through the years that their method of grief was also very personal. Even though we loved each other as brothers, a man's cancer is his alone according to men raised in the south. They knew two things for sure: First, that I would become a mere shell of what they had known for over 20 years and would not want to see me that way; Second, that I would be the one who would pick up the phone when I needed them. Phone calls came early on and then tapered off when my throat became so swollen that I couldn't talk. They called every so often but knew it hurt me to talk. I didn't see them for a couple of months. Ordinarily some people would take offense to that. But after 20 years of friendship, and true to the unspoken truth, they knew that I would just as soon not have them see me in the state I had become either. They would worry about me, and I simply did not want that.

Monday, October 7, 2013: Second Chemo Treatment / Third day of radiation
Having spent the weekend experimenting with different foods that I could eat, planning a menu ahead so that I could have something prepared to eat when I felt like food would stay down, and wondering if a feeding tube should be considered. For one thing having surgery under anesthetic again was weighing heavy on my mind. Truly though it was a simple matter of hatred knowing that I might need this apparatus to function as a live human being.

Upon entering the oncology office, I picked the same chair in the waiting area that I had occupied the previous Monday. Oddly enough, I felt the need to do that with some conviction of good luck. Though I was not comfortable with what was about to happen, space, my space, in that room was sacred and therefore calming. Shortly I was ushered back into the phlebotomists' chambers where four tubes of precious blood were drawn. No words other than "good morning" were spoken. So many waiting, so many to follow throughout the day.

A short time after that, Elizabeth, the staging nurse walked me back to the digital scales, and I hoisted myself onto the platform and saw "158.7". I felt good about that and was buoyed by the fact that I was still very close to my normal mid-150's weight. Across the hall to the question and answer room: name, address, social security number, birth date, meds currently taking (Zofran for nausea, oxycodone for pain, Zocor for cholesterol, Ambien for sleep aid, Benazepril for blood pressure, and of course Cisplatin for cancer), allergies (clams, oysters, mussels, penicillin), questions about my bowel movements and let's take your blood pressure.

Of course, I lied about the bowel question. And then across the hall, we went to wait on Dr. Ken Kotz, my oncologist.

Our discussion this Monday, my second chemo adventure, centered on my blood readings just rendered seconds before he entered the room.

"Everything looks good. Only a slight drop in some of the vitals but nothing to be concerned about", Dr. Kotz mused. "How are you doing with the after effects of last Monday's treatment?"

"I had a little bit of touch and went on Wednesday, pretty nauseous on Thursday, no appetite at all on Friday but by Saturday at noon, I was back to normal," I replied.

"Excellent! Let's get you back to the chemo lounge and get you started so you can get out of here."

Today was my introduction to Nurse Betty. She instantly became my favorite. Around mid 40's, Nurse Betty was a Mom. She soothed any trepidations simply by patting me on the bald spot on my head and talking is a compassioned whisper. She went about the same procedure that Good Golly Miss Molly had, all the while extolling the virtues of ice cream and how it was the panacea for all negative issues chemotherapy would provoke. She asked where I lived and when I told her she named off all the places en route to my house that I could stop for ice cream. Dairy Queen was her favorite stop. Blizzards were her favorite treat. Especially one with peanut butter. That's where she lost me.

I was never much of an ice cream person. However, after cancer, I found that ice cream was one of the few foods that I could endure during and immediately after my protocol. To this day, DQ is my go-to ice cream establishment. Choco Cherry Luv, thank you very much.

After the two and a half hours of chemo, I drove the few blocks to radiation oncology for my third of 35 sessions of radiation. We did some planning for scheduling, and I had decided that I wanted radiation to happen as early as I could get it. After all, I was still dealing with the day-to- day grind of running Perfect Network, so getting everything out of the way early set me up for the rest of the day. Besides, who wants to sit around all day fretting about radiation??? So for the next 32 treatments, I was scheduled as the first patient every weekday. Pete, the chief radiation technician, popped his head through the door and yelled out "L-Dog!" and back we went.

I had remembered to wear a shirt with no collar so that the mask would fit properly. Pete fetched my mouth guards, and I snuggled my teeth into both of them until my lips resembled a fighter getting ready for the bell, all puffed out and totally ripe for abuse, helpless looking even without the mask, and exponentially more dependent with the mask pressed down on them as if there were a Mack truck on top of the mask. My eyebrows even hurt. My ears were pinned so close to my head that I thought they were per-manently affixed. The dimple on my chin became non existent as it melded into the rest of my jaw. I could feel the waffles etching themselves on my forehead. My Adam's apple was pressed into my voice box so hard all I could do to communicate was to use hand signals. They folded a warm blanket over the top of me for which I was forever grateful. Numbers and letters which meant nothing to me and everything to them were called out and repeated as if we were on a submarine preparing to dive. All done very quickly and efficiently.

Pete uttered the already famous words, "Raise your leg if you need us to stop. We will cease immediately and get you back on track. But try to remain still."

And then the next question I would hear 30-some more times, "Blondie or Huey Lewis?"

They never told me that I should not open my eyes. But when that machine began its 8-10 minute circumference around my head I never once opened them. Not one time. If there was anything I knew for sure about this process, which wasn't very much, there was lots of danger in what they were doing to me, evidenced by the rigidity of the position I was in. No movement, please!

Not even an eyelid as far as I was concerned.

Again I felt no pain as the equipment bobbed and weaved. I came to know exactly where it would go, how long it would dwell in an area, and what sounds I would hear. The music which should have been evident never made it to my ears. I was on a metallic island, stranded and pinned down so that I could not have moved if I wanted to. And on this the third day of radiation, I realized for the first time that I was never going to be the same.

CHAPTER 11
THE KIDNAPPING

Joanna and I celebrate two wedding anniversaries each year, one in February and another in October. In October of 1991, our inked ribbon manufacturing company, Wordata Inc. in Middletown Ohio, marked the move into its new 26,000 square foot facility with a gala grand opening. Vendors whose nylon fabric, printing ink, packaging products, molded plastic kits, and other items used to manufacture printer ribbons came from all regions of the states. Customers from Los Angeles to Boston and Seattle to Miami made their way to southwestern Ohio for the weekend festivities highlighted by our "Made in the USA" themed stage show on Saturday night. One couple from Oklahoma missed everything. They only surfaced for food. They appeared to be pretty worn out, but euphoric by the end of the weekend and had broad smiles on their faces as I dropped them off at the airport in Dayton for their return to OK City and their three small children. Their fourth child, a girl, was born about nine months later. They named her Middie, which was the mascot of Middletown High School. My sister, Madalyn had written and then rehearsed a review cast by our entire crew of forty men and women who worked our three shifts. One of the songs was Madonna's "Material Girl". Instead, Joanna sang "Raw Material Girl".

We ended the show singing to the background from Lee Greenwood's, "God Bless the USA". Criminal Defense Attorney Frank Schiavone rode in on his Harley as Neil Diamond was singing "Coming to America".

Of the 140 or so guests that were with us that night (including a young freshman in the U.S. House of Representatives named John Boehner), was a gentle giant by the name of Detective J. C. Christenoff. He was our guest of honor. J.C. was in his mid-40's, stood tall at about 6 foot 5 inches and weighed 260 pounds. When you got past the kindness of his eyes, you saw a massive set of shoulders with a chest of granite, am imposing figure if there ever was one. If you look at his name carefully and read this story that follows about how J.C. Christenoff was awarded such an honor, you would be in the same situation as our guests were, for they too knew not why he was there.

Joanna and I were married by the Mayor of the village of Waynesville, Ohio, which was located between Dayton and Cincinnati, in February of 1990 in a small Victorian chapel. The tiny multicolored chapel, barely able to hold 30 praying souls, sat quietly on a hill, hidden from the bustle of the downtown area at the north end of a city street and down a gravel lane bordered by neatly trimmed landscaping. It was out of a scene that could only have been painted by Joanna. There was just the two of us and Norm and Kelly Wagner, Joanna's longtime friends, and of course the Mayor, who was a delightful, soft-spoken, attractive woman in her early 40's. Waynesville was a small town known for their rows of antique shops and eateries that drew scores of bargain hunters throughout the year. It was horse country with farm fields full of corn stalks and soybean rows on the outskirts of town and included a large man-made lake, Caesar Creek, where fishermen would launch their bass boats mostly loaded with youngsters out for a day on the water. They shared that pristine space with water skiers and folks who just wanted not to be land locked for that day. Huge stately 100-year old sycamore and oak trees lined the sky with their majesty. We spent the night in an 18th-century three-room Bed and Breakfast where we were the only two people, deeply in love and hungry for each other. We returned home to Tayleigh the next day. Our wedding in October of the same year came one week after Joanna had her braces removed. All three kids were in the wedding, our parents were there, but it was not a big wedding. We were married on the 18th green at Wildwood Country Club in Middletown, where we used to play golf together.

Our son, Steve, at the time of the wedding was eleven years old. Joanna had transformed him from a shy kid with coke bottle glasses, white adhesive tape on one of the bows, and not a clue as to what a Best Man was supposed to do, into the best Man anyone could ever have. Fitted with his new designer glasses with newer technology of thinner lenses and a classic set of long tails, Steve and I stood side by side each proudly in matching tuxedos. His long shaggy blondish hair had been trimmed. He felt as though he was no longer a kid, but now a handsome young man. And so he was.

Officiating at that wedding was my great friend, Attorney Vince Walsh, who was two years my senior. Vince had been born in the early 40's, a victim of the fertility drug, thalidomide. His life began having no arms at all with just proud shoulders which would always be neatly covered by a modest sports coat. Vince learned how to write with his feet, and usually, eat with his feet and in the early 80's passed his driver's test using only his feet while driving a standard issue, Chevrolet Monte Carlo. He would use his left foot for each of the pedals and his right stocking foot to grab the steering wheel with the big and second toes, which incidentally also served as pinchers which could bring you to your knees with pain if he so desired. Wordata rented space from Vince's law firm early on, and Vince would come down from his upstairs office every so often and pose his favorite question to me, letting it roll off his tongue just to entice me, "How would YOU, Larry Davis, like a cigarette?" And so we would take a break and have a Winston. I didn't smoke then, per se. And the only cigarettes I ever bought during those days in the early 1980's were those for Vince. Years later when first diagnosed with cancer, I remember one of the first questions asked was "Do you or did you ever smoke?" Looking back at the time I spent with this most amazing man, and even though it may have been somewhat contributory to my disease, I wouldn't give up those years with Vince Walsh as my friend. The most arduous task for Vince was going to the bathroom, and so any of his buddies would answer the call with him whenever needed. When all of us guys would go out to eat periodically, and in all the years during that time which landed us in various restaurants, the only time we ever had a problem having Vince with us was at a fine dining establishment in Glendale Ohio, The Grande Finale. Vince sat at his customary end of the table spot and responded to the question, "What would you like to drink?" with his standard answer, "A fair measure of your cheapest gin...in a tall glass with a straw". Halfway through our dinner, a rather large man at an adjacent table began taunting Vince, and it escalated to the point where this obviously over-his-limit buffoon started throwing dinner rolls at Vince. This insensitive idiot was upset because Vince had his bare feet up on the table. To Walsh, it was simply business as usual. He was in his 60's and had long since been immune to such nonsense. After all, thalidomide had rendered him armless at the shoulder. It was so evident that he did not have a choice. The irony of that situation was that Vince was impeccable when it came to the use of his toes. The only thing he could not do is move a zipper. Oh, the things he COULD do, though...

When Tayleigh was four years old, I came home one Friday evening to our home on Croydon Lane in Middletown Ohio to find huge, long boxes in the driveway in front of the garage. Tayleigh came busting out of the front door squealing, "We got a swing set!" Uh-oh. I knew what that meant. My Saturday morning was going to consist of erecting this monster. I had forgotten to tell Joanna that Vince was scheduled to make the 13-mile drive from Hamilton and pay us a Saturday visit. What ensued were my taking orders from Walsh while he and I put the set together. There he was, Winston dangling from his lips, sitting on his butt, socks off, and toes working miracles with their dexterity. Nuts and bolts... poles and clamps...chains and seats...Vince Walsh did it all right with me. Every once in a while, I would look over at Tayleigh, who never left his side. She was mesmerized with her new friend...and he with her.

That night at the restaurant was both the most demeaning episode in Vince's life that I witnessed, and also a shining example of the camaraderie and friendship that befitted Vince's relationship with his buddies. The smallest of us, Steve O'Neill, a feisty Irishman, decided he had had enough and invited this fellow and the rest of that table to join us in the parking lot to defend the honor of our friend. We all piled out into the parking lot of The Grand Finale. All of us except Dr. Bob Lerer who decided since our food had been delivered that someone (he volunteered) needed to "guard the food". No punches landed, and no shots were fired (guns were hidden away back then) and we only ran their asses off in disgrace.

And there Vince Walsh was, all decked out in his best suit, sweat pouring off his brow, asking once again if I would take Joanna's hand in marriage. My father proclaimed that this was the LAST wedding of mine that he was going to attend, as this was the fourth of those venues.

But that's another story. Putting all of this into perspective, there were going to be no smiling wedding pictures of Joanna in February wearing braces. So we did it again in October.

After our second wedding, Joanna and I left the next day for a honeymoon in Hawaii after saying goodbye to Olivia, Steve, and Tayleigh the next morning. The older kids were staying with their mother and Tayleigh was at home, within walking distance of her kindergarten, and was in the care of Charlene, our 60'ish sitter who had been with Tayleigh on many occasions and even for a weekend once or twice over a period of nine months. She was supposed to be staying with her father while we were gone, but of course, he canceled two days before our departure to San Francisco and Maui.

Joanna and I were having a wonderful time in Maui and were just getting used to the time change, having gone to bed on Maui time for the first time when Joanna sat straight up in our bed around one am Maui time. Breathless and agitated she blurted out, "Something is wrong with Tayleigh!" Apparently, I thought she was dreaming something vivid enough…but this was different. Her tone was desperate. Quickly she set me straight, "This is not a dream. A voice said to me, "Tayleigh was in trouble." The time difference of 6 hours put Middletown at about 7:00 a.m. We immediately started calling the house, and there was no answer. Tayleigh's school opened at 7:00 also, so Joanna called the school and was immediately transferred to the principal who exclaimed, "We were just getting ready to call you. She had not been at school for the last two days."

Joanna insisted that I call Madalyn at the factory and ask her to check on Tayleigh for us. We didn't sleep another wink that night. When the light of sun came up hours later, the school principal even walked up to our home but found no evidence of anyone there. Madalyn, a mother of three superstar kids, flew into action by notifying the Middletown police of a missing child. And now Joanna knew something truly was terribly wrong. While she threw our clothing into our suitcases, I was on the phone with Delta changing our flight to an earlier time and handling the connections in San Francisco back to Dayton. I remember they were very gracious and generous to us. I honestly don't know how

Joanna kept everything from boiling over, but we just huddled together the entire longest six hours of our lives on the flight to the mainland.

When we landed, and with tiny portable telephone technology back then, Joanna sprinted for a pay phone to call Detective Christenoff. When J.C. picked up the line, she heard him softly say, "We found her."Joanna collapsed onto the floor of the airport later telling me that she had thought that her daughter was dead. I grabbed the dangling phone, "J.C.!"

"And she is alive!"

Tayleigh was born in 1986 in Dayton, Ohio, daughter of Frank and Joanna Long.

Approximately six months after her birth two events took place, one which would bring both she and her mother sorrow, and the other such overwhelming joy. In December of that year, Margaret Henry the maternal grandmother was terminally injured in an auto accident in Monroe, Ohio. As she clung to life, the victim of a drunk work-release prisoner, her daughter, my Joanna, wept day and night except for the times that she held little Tayleigh in her arms. Though Margaret's granddaughter would never know her mother, Joanna focused all her love and devotion into Tayleigh's sweet brown eyes, telling her stories of how she and her grandma were going to leave their husbands and disappear to the Carolinas and open salon/gift shop. Had that happened, I have no doubt of their success, as Joanna's beauty was eclipsed only by her mother's. Eleven days after the accident, and just before Christmas, all life support was removed, and Margaret became one of God's angels, only to reappear on several occasions in Tayleigh's mind during her early years. Tayleigh's father, Frank, decided to book himself a ski trip to Lake Tahoe, leaving the two girls alone on Christmas through New Year's, which foretold of the joy of divorce to follow. A huge man, Frank would tower over Tayleigh, had a booming voice which shattered any calmness a baby could have, felt intimidated by the fragility of this young child, and fought with her mother on a daily basis. He shouldered no responsibility for his daughter's day-to-day care, even though Joanna was working full time for Coldwell Banker Real Estate. Eventually, Joanna had had enough and ended the marriage shortly after Tayleigh's first birthday.

"They've got her Joanna! Tayleigh has been found, and she is OK!!!"

Between the time when the police found our daughter and when we home back in Middletown, Madalyn had gone to the police station and met Detective Christenoff and took Tayleigh back to her house in Hamilton. When we finally reached my sister and sped over to her house to wrap our arms around Tayleigh, we all sat in the living room and cried. The story of the rescue was unfolded.

Madalyn, a consummate storyteller, said, "After I had contacted the police, I received a call from a detective J.C. Christenoff. He came out to Wordata to gather as much information as he could along with a picture of Tayleigh. I didn't have much information on Charlene, I'm sorry," she said. "When he left, Detective Christenoff mentioned that he had authorized having an officer camping out on Croydon Lane hoping Charlene would return with Tayleigh. They didn't have to wait long. Under the cover of darkness that first night, a car pulled into the driveway. Charlene ran out of the car and into the house, leaving Tayleigh alone in the back seat. The officer approached the car and immediately pulled her out of the car while his partner detained a returning Charlene. As it turned out, Charlene and Tayleigh had been gone for a day and a half but in her haste to get across the bridge in Kentucky on her way to Florida, Charlene had forgotten Tayleigh's suitcase full of clothing and had to reverse her course and go back to the house to pick it up. That means that the collision of events leading up to that encounter hung on a mistake by Charlene and astounding police work. What made it even more amazing is that we would learn later on that for all those nine months "Charlene" had been planning this kidnapping, Tayleigh had been warned not to tell us about anything about what had been going on for even a few months before all of this horror. As far as we could tell, devil worship was one of the activities during Charlene's time with Tayleigh. Thank God there did not seem to be any abuse other than threats for spilling the beans. The penalty was that Charlene would kill our cat, and then Joanna and me. We were sick to hear this from her therapist later on. Charlene, of course, was not her actual name. Even though all of her references had checked out, this was a woman who had a record of similar incidents. Doctors, lawyers, and businessmen all had high praise for her. But we didn't have the internet back then, and there was no other medium to rely on for references. She was a quiet, shy, grandmother who even brought her grandchildren over from time to time. I guess they were her grandchildren...

And so it came to pass, on that Saturday night at the grand opening of our new factory, our associates from faraway places and our friends and family close to home discovered that a real live hero was in our midst, Detective J. C. Christenoff. As I told our story, and with Joanna and little Tayleigh at my side, we introduced J.C. to a thunderous applause which crescendoed as he made his way up onto our impromptu stage. He bent as far down at the waist, while Tayleigh, who was dressed in a gown of red, white and blue stars and stripes which her mama had made, draped a medal over his head and onto his massive shoulders. J.C. swooped her up in his strong arms, accepted my invitation to speak, and waited for the crowd to sit down. As a hush fell over everyone, Detective Christenoff looked at Tayleigh and then to her mama and said, "Thank you for honoring me with this medal tonight." As he looked at our little girl who sat on his left arm while she hung onto his neck, his voice was loud as he spoke, "But tonight the best honor of all goes to the men and women of the Middletown Police Department. When we got the call that Tayleigh had been found, the whole place went crazy. In all my years with the department, I have never seen anything like it."

Tayleigh will sometimes ask her mama to tell her the story of our honeymoon, trying to piece together events which are still fuzzy even now. No matter what version unfolds, it always has a happy ending.

CHAPTER 12

Through October 9th2013

BIG DOG AND BIG CAT

The first nine days of treatment consisted of two Monday's of chemo therapy sessions lasting three hours each and 6-10 minute radiation doses each weekday. That was the plan for the next six weeks. Though the first few days were relatively uneventful as far as physical unrest, the psychological war had progressed to a point where it reigned supreme in my thoughts and I really thought that if this was "it", then I was going to be fine. In fact the second chemo therapy session had gone so well, I was convinced that the Zofran cocktail that was administered through my port prior to the chemo concoction was a wonder drug capable of negating any nauseous feeling I might encounter. Modern medicine had come a long way in its treatment of upset stomachs. The actual process of blistering radiation was truly not painful but overcoming the intense pressure of the mask had become a symbol of triumph over all the other maladies previously thought to be grievous. I was about 20% of the way through the protocol and other than a diminishing appetite, I seemed to be weathering the slowly developing storm. Each day I would look up at the sound of Pete barking out, "L-Dog?", as he opened the door to the staging area. I felt as though I belonged to this mess cancer had thrown me into. I felt a sense of accomplishment and even savored a few supposed "wins" along the way.

One such win came few days before the first chemo session when I had erected a sheet of white poster paper about three feet square onto the wall in my office. The paper was a calendar which started at 35 and progressed down to 1 and became another symbol of things accomplished as well as the miles to go until I completed the whole shootin' match. Big Dog stopped over the afternoon of the first radiation day to wish me well and give me a big bear hug. I had returned from Dr. Neal's office and it was fitting that Big would knock on the back door because he and Dr. Neal had been buddies for a number of years. Oddly enough Tayleigh had matriculated through John T. Hoggard High School with Dr. Neal's youngest son and Big Dog's daughter, Bryn. The stars were lining up for the whole experience to be a no-brainer. Unbeknownst to Big Dog I had a special task waiting for him as he joined me in my office. I had a huge red leather chair in one corner and he felt right at home with the color as he plopped his large frame down in the NC State-colored furniture. Big is a man of few words unless he was telling a story; in that case, you needed to bring your lunch. But on this day he was prepared for a quick in and out as the uneasiness of the situation didn't set well with him. We talked for a few moments and then he got up to leave. "Big Dog, would you do me a favor?" I asked.

"Anything Little Dog. Anything you want."

Even though radiation had not begun, I reached over to get my black magic marker, "Would you take this and mark a big-ass black 'X' over the number 35 on my calendar?" For a quick second I thought I saw some watery eyes on this proud, battle hardened friend of mine and he turned away to look at the wall. "I would be honored…and I'll be back for number 1."

Whoa! When I woke up from my Wednesday afternoon nap, I was shocked into the reality of all encompassing nausea. My eyes flashed open in fear that I was not going to make it fast enough to the bathroom from our bed, and those fears became reality with such urgency that I was totally unprepared for the force that my digestive system could throw itself in reverse. Not only did I did not make it all the way, my only alternative to laying waste to the entire path from bed to bathroom was to fling open the French doors and spew onto the tile. The entire inside of my body was in full-scale revolution from what I had forced upon it. Wretched, ugly vomiting changed the nirvana of patting myself on the back with confidence to a conscious realization that what had been foretold about chemo nausea was a truth not to be denied. Joanna and I were both completely grossed out to the point that I sent her away so I didn't have to hear her crying. This was different than the tequila hangover I had at Dad's weekend with Olivia in 1994. The chemicals, Cisplatin to be specific, were still inside me. That meant there was more to come…Oh what an understatement.

Thursday, October 10, 2013
At an hour or so before dawn I arose and immediately rushed to the bathroom with dry heaves which would stop the beating heart of a horse in its tracks. I was begging,
"Please let me throw up", but there was nothing left inside. Holding onto the sink with both hands and bending at the knees I lost all sense of control as the heaving continued for the better part of an hour. At one point I thought I was going to throw my back out, they were so powerful. I couldn't even take any pain medication to get me through it since there was no way I was going to be able to let any liquid pass over my lips. I was lost in a downward spiral of the kidnapping of my stomach, and the failure of my resolve to rescue it back. (These crushing sessions were to continue

each morning until deep into my protocol.) I had no choice but to gather some sort of normalcy and dress myself in between episodes of dry heaves so that I could make my appointment for my radiation treatment. This new morning ritual changed the course of my days and nights as I scrambled to rearrange everyday habits and schedules to try to combat nausea.

Soon my normal daily routine had intermittent interruptions of raging stomach mutiny taking center stage over anything else I may have planned. Visits from friends dropped off drastically as Joanna had to decline most invitations for anything happening outside the home as well as eliminate any visitors by passing the word that I simply was not up to seeing anyone. Headaches accompanied the nausea and my torso ached from the incredible power of the heaving sensations of a digestive system run amuck.

This new villain also signaled the beginning of an inconsistent sleep pattern which altered my demeanor to the point where I became belligerent and unruly, especially toward Joanna of all people. Naps became more of a salvation during the day and nighttime sleep on many nights was nonexistent. Nausea not only messed with me physically, my mind raced to try to find a way to get back to normal but it was no match for what cancer was throwing at me. I just couldn't get it together any more. The only true salvation I had were the painkilling drugs that took me to a nether land I called "the planet Octron". Taking so many of them led to other problems in my lower tract. Weight began to drop off at an alarming rate of a half-pound a day. No longer was I concentrating on winning the war against cancer; I was concerned only with getting through the hour-to-hour battles.

How I made it across town by 8 is a mystery to me. By now I had figured out the fastest route to get to the radiation office and knew that if I didn't leave the house by 7:25 I was going to be late. My body was shaking down to my socks and when I had looked in the mirror while brushing my teeth I saw a ghost instead of the "me" that was there only 24 hours earlier reveling in the fact that I was feeling so good. Gripping the steering wheel of my 2005 Acura MDX with my damp, clammy hands, I was fraught with fear wondering how I was going to make it through the mask. The resolve of not letting any of the madness caused by chemo therapy to upset my routine, let alone my confidence, had disappeared and was replaced by fearful, gripping thoughts of "the next step". "What's gonna happen next?!" "How bad is it going to be?" "Can I make it through these mornings of chaos to keep the schedule the docs had laid out for me?" Even at this early stage, the control I once had was slipping away to a distant memory. How was I going to make it across town that morning was the first question I had. The second was a thousand times more scary, "How was I going to endure the mask?!"

"L-Dog", Pete yelled out. It was 8 o'clock and I was moving really slow. "How y'doin' buddy?", Pete asked probably not wanting me to answer judging by how bad I looked."I'm feelin' pretty green today, Pete." And that's all that was said that day. Suffocation and claustrophobia slapped me into reality almost immediately after the mask was snapped into place. The pressure on my lips, the teeth guards pressed up on the inside of my lips to the point of numbness almost immediately. Breathing through my nostrils was impossible, leaving only a rapid series of short breaths through the mouth as the only alternative. The sides of the mask pressed my ears hard into my head. I wanted to swallow but there was nothing there to facilitate that. My entire head was under assault, and clearly they did not want it to move at all. I realized that it was all too clear: for the next 7-8 minutes I was effectively going to remain motionless. This after heaving my guts out for an hour, having no food whatsoever in my stomach, or anywhere in my digestive system for that matter, and wanting desperately to vomit. I could not move! The anxiety was overwhelming. Pete was on my side though. He plodded on with the exact same routine, knowing that the only possible positive outcome of this day's session was to get me in and out quickly. As he tightened the screws to the table, I heard him tell another tech, "let's forget the full X-ray today and do it tomorrow". Every so often they would do a full X-ray of the entire area to compare with anything previously seen. That would tack on another 3-4 minutes of hell. Not today, L-Dog. Not today.

Thursday, October 10, 2013
Mornin' Tom. My appetite started to go downhill as the nausea built up yesterday. Prior to that I was getting the 64 oz of fluids and 2500 calories each day. I'm worried mostly about food these days. How in the heck to get 64 oz of liquid + 2500 calories in my stomach at the same time is mind boggling. Thinking more about the feeding tube option as totally viable, but not sure that provides everything I need. When I first tried Boost a few weeks ago I was OK but now it is difficult just thinking about it, besides it smells something awful. I think I need someone to slap me around and get me out of this funk.

Radiation is now set for eight o'clock every morning until the end. I have 29 more radiation treatments to go after this morning. I opted for that time so that I could have the whole rest of the day to work on everything else. Bedtime has been moved up to 8-8:30 p.m. and I arise normally around 4:30-5:00 a.m. and sleep consists of a series of short naps. Feels really weird to be up at that time...and pretty lonely. Joanna needs to get away from me for a couple of days and I suggested she drive to Richmond for a few days to see Tayleigh. I find that I am more frustrated with her offers to help me which pretty much pisses me off that I feel that way. I love her so much. The food wars, however, have started and the participants are all dug in. She is constantly on my ass to eat every second of every day, and indeed that is where most of my ire is cast.

I get the shakes most every day. It's not debilitating just a nuisance. Not sure if that is a reaction to oxycodone or the wracking dry heaves I go through or the toll cisplatin is taking on me. Probably a combination of everything. Seemingly have the lower tract in manageable condition, but it's still day-to-day. Chemo locks me up for sure but the softeners and probiotics seem to have mitigated those troubles somewhat. Soreness creeping into the mouth but so far it is manageable and the pain meds keep me calm enough that if this is as tough as it gets then I will be OK. The nausea and dry heaves are a huge problem. Our cats, Lacy and Heartly sense something is amiss. They seem to know when to rally around me and when to stay away. They certainly are not used to listening to me yell at Joanna. Together our felines cost $700, and Heartly was free! Lacy has piercing blue eyes to go with her snow white fur and quite frankly is much smarter than I am. She is the caregiver of the two, lying next to me as I prop myself up in the chair for a night of interrupted sleep. It is such a calming effect to get that kind of love.

Heartly, who is my favorite cat of all time, is 20 pounds of fraidy cat. He is suspicious of everything that moves and even of some things he just thinks he sees. Not one to cuddle because of his girth, Heartly will hang around a short distance away and talk to you on a regular basis.

His idea of taking care of me is for me to take care of him.

We are cat people. That does not mean we don't love dogs, too, evidenced by Joanna's 40-minute walks around The Loop at Wrightsville Beach turning into an hour-long dogfest. We would stop for every dog, big or small, and they loved her instantly. Working at home most of the day somehow led us to having cats. The precursor to Heartly was a sweet, loving Persian, Roxie. Joanna and Roxie were as close to sisters as there could be while Lacy, the Ragdoll was much more aloof. Roxie developed a rare form of feline leukemia and her passing was really difficult for Joanna, and me too. We had her cremated, so Joanna went up to the vet and walked in to pick up the ashes. While waiting, she strolled over to the cages to look at those up for adoption. One tiny gray tabby looked out of place, but cute as could be. So Jojo opened the cage and lifted him out for a brief moment of freedom and lovin'. One of the assistants said, "That's the one for you.""Oh, I'm just here to pick up Roxie's ashes.""Oh, your're Roxie's mom", she said. "Well, this little guy is for you. He's the one to heal your heart. He is the last of 7 brothers to be here. Everyone, including one of our vets who adopted one of his brothers, has told us that they were the most friendly cats they had owned."

Joanna looked down at his little white face and there in the middle she saw his pink heart- shaped nose quivering back at her and he not only healed her heart, he stole it right then and there. And so, Heartly the cat was born, and true to his pedigree, he was a great buddy to have.

I had found that sitting upright in a comfortable chair was the only way my mind would let me fall asleep. Already the combination of the taste of nausea at the bottom of my throat and the trickle of mucous entering at the top made it impossible to even will myself to sleep lying in bed. I was afraid that I would choke on either of those awful substances. Inevitably that gave way to waking up several times after I did get to sleep, but at least being upright kept things at bay. My spot was upstairs in the TV room and many nights when awakened I would turn on the TV with low volume trying anything to keep my mind off choking and allowing precious moments of sleep to take over. I had a prescription for Ambien, but the fear of going into a deep sleep overruled any guarantee of a few hours of sleep. Most nights I would swallow a couple pain killers to set me apart from the reality of the approaching horror that was obviously coming because let's face it…this was only the beginning. The thought never crossed my mind that I was popping 8-10 of these daily now.

With cancer, your thoughts are synonymous with uncertainty and fear. Pills took away the uncertainty and replaced it with hope...the hope that brighter days are possible. If you took enough of them, those good ole days became probable, and that's what a cancer patient is looking for, the ServePro effect..."Like it never even happened". It wasn't really fair to call them painkillers, because the pain simply wasn't that bad yet. And yet, calling them "painkillers" gave them credibility, and so it was OK.

Friday, October 11, 2013
Good morning L-Dog. I've got just a few moments here before I have to go into another endless meeting day. I remember those awful days of an unsettled digestive tract as if they were yesterday. Truly none of the drugs prescribed for nausea did me much good. You have to remember that I had 50-60 pounds of fat that I had carried around for years, so I did not have the worry over losing weight to the point where it became dangerous. That didn't stop the family from tag teaming me to eat. Hard as I tried I could not get them to understand the futility of their pleas. I know they sat around the dinner table when I was not there and wondered why I was being such a bastard when it came to food. My staples of chocolate milk and ice cream would be all that I would eat for months and even to this day when I am holed up in a hotel room, there is always a half gallon of chocolate milk in my room fridge. It never ceased to amaze me that they could not grasp the fact that the process of eating was not only a function of actually having the desire for food but also the ability to swallow. The chemo took care of the former and the death rays did the same for the latter. I don't remember suffering from the shakes very often other than feeling freezing cold all the time even here in Orlando. The docs told me that lots of patients complain of being cold and chalked it up to the chemo in the bloodstream.

Something about metallic components. I would walk around with 5 or 6 layers on and still be freezing cold.

Have you made any decision about the feeding tube? I know it is a step that you don't want to take, but if you are losing weight now in just your second week, you may well want to go ahead and get it done. I simply am no help to you in that decision because it was the one thing that I did not choose to do, even though everyone was pissed off that I opted out. Whatever you decide, you know I will support you. You might as well get it done just to get everyone off your back!

To hell with the feeding tube. That steps over the line.

CHAPTER 13
NO TASTE

Saturday, October 12, 2013

*G*ood morning, Larry. I've been on the road...down in South Florida with one of the guys that works for me. It was a two-day conference, and we are one of the big sponsors. And now that Florida has passed the no texting while driving law...I didn't want to get caught returning your email while doing 80 mph on the Florida Turnpike.

I know what you are going through with the drop in appetite. Mine still hasn't come back to what it used to be. Just the thought of 8 glasses of liquid per day even when I was feeling good was a hard one to swallow (no pun intended). But as the Doc kept reminding me...you have to flush all that bad stuff that the chemo and radiation are killing out of your system. I tried every brand of energy drink...Boost, Ensure, etc. and for some reason, they all tasted like chalk. But remember, unlike you, I had all of that ugly fat to live off of. So to whatever extent you can...force yourself. Because I got real ugly with living family members that tried to "force" me to eat/drink. I know exactly what you are talking about when you refer to the frustration with "offers to help". I remember it like yesterday..."Tom, can I get you something to drink...the Doctor said you needed 64 oz per day". And my response was a curt..."just LEAVE ME ALONE?

Unfortunately, it wasn't until I was really feeling good again, that I realized how much everyone else suffered along with me. Linda and my kids all told me how hard it was to watch me suffer knowing how helpless they were to do anything about it. They said how difficult it was to even look at my burned face…holding back tears until they left the room.

For me, it was only Joanna, as I had no other family close to us and none of our friends got into our routine. And it became a HUGE deal. In fact, "food talk" was the only part of our ordeal that brought ill feelings, outbursts from both of us (but mainly me), and reasons for Joanna to take her sabbaticals to who knows where we the banter got too graphic and disrespectful. Once again, arch enemy cancer took aim on something that I held dear. No, it took aim on the one that I hold dearest of all. Up to that point in our marriage, I remember only one or two outbursts when things went south with Wordata and all the kids were in our little home in Hamilton Ohio. As Tom Haas said above, three months later the memories of those arguments about food, though distant, made me realize that I was the antagonist, and that made me somber for a good long time. Fortunately for me, I only had to endure the food fights for a couple of weeks.

I did the 8:00 a.m. time slot too. The hospital was on the other side of our downtown, so if I left my house at 7:15 a.m. I would miss the bulk of the traffic and by the time my radiation was over, so was the most of the rush hour. The group in the radiation department ran a very timely operation, and I was usually ushered into the death ray room within 5 minutes of my appointment. I was never a very patient person when it came to waiting rooms. Their being on time gave me one less thing to be grumpy about.

I was cold all the time. And it got worse as the treatments continued. Several years ago, I was giving a light weight long sleeve shirt made by Patagonia, the Sunchilla Fleece Shirt (not jacket). I never got to wear it much in Florida but found it to be one of the warmest, most comfortable garments I own. Linda and I went out a bought four more of them because that's all I wore. During the peak of my darkest days, I had 2 or 3 of them on just to stay warm along with a heating pad. I even pulled out an old

Green Bay Packer stocking hat I kept from my days as a Milwaukeean 30 years ago and had that on to keep my body temperature up. Starting at week 5, I was getting so dehydrated that I would get a one or two-liter I.V. of fluids following radiation every day. I swear they kept that solution in the freezer until they were ready to administer it.

Even with three layers of shirts and 2 or 3 of their hospital blankets covering me, I was still cold. So bottom line: it's going to get a lot worse before it gets better.

Another of the side effects of Cisplatin was the ice-water-in-the-veins sensation. Toes and finger tips were like dry ice, cracked and cut open and freezing to the touch. At night when I was not moving around, I would sleep with a thick pullover hooded sweat shirt. I had a couple of them, one gray and one black. In the beginning, I used the gray one as it was my favorite. In an almost inexplicable subconscious move, I soon switched to the black one sensing my spirits becoming challenged and my mood growing darker. Pain killers had to be rationed in such a way that I could mitigate the pain without getting so high that I couldn't fall asleep. Many times when I woke up during the wee hours of the morning, I would pull that black hood over my head and watch graphic episodes of Criminal Minds. I was sinking into deep depression and was powerless to stop it.

How is the Miracle Mouthwash working for you? I found that it was helpful in that it gave me about a ½ window of opportunity to swallow something. I was able to make high- calorie milk shakes (room temp) and get them down so I could have some nourishment. At some point...and I don't remember when exactly, my taste buds got fried and the ability to feel "sweet" went down the drain. That certainly made the shakes less appealing. But like I said, it was one of the ways to get some nourishment.

Larry...one of the things that kept me going was looking three short months down the road knowing that it will be all over by then. There is no way to "sugar coat" what you are facing. It's a road that I know you will hope that others will never have to travel. But I honestly believe that tough guys are given tough assignments in life because we have what it takes to fight them. And with the support of your wife, family, and friends, we'll be raising a toast to New Years to your good health. Our two glasses, yours and mine, will probably have grape juice in them.

Keep up your nourishment as much as possible, and vent to me as much as possible. I understand! Enjoy the weekend!

This message on October 12th was the first time for a lot of things. I believed for sure that food was a critical issue. Sure the Doc's told me about what was needed to stay alive, but they didn't tell me how to deal with it. As time went on, I came to realize that doctors know how to best cure you, but they are very reluctant to clue you in on the ways to mitigate the problems associated with your disease. Their reasons for this are obvious. Every person's DNA is different, as we have learned from the many cop shows on TV. To answer every patient's questions about "when," "how", or "why" is just impossible for them to think even of attempting. I didn't get it then, but I get it now. Joanna has long wondered why none of the doctors on my team had a nutritionist on their staff to answer the questions about survival from a food standpoint. But then again, I never asked for one. That, of course, goes back to the "I can do it by myself" syndrome. So you can see what an invaluable asset Tom Haas was in my quest to understand, even early on, the problems food posed. His windows of wisdom prepared me for the inevitable and helped me make a huge decision around the beginning of my 3rd week in treatment. Get the tube you dummy!

The reference to Miracle Mouthwash was a potion that could be mixed at a pharmacy that would cut through the thick mucus that was beginning to form in my mouth, as the radiation treatments started to annihilate the salivary glands. While at the same time, mutilating mucous membranes to the point where they were functioning on overtime trying to fight back.

Unfortunately, that solution did not work for me as it merely contributed to my nausea and therefore was relegated to a negative issue. But just by Tom mentioning it, I believed right then that mucous was going to be a huge problem for me.

Losing taste buds scared the hell out of me. Internet research indicated that sometimes those things just don't come back. No matter how you look at it, first it's your lips and then your tongue. Those two bodily parts start the digestive process and without the taste buds, worried the crap out of me. It made me believe that this cancer was curable but at the same time I realized the cure could leave me in bad shape.

When Tom wrote the no "sugar coat" comment, I confirmed what I already knew: that he would always tell me the whole truth. It gave me a sense of calmness knowing that I could most likely be forewarned before anything bad was going to happen. One of the most compelling reasons for writing this book is to inform those who are diagnosed with any cancer which affects eating was to make sure they know what to expect. Many of us who have cancer don't want to ask questions about the future. Maybe it's because we think "that's not going to happen to me...", But more than that I think it's because all too quickly we find ourselves in a very precarious circumstance on so many fronts. Getting answers to questions directly added to that conglomeration of fear and despair.

My serenity was only the outside façade. On the inside, that increasingly frail body was revolting in so many areas. I was not prepared for all of this to go wrong this early and at the same time. On the inside, I was WAY more scared than calm.

I was beginning to get a sore throat. Not like the ones I had in the past lifetime, but deeper and wider spread than something a cold or the flu would bring on. I had filled the first prescription for 75 oxycodone tablets at Costco, and they were rapidly being consumed. My previous experience with drugs of that sort was almost non-existent. I do remember about the time Sugar Ray Leonard was boxing his was toward a detached retina that I experimented with a pain killer or two. It seemed like so long ago, and I hardly remembered the feeling other than I know I was high. And yet there had been 75 of them lurking on my makeshift nightstand next to my comfortable chair in the TV room upstairs, just in case I might need them now and then to help sleep. At least, that was my intention for using those drugs. In reality, I had moved the bottle of pills downstairs into the kitchen when their visibility was apparently heightened. The frequency of popping one or two oxycodone had morphed into an "every four hours" routine, regardless of what was going on inside of me.

Now, at the end of the second week of my protocol, the nausea was uncontrollable. I found myself waking up numerous times each night and sprinting to the bathroom. Most of the time it was dry heaves, not that those were any consolation. The bare fact was that there was nothing there to throw up. The sound would inevitably permeate back into the bedroom and Joanna's sleep, so precious a commodity to her, would be interrupted. I knew the promise my doc's had made early on: "you will lose a lot of weight if you don't keep eating. You need at least 2500 calories a day to stay healthy."

Adding to this carnival of disgusting changes celebrating inside my body was the continuance of the body's ability to produce an infinite amount of mucous. I never did figure out if it was on my tongue and transferred to the roof of my mouth or vice versa. Whichever way it was, it was prolific in its quantity, its viscosity, and probably the only thing making its way down my throat and into my digestive system. When it did "come back on me", it was a murky looking substance with a consistency of Elmer's Glue. As the days wore on, the color became darker, and the glue became congealed grease-like, the taste of which in and of itself would send me reeling to the bathroom dozens of times per day. Laying down to sleep normally was dangerous due to choking caused by the mucous. The only time I allowed that was during nap time when I knew it was only for minutes that I would be out of control of my breathing, not hours. There was no question at this point: Mucous had overtaken nausea as enemy #1.

So OK. It was time. I began to build into my daily routine, a systematic and scheduled regimen of pain killers. You may know it as Percocet which is a tablet of oxycodone plus Tylenol. In reality, the Percocet pills are so large that Dr. Neal, of course, knew before I did that I would be unable to swallow something that large, so the prescription was for Oxycodone by itself, a much smaller pill.

The first by-product of this new phase was a lock down in my colon which produced, at one point, a single bowel movement in the space of 13 days, followed by another ten days of nothing coming out.

The second was sneaky. This stuff was habit forming...

CHAPTER 14
ELEPHANT TRUNK

Sunday, October 13, 2013

*G**ood evening, Larry. Just a suggestion when you go in for your radiation treatment on Monday. If you still don't have your Miracle Mouthwash, ask one of those lovely death ray technicians to ask the doctor if he has any sample bottles of Lidocaine for your throat to hold you over until your order comes in. My doc gave me 2 or 3 small bottles that I liked better because it didn't make me gag as bad as the Miracle stuff.*

File this (below) in the "information you would never have been interested in knowing unless you were diagnosed with throat cancer" file.

The most famous formulation of magic mouthwash contains viscous lidocaine as a topical anesthetic, diphenhydramine as an anti-inflammatory, and Maalox to help coat the tissues in the mouth. Other formulations include antifungals, corticosteroids and or antibiotics:

- *Diphenhydramine: an antihistamine to reduce inflammation*
- *Glucocorticoids: to reduce inflammation*
- *Lidocaine: a local anesthetic to relieve pain*
- *Xylocaine: another local anesthetic*
- *Maalox: an antacid formulation which acts as a coating agent*
- *Nystatin: an antifungal for candidiasis*

- *Sucralfate: a coating agent*
- *Tetracycline: an antibiotic*
- *Erythromycin: an antibiotic*

- Tom

Thanks so much, Tom I have included Joanna on this, I hope you don't mind. I did re- read your comments to ensure I wasn't sharing anything too personal. I am meeting with my gastroenterologist in about a half hour to schedule the feeding tube. I figure I've got three main things to worry about: pain in my neck, ways to get nourishment to my body, and nausea. With the tube, I can satisfy the nourishment to some degree, so I'm ready for the tube. My docs all agree. I get one bag of fluids each Monday with the chemo and I am scheduling another on Friday mornings. After Monday's chemo, I am half way home on that ordeal. I'm kind of thinking that the shakes may be from dehydration as well as from the cold sensation. Yes, I get cold too. Thanks for the warning. I know Joanna will see your comments of the Patagonia and her first thought will be, "I need to shop!"

"Sweet" is like a Kelly Clarkson song, "Already Gone". Everything seems to taste like salt water to me. I did have a frosty today, and that made it down the hatch. I look forward to New Year's Tom. You are such a good man to write.

Thanks again, Tom. L-Dog

Amid the reports from various sources on the internet, WebMD. com is one of them. The taste buds are the bell ringer for good things to come for a neck cancer survivor. By far the most debilitating after effects of chemo therapy and radiation oncology, mostly the radiation, are the inability to swallow, chew, salivate, and clear copious amounts of mucous from the total mouth/throat area, and taste without connection to the food source. The typical mixture of mucous and saliva allows for the digestive process to start once food has entered your mouth.

All of those effects are critical, but if you think about it, taste starts it all. Taste sends a message that you either like the food or dislike it. And if you like it, then the process of mixing the food with the mucous and saliva proceeds normally. It's a pretty simple procedure and one we always take for granted. But just like anything else we take for granted if any of the processes are short-circuited eating transforms from an enjoyable, regular occurrence to something else entirely.

Taste becomes a life and death situation...

After receiving Tom Haas' email on Saturday morning, there were several hours of soul searching about how to resolve the food issue. On the one hand was the feeding tube, about which Dr. Neal had exercised his authority early on in pronouncing the tube as a certainty. It was another operation, another trip to the surgical wing of New Hanover Regional Medical Center, another intrusion into Joanna's day, another dose of anesthesia, and another doctor entering the fracas. On the other was damn near everyone I knew telling me I had to eat.

Though I had consistently eschewed (ala Howard Cosell) anything having to do with a feeding tube coming out of my shell-shocked body, Tom's words battled back and forth in my mind.

Though he never had the tube inserted, I read between the lines of his email and realized he was telling me to get it done.

I got on my digital scale and sure enough, predictably, I was down another pound.

That night Joanna rushed me to the emergency room when I passed out while sitting on the toilet. What a sight that must have been. I can't remember whether or not I was "finished" and this is the first time I have even thought about that. The shakes indeed had been a warning sign to take fluids because as it turned out I was severely dehydrated. After about 4 hours in a little room with a bed in the main ER, having blood work drawn and read, taking two giant bags of saline solution through an IV, and a good old fashioned tongue lashing from the ER doc, my fluid levels came back to life and my color returned. It was at this point that I vowed to have the feeding tube installed as quickly as possible.

Monday, October 14, 2013...1:45 AM
Well, Tom, as you know this life's event is a series of ups and downs. This past week was by far the most challenging for me. I began Monday finding it impossible for me to swallow the time-release capsule for omeprazole, which I had been taking every morning for ten years or so. I put off seeing Dr. Kittenger, the gastroenterologist until after the tube was inserted so that he could tell me what alternatives were available. Big mistake. By Sunday I was so dehydrated that Joanna had to run me to the emergency room after I collapsed in the bathroom, which was now being called the "annex" to my home office. Plenty of tests were taken to eliminate anything else other than dehydration, so the ER doc called in a prescription for omeprazole in tablet form which I could grind up and wash down my tube at the morning feeding.
Another crisis averted. What next???!!!
L-Dog

Didn't have to wait long for the answer to THAT question...

Monday, October 14, 2013...3:35 AM
Tom: Throat totally closed now. Barely able to take meds. Haven't eaten anything of any substance since Thursday. Weight down from 162 to 147. Appointment with both docs this morning. Tube in Tuesday afternoon and hopefully I can make it until then before everything starts to shut down. Man, that was fast. L-Dog

After the 9th radiation treatment and my third chemo therapy regimen, I made the call early Monday afternoon to Coastal Carolina

Radiation Oncology to refer me to Dr. Kittenger for insertion of the feeding tube, and Dr. Neal's nurse asked me if Jim Wortman was still my internist. The chain of command in cancer protocol reverted back to the beginning as Dr. Jim was summoned to turn the matter over to his long time contemporary, Dr. Joe Kittenger, my gastroenterologist. Dr. Joe was a man of my age so he was a throwback to a time when doc's made house calls and considered you to be family. He had a gruff voice which belied his kind demeanor and had performed several colonoscopy's and an endoscopy for me over the 10-12 years that I had been seeing him. The only continuous interaction I had with his office was to refill a prescription for Omeprazole which was for abating acid reflux.

The decision to have the feeding tube was a real no-brainer. Even after finishing only 30% of my radiation treatments I knew that swallowing was going to be a problem...a huge problem. My weight had already dropped from 162 to 147 so there was no time to waste. I would be asleep during the 20-minute procedure and ready to go home right after it's done. The formula that became my "food" was something made by Nestle' and all they had was vanilla. To this day I cannot stand the smell or the taste of vanilla anything...except for Dairy Queen blizzards. Each portion had about 500 calories in a 10 oz serving and you fed this liquid down through a rubber tube about the length of a football field. Well, ok, a little shorter than that, but I felt like an elephant in the shower. Note that this decision was made so that the insertion of the tube took place on a Tuesday which was normally the calmest day of the week because along with the Monday chemo I was given a bag of anti nausea drugs, therefore the nightmare of begging to throw up had not started yet for that week. Joanna was going through menopause and so she was hot all the time. I was going through chemo therapy so I was always cold. That dichotomy and food dilemmas made for a house divided and it would have been were it not for Joanna. Let me put it this way: the exhilaration we used to feel with making love, prior to the diagnosis, had been replaced by simply getting though a day with smiles and kindness instead of my casting aspersions toward the love of my life. To say that I could be an SOB during all of this would be laughable. I was a real asshole sometimes and Jojo would calmly grab her purse and take a drive for an hour or so to collect her thoughts and feel strong enough to withstand any further barrage of hateful verbiage. Cleaning up vomit was no fun either, but she kept going nonetheless. Joanna appeared to be fearless and methodical but later admitted episodes of sobbing so hard that the bed would shake as she slept alone, night after night, wondering if I were choking on mucous or fighting the dry heaves in the wee hours of the mornings. For a time, I never gave her ordeal a thought, so focused on getting by minute-to-minute for days on end. The oxycodone began to rescue me from being so hateful and it became my go-to friend to alleviate most anything bothering me.

Dr. Kittenger's office called me around two o'clock on Monday, the 14th and I went into the office almost immediately. When I checked in at the front, I was told that Dr. Joe was on vacation and that his PA would see me. While in the interview room with her, I was not at all comfortable with an unknown associate doctor performing the tube insertion operation. The PA got a beep and left the room for a moment. Once again, the course of my protocol took an unexpected turn and started back down the road already occupied by so many friends rooting for me, always ready to rescue me.

The door to the examining room opened, and as I lifted up my forlorn face, there was Dr. Joe. An avid mountain biker, he had been on the way to the mountains in western North Carolina for a well-needed vacation with his wife. The October flora and landscape of that area were in full-scale season change with the brilliance of colors and smells. Not so fast! This good-looking man turned his car around and walked into my room with tears in his eyes and a bear hug only he could provide. I shouldn't have been, but I was stunned. And humbled, too.

"I thought you were on vacation," I questioned.

Dr. Joe Kittenger replied, "I could not leave without seeing you and making sure you understood what was going to happen. You are one of my boys, and I love you." He told me that I was one of a handful of his "boys" who had been diagnosed with this type of cancer over the past few years and that all of them had fought the tube, but wisely decided to fight it no more. We were already scheduled to have the operation the next morning, once again in the early hours of dawn. As he got up to leave the room, he grabbed me and kissed my cheek as he hugged me tight, and then whispered in my ear,

"And every one of them were cured."

Monday, October 14th…9:17 AM

Larry, My heart goes out to you. Praying that all goes well with the tube insertion. You are charting new territory with the feeding tube. When you're up to it, I'd like to hear what you had to go through. That weight loss is significant, and I'm sure your Docs will do everything in their power to keep you healthy enough to fight. I had several of the meds that I was taking prescribed in liquid form. One of the biggest blessings for me was the liquid hydrocodone. It did burn a little on the way down…but seemed almost instantly to numb the pain. Then it provided a few hours of relief.

The Big Guy upstairs gives tough assignments to tough guys. Just from the short time I've know you, I sense that you are the individual that isn't going to let this damn cancer get the best of you. I know it's going to be hard to keep a positive attitude with all the crap you are going through. The most difficult part was knowing that there was still more to come. Just remember, you have a beautiful wife and lots of friends pulling for you. We won't let you down!!!

Tom

So I upped my pain medication, adding a dose of two tablets in the middle of the night. I was awake half the night anyway. My choices in TV shows had changed from sports programs to real life cop shows with plenty of violence, and hard-hitting stories of drug deals went wrong, and murder suspects hunted down. I found myself hardening a bit, with an outlook that bordered on desperation. I couldn't tell if the inability to talk stemmed from the swelling inside my throat or the buildup and caking of mucous. This after only nine radiation treatments, which were, in fact, a lesser amount of radiation compared to the final nine treatments.

Monday, October 14, 2013...Noon
Thank you for your uplifting email, Tom. I'll certainly give you the update. As far as I know now, I will be given the same pain med and anesthetic as I had with my biopsy...out a total of 20-25 mins. RN service will then give me instructions and comments on how to use and clean the tube. ¼ inch incision.

Already have the liquid hydrocodone waiting for me at Costco. I also got liquid Tylenol and liquid Miralax. Lack of bowel movement for five days is now the culprit and today's procedure in not going to help that. There is just nothing in the colon of any substance, and to find out that it was the Thrush that was causing it is a bummer. The radiation dude gave me antibiotics for Thrush in my mouth and after two days of 7 total, I am 110 times better. I wanted a hamburger this morning but of course, the standard "nothing to eat of drink after midnight..."before the procedure. So I will be starting the tube without being desperate. I feel that's a good thing.

God has been blessing me since birth, through bacterial meningitis at age 4 (back in the dark ages of medicine) and Viet Nam, failed Marriages just to get to Joanna (23 years and two days ago), Tayleigh my adopted daughter and our son Steve and his family out in Denver. The list is endless on how God has been Good to me. He's not going to stop now.

*And friendships, oh yes, more that I could have ever hoped for. Thanks
for joining that bunch. Take care and let's both kick some ass today. L-Dog*

I missed radiation that day. Although I was sure I was the only person to realize the urgency in the timing of the tube insertion operation, it soon became evident that the doc's knew the same as I
did that the nausea from Monday's chemo was going to rear up on
Wednesday, so this operation was quickly inserted into the operating schedule at the hospital. I awoke to the normal dry heaves and
mucous attack around 3:30 and at the time it was ready for us to
drive across town, I was shaking profusely, both from the freezing
cold sensation of Cisplatin being in my veins again, and from the
violence I had just afflicted on myself hanging on to the sink and
the bathroom. Hoarse and sore everywhere, I had quickly made
my way to the kitchen for relief.

The routine was the same at the hospital, except for one little
ditty that usually would have rendered me angry but this time only
initially sad. After checking in at the Medicare desk, Joanna and
the assistant walked ahead of me and I heard the lady say, "How
long has your father had cancer?" Now the age difference between
Joanna and me is 11-1/2 years, but I had never been labeled old
enough to be her father, except by some of my buddies of course.
By the time we reached the prep room, however, I was at peace
knowing that Joanna, my bride of 23 years, honestly did look like
she could be my daughter. The fact that I looked and felt like crap
just did not matter anymore.

The oxycodone had just kicked in. The insertion of the tube
was a 20-minute success. Joanna and I drove home in silence, the
anesthesia still working on me. I felt both defeated and relieved at
the same time knowing I indeed had crossed over that imaginary
line again. Control of my bodily functions had been transferred to
a two and a half foot apparatus which resembled the plastic tubing

you could buy at Home Depot for irrigation. It had a bulb on one end of it that clung to the inside lining of my stomach while at the other end there was a tornado shaped cap which fit into the hole, ostensibly to stop anything from seeping out. My "food", cases of which had already been ordered and delivered to the front porch of our home by Walgreen's, were stored away in the pantry. Eating was the last thing on my mind.

I was told to stay out of a shower for a day or two and to keep the hole in my skin around the tube dry and free of blood. This procedure of keeping that area was way more easier said than done, for in the wee hours of every morning, the dry heaves tried valiantly to pop that tube out and onto the floor of our hall bathroom. The trauma around the hole in my body, just north of my belly button, precipitated seepage of God knows what coming out of my stomach making cleanliness and dryness impossible. I wrestled with that situation for 3 to 4 weeks until finally the scabs and the droplets gave way to a pink halo around the tube.

My first foray into feeding myself with a vanilla flavored liquid was a disaster. I was a novice at positioning the funnel onto the tube and as I poured the first 12 ounces of liquid food into the funnel, it disconnected from the tube and went all over the place. I yelled and screamed perhaps the worst time ever simply pissed at my inability to perform such a routine task. The entire kitchen eating area smelled like formula for the next few days. Just what I needed: another reason to throw up. The food contained 500 calories and enough vitamins to keep me functioning. At first I would supplement that box-like container of vile smelling food substitute with Boost or Ensure, but as the days wore on, I didn't bother with that. I became so disgusted in those early weeks of the tube that my demeanor crashed to a new low. My friend, the oxycodone, helped me forget some of that depression, but every time I would reach for the syringe-like funnel to plunge into the hole in the tube I simply became more and more numb to the situation of watching others eat normally while I poured liquid into my body right in front of them.

What to do with the tube when I was not using it to give my body nutrients? It was just another battle in the war. Tie it up? Roll it up? Tape it to my body? Put it into my pocket and cover it up with a shirt tail? I even for a while ran the stupid thing down inside my underwear and onto my inner thigh. At first I was protective of the little bastard, knowing that my life depended upon its intended function. I had read on the internet that about 30% of the time the tube had to be removed and reinserted by surgery and I did not want to have that happen, so I babied it somewhat as to how I handled its downtime. In the beginning, sleeping with the tube wasn't that much of a big deal because I was sleeping sitting up, but in the later weeks, that became just another sleep robber, trying to make sure it was not disturbed. At first, when taking a shower I had made sure that the tube was taped up to somewhere on my chest so that it would not get in the way of sensitive areas while I washed. In the end, I just let it hang like an elephant's trunk. By that time it had become a part of my life just as throwing up, locked up bowels, staggering weight loss, hair falling out, neck burned to the crisp of bacon, intermittent rashes that looked like red sand paper, and mucous, oh my God the mucous that would fill a 55- gallon drum every other day.

Oh what the hell, just take another couple of pain killers here and there and move on.

CHAPTER 15
DR. KOTZ AND HIS ANGELS

Dear Dr. Kotz,

I know you asked me to call you in five years and let you know how I was doing, but there simply were just some things I had to say now. The first of course is how much your caring for me in my time of need meant to me. I cannot begin to tell a story about my chemo therapy team without tears forming in the corners of my eyes.

The experience starts just by walking through the doors of your facility, noting the somber atmosphere in the waiting room, and hoping to find a smile at the check in desk. I was never disappointed. Though one of the mainstays in that area has since retired (coincidentally the same day I finished my treatments), the greeters always had that smile, and it was usually accompanied by a lead-in to some sort of banter about something funny. That sent me to my seat with a feeling that this just wasn't as bad a place as I thought. I always sat in the exact same seat near the front entrance, just in case I wanted to bolt. No, that's really not the reason. I guess I just felt safe sitting by the window, knowing that my car was just outside, and that I would be back behind the wheel within a few hours.

After a few minutes I would be summoned to the vampire quarters where silent phlebotomists congregated waiting to draw the barometers of health, aka blood samples. They had little teeny tiny voices that conveyed orders just above a whisper; and, what would any sane person expect from them? After all, they were sticking needles somewhere every time. I had come to realize that I did not mind the stick, as long as I didn't look; I didn't mind the tourniquet, as long as I didn't look; and, I didn't mind the 4th vial, as long as I didn't look. They were very business-like in that room and in that instant all of us, the patients, were afflicted with the same malady.

On the days that I would be seeing you, the next step was the call back to the inner sanctum and the dreaded weigh-in. Being a light weight anyway, it was always a shock to see more weight had been lost, especially after the feeding tube was inserted during the second week of the seven weeks' procedures. I developed the "No Assatall" disease, which my wife says started before the cancer diagnosis. Still, it seemed to me that my jeans were going to fall to my ankles on a moment's notice. From there we were ushered to the first of two examining rooms, which I came to know as "staging". The only other time I heard staging referred to as a preliminary billet was the two weeks prior to debarking for South Vietnam as a Marine in 1967. This was much better because instead of a drill sergeant, I had Elizabeth.

Then came the barrage of questions which didn't change one iota from the first time to the last. Birth date... list of meds...changes in meds...bowel movements...eating habits...schedules...blood pressure (please uncross your legs)...temperature...earlier blood work results... Please understand that I'm not being flippant here. But similar questions were asked at every doctors' visit no matter which physician it was that I was seeing. I came to realize that the answers to these questions were telling the story of my progress or my demise, and so I became just as interested in the answers as Elizabeth was. As I sat waiting in the second examining room, I was able to read and re-read the story of the physician who I believe was your grandfather and his ground-breaking achievements in the field of medicine at Johns Hopkins (I think). I always had a smile seeing that hanging on your wall because it conveyed a sense of family to me. I think cancer patients seek out and thrive on those who we feel can be considered family. The emptiness of the disease is transcended by the kindness one's "relatives" extend at the time of need such as this. There was a blending of the Kotz and Davis family for that fleeting moment.

That first week's meeting with you spawned several emotions. There was the feeling that I was certainly in capable hands, although your top notch reputation had already preceded you. I think that first time my reaction was that you were all nuts and bolts, that you had seen this type of cancer so many times that all those stats and prognoses were imbedded in your mind to the point where individual cases simply fell within the curve so to speak. As the moments clicked by, the kindness in your voice and in your eyes put all that to rest. No, I was not just another patient in the mix, I was special and you were going to make sure that I was treated that way. And, when you uttered that most special word of all: "cure"...well, I was on your side just as much as you were on mine. You had me, Dr. Ken. Do with me what you will and you would hear nothing negative from me. Let's get started.

Joanna and I had toured the chemo room the week before and knew the layout of the lazy boy chairs. I remembered trying not to look at the faces, nor the I.V. stands, nor the bags hanging from those stands during the tour. But today, the stark reality that this was now going to be as much a part of my life as it was of those who were there last week and this, shot through me like a knife through hot butter. I wondered how in the world I was going to get through this madness, and yet, there was a sense of serenity in that large room full of mini stations. In that first instant I laid that blame on the patients who were as fearful I was and our inability to totally comprehend what we were there to do. Oh my, how wrong I was once again...

There were a handful of true superstars there that day. No, not Labron James, Tiger Woods, or Taylor Swift. Except for the unique surroundings, they could have been mistaken, at first glance, for people there to fix a leaking pipe, or to replace an electrical switch, or to don a screwdriver or a wrench to do almost anything other than their intended purpose. They were guiding rolling Craftsman tool chests all around the room, stopping here and there sometimes for just a glance, most times for a long pause. There were no uniforms or smocks which would give them away. There were no normal tools in there tool chests but they indeed were there to fix things. They were there to fix me.

Your nurses in that room came to be the most extraordinary people I have ever met.

Totally unassuming, caring, professional, loving, roll-with-the-punches, cosmopolitan, comprehensive, laughing, crying, sensitive, and clinical, all rolled into uniquely different packages but all part of a closely-knit team of nurses. I know now, beyond a shadow of a doubt, that these wonderful angels played a huge part in saving my life. Above anything or anybody else, they kept me coming back to the oncology center. They all knew who I was, why I was there, what was going to happen to me in perfect chronology, and from the start, they all knew precisely how to handle me. It became as natural as meeting at the same place at the same time with the same friends for lunch, a Bible study, or a game of Gin Rummy. As time went relentlessly on, I was at peace with my plight in the chemo room.

Sometimes when I want to say nice things about people I get fearful that I might omit someone deserving of my thoughts, and if this is the case today I hope that person will forgive me. But there is too much truth in some of my memories to not tell some stories about Betty, Crystal, Molly, and Brittany:

Crystal attended to me the last day of my treatment, though at the time we did not know it would be the last. It was also the first time I had been under her care, although I felt as though I knew her anyway. I had watched her pretty face float from chair to chair all those many hours of each session. Curiously I had not seen much emotion from Crystal, though perhaps it was just because we did not know each other. But this day, we opened up to each other. I saw pathos and caring as well as a hidden sense of humor that made me laugh repeatedly. She grabbed a stool and sat down and talked to me about life in general and what she wanted from it. It was clear Crystal had experienced an emotional roller coaster as an oncology nurse yet hiding it was part of her soul. Evidently my laid back approach to life was something she needed that day as we clicked immediately. As my time ended on that Monday morning, I turned to leave. I felt a gaze on my back and turned to see Crystal with her hands on her hips. It was one of those bear hugs, unexpected but not unwanted. It conveyed love and hope for the future from one human being to another whose lives were touched under the most threatening of circumstances. I carry that feeling with me to this day.

Good Golly Miss Molly! Could have been Cousin Molly. Could have been Aunt Molly. Could have been Sis. Molly was the first nurse to administer the chemicals to me on

Day One. It was as if God said, "let's make sure L-Dog comes into the family right away". And almost as I took my second breath, I was already there. Maybe Molly was the care giver for every one's first time. If she wasn't, then she should be. From the instant she wheeled her tool chest in front of me, she began the litany of instructions and explanations of what it was, where it was going, what it was going to do, what I should expect, what I should do, how I should handle it, how long it would take, what I would and would not feel, how great it was that I had gotten a port in my arm, how much easier that would be on both of us, and of course, what was the date of my birth! We were off and running with the Zofran anti-nausea, another anti-nausea bag, and the CisPlaten (sp) chemo drug. She told me that the Zofran would get me through this day and probably the next two, which would take me through Wednesday and help with the nausea that normally comes with Chemo Therapy. Unfortunately I remembered those words for the next 6 weeks, because when Thursday rolled around, it was brutal. She told me to not be timid about coming in on Thursday and getting a big bag of fluids, but for the first few weeks I was just too far gone to risk making a mess of the area. Molly was my leader of the pack, and I never wanted for information, nor had to inquire about what was happening to me during those weeks of chemo therapy. I knew because Molly trusted that I could handle knowing the best and the worst.

Brittany was as cute as she could be. She is so young I don't think she quite knew what to think of this old man in week 2. I guess I came across as too confident after being schooled by Molly the week before. So not much was said through the first half-hour of prep and set up. I noticed there was no ring on her finger, so I decided that I should break the ice so to speak and ask Brittany a personal question, "What's wrong with all those men out there that you're not married and starting a family?" Yes, that's what us traditional old guys think. And her answer was priceless, with hands on her hips she said, "that's what I want to know!" We laughed and the ice was history. There is not a more gentle soul on the face of this earth than Brittany. Nor one that is more driven for success and career in her chosen field. For someone so young to be so wise about the serious nature of her profession seemed unusual to me. Maybe that's what makes those stupid guys shy away. But I learned that this young woman had passion for the well being of those she treated. And, once again, there was validation for why I was there and what the outcome would be.

Ice cream and milkshakes. That's what got Nurse Betty and me off the ground. For the next three chemo sessions I was hers and she was mine. Betty was so soft spoken that it was difficult for me to hear through my tinnitus some times, but undauntedly she would repeat every time the words of wisdom she had about my stopping at one of her favorite fast foods places for a milkshake on my way home. It was as if she was telling me that my caloric salvation was hidden in the fruits of those shakes and that it would make all the other doctors and nurses at all my other stops along the way not have to say, "you need to gain some weight!" But halfway though those three weeks something changed. It was as though Betty sought me out, and maybe even more than that. Perhaps the scheduling lady at the front desk inside the chemo room had been told, put L-Dog in Betty's station. Once again, we were family. More than that, we were close family, the best of relatives, the favorites. Betty would hug me as soon as I sat in the chair. She would kiss the bald spot on the back of my head. She would grab my hand and just hold it for a brief moment. She would whisper words of incredible encouragement in my ears. Nurse Betty is one of the kindest, most genuine persons I have ever known in my lifetime. The impact she had on me has carried on deep into my recovery period as I remember her building blocks of positive reinforcement on days that negativity seeped into my mind. I think if I had asked Betty for anything at all, she would have found a way to give it to me. It was not a romantic love between us. It was simply love uncluttered and pure. Under those circumstances, she was mine and I was hers. Isn't that the way you want it to be when the breath of life is on the line and nothing else matters in that instant? I think it is.

And, Dr. Ken, that brings me to the story that foretold the writing of this letter. The week you cut me loose, one week early, and I was allowed to go back to the chemo room to say my good-bye's, Betty was in the mixing room, all garbed up with the whites and the gloves and the mask. When she saw me she fortunately was just finished mixing a bag of chemicals for someone and began to shed those outer garments. She came out of the room and we embraced for a moment. I told her that I truly loved her, just as I had told all the others moments before.

She looked up at me, touched my arm and motioned to a young woman seated in a chair close to us hooked to the chemo therapy drip line. Betty said that this woman had just had her feeding tube inserted and she asked if I would sit with her a bit and tell her of my journey and answer questions she may have. As I touched this woman's stocking feet I felt a sense of calmness come over me and could tell she felt the same. I told her that the feeding tube was both a badge of courage and a sign of extreme desire to beat her cancer. She asked if I had ever been embarrassed feeding myself in front of any one and I laughed and told her that I always believed that I was the lucky one because I knew what was wrong with me and I made the decision to help with the cure. I was proud of my desire to do the one thing that could help myself beat it. I feel I left that young woman with a more positive mindset for the next few months.

So I have realized that I want to give back. If there is any way that my presence in the waiting room or the chemo room, or my help on the phone or by email, could make it easier for someone in your care to cope, I would like to have that opportunity to do it. All you have to do is have someone get in contact with me and I will be there for you and for them.

I wish you and your family the best in everything you do as time marches on. All of you have given new meaning to life to me. I couldn't be more thankful.

Sincerely,

Larry Davis

CHAPTER 16
OUR SON STEVE

I almost missed the event at Riverside Hospital in Columbus, Ohio on July 17, 1978.

After all, it was only three years earlier that my daughter Olivia took enough time for me to drive to Columbus in a rainstorm, end up with a sheriff's escort for the last 10 miles to a waiting commercial airline at the Columbus airport, fly to Northern Kentucky, take a taxi to Christ Hospital, and wait for another 9 hours for her delivery. Labor with Steve lasted 30 minutes.

For the longest time, I worried about Steve. As an infant, he seemed to be overshadowed by a big sister and yet was entirely satisfied to be in that role. Madalyn, my older sister, certainly had that effect on me. As a youngster, he wore coke bottle glasses, most of the time with white tape on the stems, a result of running head-long into God knows what. Fully clothed, he might have tipped the scales at 80 pounds by age ten. I weighed 130 pounds when I was inducted into the Marine Corps, so you can imagine what I looked like at age 10, and so in that regard, he was shadowing me. He was an excellent but not motivated student and an adequate sandlot ball player, no matter what sport. Again, ditto for me.

When Steve was almost eight, about a year or so after my divorce from his mother, I had gone to pick him up after he and his friends had spent most of the day at the pool. The walk to the car was about 200 yards across a lawn. When we had walked about half way to the car, Steve suddenly dropped to his knee and began to sob.

"What's wrong," I asked.

Through gasps for air, he replied, "When are you and mom going to get back together?"

After all that time, this little guy had been carrying that around inside him. I felt pretty low right then. So we sat right there for about a half hour as I explained that the divorce was not a result of anything he or his sister had done. As he sat on my lap with his little head on my chest telling me how much he missed me being there for him, my heart was breaking. Steve was brutally honest and, to speak the truth, he is the same today. Somewhere along the way of his life he had made the decision to be a truthful person, hiding nothing as an ulterior motive. On that day and in all the days since, I spoke not one ill word about his mother In all honesty it was mostly my fault that my second marriage, though lasting almost thirteen years, was a loveless union between his mother and me. It was at that point in my life that I realized the being a dad was much, much more than I had been willing to give. Olivia had seemingly been able to handle the breakup, but now I knew Steve had not. I was concerned that Steve may have some permanent issues since this was, after almost two years, the first time he and I had ever talked about such things. Big mistake on my part.

I did step up my game to the point where I did not allow traveling to interfere with the days and weekends that I would be with Olivia and Steve. The relationship between son and father had begun to blossom as he took on more responsibility to fight his demons of loneliness and perhaps sometimes hopelessness. During family planning with his mother years earlier, she had made it abundantly clear that she did not want children because it would interfere with her employment as a medical technology. This attitude seeped into motherhood and Steve eventually felt left out by both parents; however, his resolve made it possible for him to function in school and at home with his friends. Friendship is where Steve found joy, as his cousin, Jay Davis, once said, "I don't know anyone who doesn't like Steve." He made it work by being the best kid under any circumstance. We never had to discipline, punish, worry about, push him to succeed, or speak to teachers about Steve. What a testament to his inner strength and his resolve to get through those young years without the guidance of either parent. At one point I thought it was a miracle. Looking back with tears in my eyes and an ever-present ache in my heart, I realize that miracle was named Steve Davis. If you knew him, you would love him too.

Though I did not understand then, his mother was always planning her future, with or without me. There was an air of distrust as it turned out, but while we were married for those 12 years, I just thought she was cold hearted. As it turned out, she was right, and I was wrong.

During a subsequent weekend that I was in charge of the kids, his sister, Olivia, three years older, was invited to a sleep over and it was going to be just us guys for the weekend. Back then, Piedmont Airlines was offering one-way non-stop fares of $39.00 from Cincinnati to New York City. It was early December, the beginning of the Christmas season, and I thought we should take advantage of both our new found freedom as well as that cheap airfare. I told Steve not to unpack his overnight bag and that we were going to do something special. We made the one hour trip to the Cincinnati airport and we boarded the plane and headed for the Big Apple. It was Steve's very first plane ride and his face was pinned, against the window, taking in all of God's majesty. The boy was so excited but you had to know Steve to understand that he was.

We started our city adventure going to the toy department of the old 6 or 7 story Macy's Department Store in Manhattan. The ancient boiler was working overtime to keep the place warm, except on the toy floor. There were so many toys in action, with lights and sounds on overload, that it must have been 110 degrees up there. Steve, in all his excitement, implored me to get him out of the store before he threw up. Down the rickety elevator we went with seemingly hundreds of people crammed in there with us. It took us forever to go down four floors. Steve somehow plowed his way through the crowd and bolted.

I realized as soon as I got off the elevator that Steve had not waited for me. I looked left and right, but all I saw were what seemed to be thousands of shoppers of all sizes and shapes. He was nowhere to be seen. I looked to my right and saw the myriad of doors at that old store. Each side of the building had a half dozen or more of gigantic wooden windowed double doors and bunches of revolving ones leading out into the streets of New York City. There must have been 25 or 30 doors that he could have taken to get outside. I was panicking. Now I was the one who wanted to throw up. As I raced out of one of the doors on the right, I heard a voice outside and behind one of the massive doors,

"I'm over here, Dad." There the little guy was, crouched down on one knee, looking pretty forlorn. Not wanting to let him think I was angry with him for running off, I gathered him up, dusted him off and said, "I'm never letting you go ever again, Steve."

One other memory of that trip: Tyrannosaurus Rex. The New York Museum of Natural History was displaying all kinds of dinosaurs that month and Steve's class had just finished a section surrounding the mystery of dinos. I remember walking into the massive front doors and looking up at least 4 or five stories to the top of Rex's huge head. It was truly an impressive sight even for me. But what I remember most is Steve's tiny hand holding tight to mine, with his eyes lifted as high as mine in disbelief. It was one of the sweetest times of my life even to this day. Thank you, Lord.

In retrospect, I remember many times wondering if Steve and I would have any close relationship with father and son. I carried a big basket of guilt around for some years not knowing how to "make up" for lost time. Or maybe I just did not take the time to make it work better. Though Steve would not admit it, he was the catalyst for the extreme closeness we enjoy now. He took it upon himself to grow up with an absentee father until a horrific accident occurred in the summer of 1990.

Worrying about Steve was a fact of life for me. I knew if he truly was the incarnation of his father, which he would have some hurdles to handle along the way. And sure enough, the summer of 1990 saw the young life of Steve Davis hang in the balance through days and nights of uncertainty and the real fear of what his future would bring if indeed there would be a future at all.

Joanna and I were enjoying a Sunday afternoon on the Ohio River drifting down towards the locks below New Richmond Indiana on our boat, the Too Deep, when Vince Walsh and Dr. Bob Lerer came fast down the river looking for us. My first reaction was wondering how in the world they found us, other than knowing the current was moving northeast to southwest.

Boating on the river is different than on a lake or any other body of water. There is a constant current which will take an unpowered boat slowly down the river.

"There's been a boating accident on Lake Cumberland," Walsh said. I knew both Steve and Olivia had gone with their mother on vacation to this Kentucky Lake, some 150 miles away from us.

"Olivia is okay, but Stephen has been airlifted to University of Kentucky Medical Center and is unconscious."

Joanna immediately jumped up, cleared the decks of our boat, and the two crafts barreled back to the dock about 15 minutes away. When we arrived, Janis Lerer was waiting to drive us the

300-mile roundtrip to the hospital. This was not uncommon for any of these friends to put their lives on hold for however long it would take to render help and love. Along the way, Janis described the accident:

"Steve and his buddies were riding jet skis off the houseboat the adults were renting. The boys started to race toward the houseboat and then, at the last minute, would veer off to the right.

What they were doing was splashing water on the adults up on the front deck," Janis, a registered nurse, relayed to us. "Stephen misjudged either his speed or the turn and crashed into the houseboat. Rescue pulled him out of the water where he was unconscious."

Olivia and Steve had just recently, at their request, moved into our tiny house in Hamilton, Ohio. We had sold the home in Middletown when our company, Wordata, was closing its doors in summer of 1992, and moved to Hamilton ostensibly to be closer to the kids. We honestly had no idea that they were going to ask us if they could move from their mother's home a few blocks away from our small three bedroom house. As we later found out, Olivia had the ulterior motive of an arrangement with her first serious boyfriend and Steve, honestly not wanting to move, went along with her wishes to have less supervision during the afternoons that Joanna and I were 13 miles north at the factory in Middletown. Steve had set up shop in the old basement, and seemed happy with his lot in life, playing video games and casting glances toward Elle McPherson whose huge poster adorned the wall opposite his bed.

Upon reaching University Hospital in Lexington Kentucky, and after what seemed like an eternity, Joanna and I were able to see Steve in his room. Had he not been unconscious he would have heard how suddenly the sight of our son would take our breath away. His eyes were a dark purple with his eyelids the swollen shape of plums. The railroad tracks of 110 stitches in his face transversed from left to right high on his forehead, dipped at right angles down to the area between his right eyelid and his nose, ran across the right eyelid, and ended around the right ear. His innocence shattered, I knew Steve had already begun to fight back, because, by the grace of God, he was still alive. We later learned from the orthopedic surgeons that his right wrist had been broken in two places, and several ribs were fractured. But the worst bone injury was to his left femur, broken cleanly ¼ inch below the growth plate where marrow is produced for the left leg and the left hip area. If the marrow could not be provided for the leg, then the leg would not grow normally. We began to hope and pray that the three long screws that had been drilled into his femur would heal it completely enough to perform its normal function.

"I do have some good news," the surgeon remarked as he got up to leave the waiting room. "One of the physicians on call when your son arrived at the ER is a plastic surgeon. The young man's face will heal in time."

What were the odds that a resident plastic surgeon was on duty on that late Sunday afternoon?

"And one other thing, the wound completely missed both of his eyes."

What were the odds that the tracks of the stitches would run right across his entire eyelid while the impact would not injure his eye?

Four fear-laced days later, Steve regained consciousness, and we were able to take him home to the house where Joanna, Olivia, Tayleigh, Steve, and I lived in Hamilton Ohio. We brought in a hospital bed, helped get him up and down off the toilet, hoist his naked body into a shower stall and wash him down. Even Tayleigh at age four would empty his urinal. It was something she could do to show Steve that she loved him. Joanna would take him to physical therapy three days a week and care for him as her son. Steve suffered various indignities for a year or so. His eighth-grade classes started in late August while he was still using a walker to get around and he endured painful physical therapy several times a week for many months. Wilson Junior High School was an ancient brick building with classrooms on two floors. To be able to make it to all of his classes, Steve would go up and down the steps on his butt, and a buddy would be waiting for him at the end of his climb or descent and help him regain his place behind his walker.

Here's the thing, though. Steve never whined or complained... not once! Cried, yes. But only to me. It was a sad cry and almost a relief for me to hear him do it. To this day, Steve Davis doesn't complain about anything. And as a middle school teacher in Brighton Colorado, he must have every reason to blow off steam!

The next steps for this type of injury to the growth plate were to measure both legs by starting at Point A with a measurement from the top of his legs to the bottom. Six months later, Point B would be measured, and then after another 6 months, Point C. What we were looking for was the rate of growth in both legs and the comparison of the two. At Point B our surgeon decided to begin discussion about how to stretch the left leg to enable it to keep up with the right leg. Obviously this meant the doctor was not happy with the 6 months' results. There was talk of installing a stretching brace at a place where the lower part of the leg would purposely be broken, attached to the stretching brace, and then tightened every week. This was an extreme measure and was excruciatingly painful. However, we all decided that we could wait three months to act on that. The discussion revolving around the stretching brace became a moot point when by the end of the next year or so it was evident that the growth plate was functioning. I'll say it was! Within a year he grew to his present 6, foot height with everything in perfect alignment. But it's more than that. Steve grew up in more ways than one that summer.

Emotionally he was much more mature and had a very high self-esteem. His life blossomed into manhood with the same calm demeanor as always, inevitably having cheated death that day at Lake Cumberland Kentucky in the summer of 1990.

Steve went on to graduate from Ohio University in 2000 with a degree in education. As was my custom, for graduation I offered to take him wherever he wanted to go in the USA for a long weekend. He never hesitated and chose Denver as his destination where a good many of his OU buddies had begun their careers. Soon after he moved out west, he met the beautiful Kristi Burns and along the way brought a granddaughter, Brynn, and a grandson, Lincoln, into the family. He is in his 15th year as a middle school teacher and has his eye on becoming a principal.

As a student, Steve was, as I mentioned, not outwardly motivated to excel. I think moving as far west as the Denver area was his way of communicating to me that the drive to succeed had always been there inside his soul; it was just not something he needed to display. Further, that was his way of coping with the uncertainty surrounding his childhood and his relationships with both mother and father. We were both "distant" parents, she in attitude and me in actual physical absence. Consequently, his self-made character has enabled him to achieve greatness as a father, a husband, and an educator. Most days Steve will come home from work and segue immediately into a dad, mentoring his two children and molding them into active, productive kids who show their love for their daddy more outwardly than I have ever seen. He started working for Outback Steakhouse soon after he achieved his Master's in Education and had toiled 10-15 extra work hours a week for ten years.

Now in his late 30's Steve has become one of my most trusted confidants because he neither judges me nor harbors any of the memories of a childhood full of pitfalls because his dad was not always there for him. Though we only see each other a couple of times a year, we talk sports and jobs, grand kids and pets, and even some politics, even though we are opposites. Of the 5-6 weekly conversations we have on the phone, Steve initiates most of them. When the abyss between his sister and me opened up in 2012, he asked me to reach out to her early on which I did, to no avail. Since that time, we have not spoken much about it, each of us feeling the loss in our way.

When Joanna told me that Steve had called her in early November of 2013 and revealed that he and Lincoln, then 20 months old, would be visiting us for Thanksgiving, I was humbled by his initiative to sacrifice serious money to fly to Wilmington and bring loving cheer to all of us. I have known for many years that Steve has lots of respect for Tayleigh and Joanna. He was able to overlook the apparent breach in his early family life and invite the love that both Joanna and Tayleigh have shown toward him and his family. Of all the memories I have of the human elements which have touched my life, I count my son Steve Davis as the brightest shining example of courage that I have ever seen.

True to his nature, to this day, Steve's love for me is outwardly understated. And yet, his embrace of our father/son relationship is as genuine and warm as any I know. Moving toward the twilight of my life, my son, Steve, has made me forget any lingering sorrows of inadequate parenting and has given back the blessings of fatherhood.

CHAPTER 17
SHOP VAC AND NURSE BETTY

That Tuesday in October, when the feeding tube became a part of my body, was the darkest day up to that point because for the second time in my life I felt as though I was on the precipice of death's doorstep. I wasn't on the doorstep yet...but I was close. At least, that was where I was, psychologically speaking. The first time I felt that dark was my first flight into the Tet Offensive of 1968 in Viet Nam. The dangers were certainly there, and I had seen the blank stares of returning crew members as they came back to base. The carnage of casualties was staggering. How could this one be worse than that nightmare? I think about it that way because, at age 21, I felt invincible. Now at 67, I felt incapable. Would cancer take me? Would I make it to the end of the protocol over a month away? Would I even make it through the next week? I decided to begin popping the pain meds at each meal. Started with 1 per dose and realized that was not enough so began taking 2 for a total of 10 each day. That seemed to get me where I needed to be. If my dosage could not be met with the pills, I would throw down a shot or two of the liquid pain killer. The pain was intense. I mentioned that to the radiology oncologist, and he wrote me a prescription for 100 pills. Geez, I thought, am I really missing something here?

Is it going to get that much worse? That seemed like a bunch to me. The pharmacist at Costco gave me a pill crusher that they had used in the pharmacy, and that became a utensil that I used regularly. I could mix the ground up pill in some form of liquid and get it down my tube. (On days that I felt horribly sick in the later stages I would mix the ground up pills into the liquid pain killer and take them both.)

At every turn, the enemy that the docs didn't say much about was mucous. The normal person worries about mucous only when a cold or flu symptoms persist or when the commercial about the mucous gremlins runs a million times during flu season. To the radiation patient, mucositis creeps slowly along the first 6-8 days. You notice some drainage and have to clear your throat more often than usual. Then you begin to see that you have to clear your throat each morning right after you get up and soon the stuff you spit out shifts from a clear and viscous substance to yellow and thicker and then to brown and as thick as glue. Any person with an ounce of sense would realize that the death rays had been pounding something to make all this happen. I surmised that radiation was destroying some mucous membranes and that they were fighting back. I learned later that wasn't it at all. Queries about that phenomenon fell on deaf ears mostly because there was not a damn thing that could be done about it...and it was going to get worse...and it was going to last long after the protocol was finished. This, I learned after posing questions about it several times. It became the same answer as the one when I asked how long after we stopped radiation would I regain the ability to eat normally. It was, as I finally decided, a moving target which moved in different directions and different speeds depending on who you were. Let's see, I was old, undernourished, all beat up, full of chemicals, had bacon for a neck, and my throat was closed.

No news was good news.

While getting fluids in the emergency room on Sunday afternoon, October 13th, I was introduced to a mucous suction machine which helped considerably. The next day Joanna called around town and found a medical supply store that had a portable one available. This little machine became a mainstay by my side wherever I went in the house, and Joanna could hear the ugly sounding motor grind away every 20-30 minutes, night and day. The color of what was coming out of my throat was indescribably disgusting. The machine's motor would bog down on occasion if it had been over an hour since using it because of the heavy viscosity of the globs. I would insert a tube about a quarter inch in diameter in between my broken and chapped lips, shove it back into the depths of my mouth, and turn the machine on. It was like a mini Shop Vac, albeit it with a low guttural grinding noise instead of the high pitched whine of the real Shop Vac. It was a Godsend for many reasons, not the least of which was that it gave me a ray of hope for being able to sleep lying down at night without fear of choking to death. Eventually, I segued into a series of nightly naps ranging from 30/40 minutes to sometimes an hour and a half. I would simply wake myself up, turn on the pump, and then go back to sleep. Normal? No. More normal than sleeping sitting up? Yes. I was at the point where I needed something that was "normal". I used that pump for several weeks and wore it out to the point where I had to take it back and get another one. Joanna would secretly clean the apparatus out when I was sleeping during the day, a task that was pretty disgusting.

If only I had known that Tuesday was a cake walk compared to what was to come...

I discovered quickly that the tube was going to get in the way. I tried to think of ways to forget about it, but that was about as easy as backing your car into a parking space with a trailer hooked on. The area around the hole in my skin was very tender and had continuous trickles of blood that eventually would coagulate and need to be cleaned off with some alcohol or hydrogen peroxide. If I didn't clean it in time, it would get crusty and then peel off, and the bleeding would start all over again. And of course, if blood was going to seep then so was that horrible vanilla "food" thereby making for just mess around the tube. This cleaning process continued for the better part of three weeks when finally the skin grew around the circumference of the feeding tube.

Wednesday, October 16, 2013

Welcome back to nausea day. Only this time I had a few ounces of liquid food in my stomach. I had made a pact with myself the day before that I needed to fight with every bit of strength I had left to avoid throwing up. I knew this pitiful excuse for food was my lifeline, so even though Cisplatin was a powerful adversary, at least on this day, and Thursday to follow, I was able to get through without wasting any of my precious calories. It was of utmost importance to keep this in my system for so many obvious reasons, including the hope that this liquid would make its way south and my lower tract would begin to come alive again. I certainly did not want to have to retrain myself to poop because of long periods of inactivity. That was a possibility and would involve further surgery, which at this point I was patently against.

It was at this point, my spirits at an all-time low, that I consciously thought of all the ways nausea could be avoided. One morning around the now normal wake up time of 4:30 I began to brush my teeth. Within a few seconds, I was once again gagging and gasping for breath at both the taste of the toothpaste and the act of putting a toothbrush into my mucous-laden mouth. Not only did it physically force a heaving stomach, but it also was psychologically disgusting to mix toothpaste with mucous. And so, for about two weeks, until I regained control over that reflex, I did not brush my teeth at all. I rationalized this stupidity with the fact that I was no longer eating anything through my mouth and therefore didn't need to brush my teeth. I felt that I had to make a decision: losing precious food v possible tooth decay. I forced myself to use the Magic Mouthwash, which had been sitting unopened on the vanity of the annex along with all the other bottles of salves for my crispy neck and liquids used for various reasons.

As I said: Stupidity.

Thursday, October 17, 2013

At 7:45 AM I arrived for my 10th radiation treatment. Ole Roy Lee was already in his customary chair in the waiting area, so I sat down caddy corner to him. I hadn't seen him for a week or so. He was a different man, no longer stooped over and gaunt. He told me he had finally succumbed to the rigors of radiation pain and had started taking pain medication. He looked tired but almost healthy. Today was his last day of radiation. When he was called back to the inner sanctum, I stood with him, thanked him for the kindness he had shown me and hugged him big time…tube to tube. A tiny bit of me thanked God for Ole Roy Lee for he showed me that a guy could win this battle of time and pain.

I never saw him again. However, his kindness and forthright-ness have stayed with me to this day.

As was usual now every Thursday and Friday morning, I would get strapped down to the metal table with the mask suffocating me at a time when I needed to throw up. As I look back on those excruciating few minutes of captivity, being in a position to not have any control over any bodily function may have helped keep me from succumbing to my urge to empty my stomach. If there was one smidgen of good associated with the mask, it was that.

The radiation was still spread over all parts of the front side of my neck. It would not be until the 18th treatment that it would be concentrated only on the left side where the original swollen lymph node had been. The skin on that part of my neck resem-bled a barbecue chicken wing with specs of brown crust forming. In the "care package" that Tom Haas had sent me were tubes of

Aquaphor and Eucerin lotions which he had used for his neck. I settled on Eucerin as my go-to lotion to try to mitigate the crust, and it seemed to do a pretty good job. It was ugly, but softer, after each of the 3-4 treatments I would apply each day.

Now well into my protocol, a collective "everyone" knew I had cancer and undergoing treatment. Most every day Joanna would answer the front door to find ladies from the neighborhood delivering delicious food in casseroles, sandwich form, or desserts. Big Dog's brother, John Musser provided a roaster full of fried chicken which we used to feed most of the folks on our block. I asked Joanna to call him and tell him how much good will he had gotten from the 'hood but please hold off until I gave him the green light down the road. John either texted me or left a voice mail for me every day until I finally tasted his fried chicken some weeks later. John and his wife Erin are stereotypical entrepreneurs who started with a catering truck and a couple of sand volleyball courts. Today they have over a dozen courts and a complete restaurant/ bar establishment that provides a place where mostly young people can go to work out their frustrations on the volleyball court. They have made it a family affair with their kids doing a lot of the work. Each year they sponsor a huge event that honors their father who succumbed to Alzheimer's several years ago. They provide a New Year's Day pig picking for all their friends. Wherever you see a charitable event which lists their sponsors, Capt'n Bill's Backyard Bar-B-Q is near the top of that list. A more generous family never existed in my life. During my illness, I came to realize what it meant to not only give but to give continuously. To this day, we are trusted friends and charting different paths to success with the same thread of giving back.

Friday, October 18th, 2013 9:16 AM
Mornin' Tom. The third week is ending up mostly like the 2nd week, save the bullet hole in my frontside. That is now mitigated and is nothing more

than a nuisance to deal with. Getting 2200 calories per day now and feel as though that is enough.

Mucous continues to be my main demon now. I think I mentioned to you that I procured a suction machine that is making me feel safer, albeit more BS to deal with every hour. It is tough to breathe in and out while laying on the radiation table, and I know that is going to get much worse. If you have any thoughts on how to combat that malady, just let me know. I'm wondering if I use the magic mouthwash just before I go in there if the would help???

Thank you so very much for your care package which arrived Thursday I think. I have been advised not to use the Biotene rinse as it could tend to burn some of the already burned areas in my mouth and throat. What are your thoughts on that? The Eucerin lotion will be a huge help. I appreciate your kindness in sending that along.

I don't usually get too far ahead of expectations or worries but still harbor anxieties about the next four weeks and the carnage the radiation is going to do. As a consequence, I got a little testy with my beloved Joanna once this week. Am now including a .25mg Xanax to my stable of meds, and it seems to keep me reined in a little more.

The lower tract switched gears mid-week from locked up to open flood-gates due to the formula I am devouring. So this weekend I have been experimenting a bit with the pain meds and the food to see if one will counter the other, and so far it is. So I'm going into the 4th week in pretty good shape all around. Throat sore, but manageable.

Chemo: 3 down and 3 to go Radiation: 12 down and 23 to go

Is there anything I should be on the lookout for from the second half of the chemo that I have not felt from the first half? I do sense a slight neuropathy in my feet, but not bad. That's about it.

Very best regards to you and your family, Tom. And, thanks again for your kindness. L-Dog

Weekends did indeed bring some relief from the onslaught of chemicals and death rays, but Saturday and Sunday only did not mean what they used to. It was like a chronic case of the flu and violent sunburn with a bit of pneumonia thrown in. Though weekends were a respite from the demon mask and chemo, there was no normalcy anymore. Saturday was the continuance of a downward spiral of resolve and Sunday was a harbinger of bad things that loomed closer with each passing hour. Extended periods of silence had permeated my life with Joanna as we skirted conversation about what was both good and bad with our lives at that time. Talk about the good stuff made me sad; conversely, any mention of the bad stuff made me angry. There was never a time where we spoke of not being together anymore, but plenty of occasions we silently wished the end would come, one way or the other.

Sunday evening of the 20th of October we both steeled ourselves for what was to come the next week. I looked at the chart on my wall and read the number "23". It was still a long way to go.

Monday, October 21, 2013...9:11 AM
Good morning, Larry. I didn't hear from you this weekend, so my guess is that this dang chemo and radiation is starting to take its toll on you. I know one bright spot may be that you have hit your one-third mark. I'm interested in how the feeding tube methodology is going. I remember it was about this time when I started being repulsed by the thought of food. The nausea meds didn't do anything, the mucous crap in my throat continued to gag me, and the pain was getting to the point that I thought it was unbearable. Unfortunately/fortunately, I found out in the weeks to come that the pain did, in fact, become unbearable...but found the strength form family, friends, and prayers to make it through another week. Well, sometimes it was to make it through just one more day.

I think I may have told you that about this time I was getting so dehydrated that I was receiving IV's every day to get some fluids back in me. It got so bad that one day I passed out in the garage as I was walking outside to get the paper. In know, your body is getting hammered beyond belief. And unless someone has gone through what you are going through right now...

they will never come close to realizing what it's taking for you to hold things together. I honestly wish that there was some silver bullet suggestion to help you out right now because I would make a trip to Crows Landing Circle right now to deliver it… but it doesn't exist. All I can promise is that there are better days ahead…and it's in my hopes and prayers that they come as rapidly as possible for you. Tom

At the point that Tom was sending this to me, I was introduced to the chemo nurse who would take me through the treatments of day four and day five. Nurse Betty was first and foremost a mom and a grandmother. Though the drill was pretty much the same, I knew that the next three Cisplatin does would be stronger each time and that I needed to be on my game to keep up with my vitamins and formula so that my blood readings could remain within the range of the living. On this day, I had been running late to get to radiation and forgot to take my pain meds before I left, so by the time I got through the phlebotomist drawing my blood and the check-in nurse, Elizabeth, checking vital signs, the pain in my neck was debilitating to the point I saw stars. So when I finally got into the recliner, I could barely speak. Somehow I managed to remember that I needed a shot in my port for pain, knowing that it would take a few minutes to get the OK from Dr. Kotz who was at a satellite office. When the relief finally came, it was unlike any feeling I had ever had. The port, of course, ran right into the chest cavity and hit my arteries in a matter of seconds. I felt the rush of painkilling morphine across my upper gums in my mouth and seconds later the pain in my neck had subsided.

Nurse Betty, all 5 feet of her conveyed serenity like an angel and this fourth and stronger dose of chemicals came and went quickly. I would doze off momentarily only to feel her sweet hand patting my bald spot on my head. Though she was in charge of multiple patients, I felt her presence the whole time I was there. At one point she had to assist several of the other nurses and one physician when an elderly, beautiful lady had a severe reaction to her chemicals. She sat right across from me and was comforted by her two granddaughters, each of whom wore the most stunning long flowing outfits I had ever seen. I sensed that the lady in distress was not doing well and a couple of weeks later was told that she had passed away. She had been through chemotherapy protocol on three occasions over a period of years. It was a very sobering time in my life as I felt a kinship for anyone and everyone going through chemo. I can still picture Miss Hallie, recovering with grace and dignity from her morning distress. Betty saw my tears, brought me a tissue, and kissed my forehead.

Radiation #13 and chemo #4 were histories, and I drove home to hunker down, knowing that my routine of dry heaves, mucous onslaught, eating through a feeding tube, popping painkillers, running the pump, sleeping in intervals, and trying to keep Perfect Network alive awaited me. I was at the beginning of a long spell without anything coming out on the other end, I was not brushing my teeth, and secretly hiding my fear of unknown hurdles that lie ahead. I knew they were there…I just didn't know what they were.

Since everyone we knew had knowledge of my condition, most of the men were supportive but distant. It was that male thing of knowing that they were there for me if I called upon them, but not a whole lot of volunteering was happening…which was all right with me. I felt as though Joanna and I had built a fortress, fighting off whatever came our way in seclusion. Beginning the fourth week, at my encouragement, she began to attend some functions with her friends and even went out to lunch several times. She told me later that she was never allowed to pick up her tab for anything. Flowers which I thought had come from our garden were present almost non-stop from this time forward, generally left on the front porch from one of our friend's gardens. No food had to be thought out and cooked because the neighbors and friends had supplied plenty for her to eat. That was a real Godsend because the aroma of cooked food drove me right into the "annex" with heightened nausea.

My customers, who knew that I was sick, sent countless emails and cards while leaving voice mail messages of good feelings when they also left orders for toner. One such message, from Roxie Dilleshaw, resonates with me to this day:

> *Good Morning!*
> *Sorry for the delay in response. It is with a heavy, hopeful heart that I am writing this. I hope you know we all came together, and each is praying for you and your family. I know it seems harder on your loved ones not knowing in concrete what God's plans are for you. I have FULL Faith that you are in good hands, His hands. Larry, what I do know about you is that you have a beautiful family that has more than enough love to travel above the moon and back and that, is sufficient to keep a light in the darkest places. Your needs and theirs will be met in abundance. Hey, you may be rocking peach fuzz at Thanksgiving :) but, to those that love and know you, you will glow beautifully as will your family knowing what a blessing it is to have each other. Keep your eye on the Prize. You've got this because God's got this!!!! Joanna is an amazing woman. That is why God chose you both for each other. Please know you all are in our thoughts and prayers.*

At another of my customers, Davidson County Schools, a middle school teacher, Cenda Wooten, became my confidant in keeping the secret that I was fighting curable cancer and that no interruption of service was expected. If there ever was a moment of indecision by DCS to continue our long relationship I never saw it. I don't know for sure that Miss Cenda had set everyone straight, but I like to think that she did and that her information was met with respect and confidence. I never heard a tentative word from any other person at DCS until I was sure enough that I was going to make it through. Joanna and I had discussed the alternative if that happened and she would make sure all the teachers at the 31 schools and all the administrators would know where to get what they needed if we could not provide it for them.

And then there was Murphy Brown. Nestled in eastern North Carolina, this customer is part of Smithfield Foods. Their stock took a nosedive in 2013 because I was not able to eat.

They make bacon. And they have restaurants that serve fried chicken and barbecue.

You may remember Ole Roy Lee, my friend at radiation. Well, the correct Roy Lee is at Murphy's along with Laurie, John, Jonathon, Alan, Mike, and the rest of the warehouse crew.

To a person, you would not find a better, more loyal group assembled in one place. On occasion, I used to drop by with some Krispy Kreme donuts, or sausage biscuits (complete with grape jelly) from McDonalds. I couldn't eat those either...hence my absence from those festive occasions for a longer than a reasonable period. That became troubling for me, so I picked the kindest, sweetest, most flexible person I knew at Murphy's and called Laurie Weston. Be advised, if you messed up, you paid. So from a business standpoint, I did not get any special treatment. But I did get encouragement and a big ole hug when I returned from my 6-month sabbatical. We never missed a beat.

I tell people to this day that cancer made me a better person. Not necessarily the disease, but rather the ribbon wrapped around the sickness. Whether corporate or neighbor, friend or just a compassioned person who knew of my cancer, the mailman, UPS driver, lawn maintenance personnel, church members, or literally anyone anywhere who somehow found out that I was fighting cancer, my life was enriched in ways I never thought possible. The qualities that came to life in these kind and unselfish people were transferred to me through cancer. There are stories throughout this book that still cause me to cry when I remember how these real heroes reached out their hands to me and pulled me through the darkest of times. They put their collective arms around Joanna and gave her someone to talk to who was not under a shroud of fear.

So if ever there is a time that you are faced with cancer or if someone you care for is afflicted, my advice is to get the word out. People feel sorry for your spouse...they don't feel sorry for the one who is sick; they fear for them. Cancer patients need strength in numbers pulling for them, praying for them, and you can't do that if you feel sorry for them.

As the lurking darkness of perpetual night closed in on our home, there were so many people to turn to, but no one could help. I knew that right then. I knew that Joanna and I were about to hit rock bottom, and we had nowhere to turn but to each other.

My angel came through big time.

CHAPTER 18

CREEPY, HIDEOUS, AND ANTAGONISTIC

Tuesday, October 22, 2013

The day after my third chemo treatment and a week after insertion of the feeding tube,

I awoke to Heartly's huge body laying next to me, sort of like going to bed with a 20 pound sack of potatoes. It was a little after 4 AM and even with several layers of blankets and the big boy nestled up to me, I was chilled to the bone. There is a certainty when it comes to felines around sickness and countless stories have been chronicled about their abilities to sense illness. I remember when Joanna's beloved Roxy was sick with feline leukemia, Lacy our ragdoll would constantly sniff at Roxy's mouth, knowing that what was exhaled in her breath was not normal. Stories have been written about cats sleeping in cribs with babies and the fear of suffocation, when in reality perhaps the cat was sensing something not right in the baby's breath. Looking back now on Heartly's actions around me, I can only surmise that he knew something bad was wrong. He was the only talking cat I have ever heard about, so I tried to tell him his life was still pretty cool, but he was having none of that…and told me so in no uncertain terms.

I threw down 1100 liquid calories, popped two ground up pain killers and decided it was time to brush my teeth, after almost two weeks without touching a toothbrush. I slept in the "guest room", AKA "Tayleigh's room" (because Joanna just can't call it anything else), and the annex was just down a short hallway in between the kitchen and my office. As I hunted for a toothbrush and toothpaste, I happened to glance in the mirror and what was staring back at me was creepy. No, it was scary.

My face had taken on a sort of macabre look of sunken eyeballs and various stages of cracked and peeling lips. My hair, thin to begin with, was best described as spotty, and more white than gray. Both sides of my neck were a light brown and rough to the touch. There hadn't been but a few glances over the past week or so since I was not doing any type of dental maintenance. I made myself very sad by just looking. And I had no idea what Joanna must have been enduring now that my very appearance had begun to mirror the situation we faced each day. The mucous really was disgusting, and there is no other way to describe it. I was waking multiple times at night and getting up for good about 4:30 every morning now with the first 40-45 minutes spent getting my mouth and throat cleaned out. I had to do that dozens of times a day but mornings were particularly disgusting. Wretching with dry heaves would take over and drive me to my knees. Throwing up just wasn't an option for me that early in the morning, nor at any time for that matter. I did not want to get started down that path on a daily basis. Strings of prolific mucous could be seen just by opening my mouth and it made me gag just imagining what gunk was lurking beyond. Joanna had purchased a couple dozen throw away toothbrushes so that I didn't have to use the same one twice. I brushed my teeth as best I could and as I was rinsing out my mouth I noticed my tongue. There appeared to be a thick layer of dried mustard-like substance covering the entire surface of my tongue. I consulted the internet regarding whatever it was on my tongue. Fittingly, the diagnosis was "Yellow Tongue", and the description was: "Yellow tongue usually occurs as a result of a harmless buildup of dead skin cells on the tiny projections (papillae) on the surface of your tongue. Most commonly this occurs when your papillae become enlarged and bacteria in your mouth produce colored pigments."Also, "the longer-than-normal papillae can easily trap cells that have shed, which become stained by tobacco, food or other substances. Mouth breathing or dry mouth may also be linked to yellow tongue." Of course the yellow on my tongue could only be a result of a buildup of mucous since nothing else was entering my mouth at that time.

So this became not only another malady caused by the radiation but also just another disgusting hurdle to leap over. I had been warned that the salivary glands would fall victim to radiation to some degree and therefore a lack of saliva would ensue. During my protocol the Zimmer Cancer Center at New Hanover Regional Medical Center had enlisted me into a test case involving my type of cancer. There were checklists and updates each week that needed to be filled out so that they could chart a new approach to dealing with this type of cancer. It was a voluntary participation and I consented immediately. The core of the new approach was to treat both sides of the neck for one-half of the protocol and then only the side where the primary cell had been found (in my case the left side) for the second half of radiation therapy. Each side of your face has identical salivary glands, with the main one being the Parotid glands, one on each side. Early on Dr. Neal informed me that the parotid gland on the left side would be impaired to a great degree and the prognosis for it returning to full operation was basically a crap shoot. Each parotid salivary gland is responsible for 35% of the total saliva, with the other four lesser glands responsible for the remaining 30%. The lesser glands, sublingual and submandibular, could very well be maimed also. So for this type of cancer, both parotid glands would be affected with the left gland taking the brunt of the punishment. Part of the study was to discover if the parotid gland on my right side would stay active since it received less radiation and of course I was rooting hard for that to be the answer.

Mucous had overtaken what little saliva was being produced and Dr. Neal told me that it would be months before we would know what damage would have to be inflicted and therefore how much I could expect in recovery. The history suggested anywhere from 50% to 80%. So my thinking was I would get closer to the 50% on the left side and 80% on the right side. Yellow tongue was a by-product of too much mucous and too little spit resulting in a buildup of bacteria. I contributed to that by not brushing my teeth. Though I blamed nausea for my reluctance to continue proper oral hygiene, the fact remains that the word that best describes my actions in that regard was "stupidity". You may remember that word from earlier in the book...

The day before, I had taken 12 oxycodones, then two more around 2 AM. Before I would travel across town, I would take another two. The pain was a hot, searing intensity now after each morning radiation therapy. After making the 13-minute drive across town, I sat in the waiting room scanning the mood. This particular morning I wasn't feeling high, but of course I certainly was under the influence. To have acquiesced to Joanna's pleadings to let her drive me over there each morning would have required two digressions from the norm. First, Joanna would have to sit in the waiting room each morning and endure the pain right along with everyone else. I simply did not want her to heap their sorrowful plight on top of what we had together. Just wasn't going to do that. Secondly, her morning routine would be totally interrupted. I knew she was not sleeping well at all, and that mornings were her best sleep times. After all, she was going through menopause and sleep was another crap shoot.

The hood of foreboding darkness which had pulled itself over my eyes during the evening and nighttime hours began to creep further down my face as the days wore on. My relationship with Joanna had become adversarial with me snapping at her way more than necessary. Initially she had tried to rationalize with me and neutralize these intermittent disagreements, only to realize that the best thing to do was to leave the house for a couple of hours. Those decisions not only saved the marriage we had always cherished, but it also may have saved my life. For as she would walk out the door and I heard the car start up and the garage door go down, the instant lonliness crept into my darkened soul and I could feel it laughing at me from the inside out. From the mirrored image to the lack of personal hygiene discipline to my deplorable demeanor around my sweetie, I had become someone else. Cancer was winning battles left and right. And I was letting that happen. The only time I felt somewhat normal was on the drive to and from radiation, somehow transcending the fact that I had consumed copious amounts of pain killing medicine. Toward the end of each week the rocking and humming of the car on the road, along with the feeling that I was in control and just navigating the familiar route, stalled the nausea long enough for me to walk in the door of the office and lingered long enough for me to get strapped in. However, once that mask clamped down on my face, and in particular my lips, all bets were off and my resolve was shattered.

God just get me through one more.

The drive also resurrected my love for music. For instance, when I was just finished with radiation #17 I could not get enough of Bon Jovi's "Livin on a Prayer" because it proclaimed "We're halfway there!". I played the beginning minute of that recording a thousand times just to pump me up. Music became another rallying point and I leaned on it for weeks during the morning drive.

Neither Tom Haas nor I were particularly religious in an evangelical sort of way; however, our faith in the Almighty was strong.

Throughout this dark time in my life, with new maladies cropping up so fast, courses of thrush, yellow tongue, constipation then diarrhea, and ever-increasing pain might cause a person with weaker beliefs want to sign off and quit. Only one time, close to the end of my protocol at a time when death came calling, did I want to throw in the towel. I knew if I crossed that line, when life itself was travelling at a speed with which I was unfamiliar, when my thought processes were no longer rational, when those around you gaze back with sadness, and when those closest to you shy away because their inability to provide comfort confronts them, that precipice of doom looms large. Just as I would get over one hump by shedding this or that sickness and jumping over hurdles, there would be another, more menacing, waiting its turn to affect its torture. I was helpless and floundering in an environment over which I had no control.

Thursday of the fourth week, October 24th, a day of intense nausea, I met Gene in the staging area for radiation therapy. Gene was a man of 55, a little over six feet tall, and built like no other giant of a man I had ever known. His chest and arms could have lifted a small battleship and his shoulders would have balanced it for hours. Gene's hands hid nothing in the way of questions about what he did for a living as they were massive mitts made of calouses and leather. I guessed he was some sort of construction worker and so he was. We talked for a few minutes about God knows what and then the conversation came around to what it was we were both "in for", almost like we were talking about prison. For Gene, this man of such strength, his plight had been diagnosed two years earlier: inoperable brain cancer. His physical brawn had been eclipsed by the demon cancer and could very well have rendered him helpless. And yet Gene was far from that. Gene was a man of God and believed with all his heart that his terminal illness, one which doctors had originally given him 6 to 8 months to live, had indeed just passed the two year mark. Radiation had become a normal part of an abnormal life with a schedule of 3 months on and 3 months off for those two years.

On this day he was flanked by his equally enormous son and a gorgeous daughter, each of whom obviously loved their daddy. Their togetherness in Gene's plight reminded me of how steadfast Joanna was with me even in the past few days of my anger and anguish aimed at her.

I vowed to never strike out at Joanna again as I watched the look of happiness on Gene's kid's faces as he walked back to the death ray chamber. They rejoiced in the fact that they still had their dad, and that every day was another of God's blessings. Dad had cancer but cancer did not have Dad. A flicker of life ran across my eyes and allowed me to peek out from under the dark hood. In that moment, just before my 16th radiation treatment, Gene's family and their faith lifted my spirits and proved that I still had the fire inside of me to beat this disease. That was Gene's precious gift to me.

As I pressed on past the half-way mark in my protocol, my thoughts drifted back to the days before diagnosis. I couldn't count the times I told those who would listen that I had the best life that anyone could have. At 68 I was able to work with top shelf people who genuinely valued me. I had a group of friends that never made me feel like I was being "used" for one purpose or another other than simply being there for each other. My two kids were tremendously supportive, almost making up for the absence of Olivia. I was neither rich nor poor on a materialistic scale. But I had my Joanna. There was no truer love on the face of the earth. I remember a few weeks past the cancer treatment regimen I was waiting in the exam room for Dr. Neal to come in and review my first month after the last radiation treatment. I still had the feeding tube in my gut but had secretly scheduled its removal for 2 weeks hence. Dr. Neal and I had a discussion about that removal and he did everything but pound his fist on the table admonishing me to leave the tube in past flu season…another two and a half months! His fear was that if the tube were removed and I went down with the flu and lost my appetite that I would be in serious trouble. My answer was pretty simple:

"Dr. Neal, I am having the tube removed on the 91st day after its insertion. And then I am once again going to lie down and make love to my wife."

The way I figured it was with all the sacrifices Joanna had made for me, all the way back to picking up and moving south, making new friends, sending Tayleigh off to new schools, starting over in business, getting through the fear and loathing that cancer forced upon us, and letting me know that our marriage was the most important part of her life, the least I could do was chance a little flu bug. How could any doc say "no" to that?

CHAPTER 19

THE HAUNTING:ADDICTION

Tom Haas opted to run through his cancer protocol without inserting a feeding tube.

Though his radiation treatments were a full three weeks longer than mine, his rationalization was that he could lose 75 of his 265 pounds and still survive. Throughout his ordeal, not only was he constantly hounded by loved ones to eat solid food, he also became dangerously dehydrated.

Though I was "eating" more than the required amount of calories by mixing supplements with my formula, my weight continued to decline rapidly into dangerous territory and dehydration became a problem for me too. The docs continued to advise drinking 64 ounces of liquid per day and due to its immediate saturation rate into the bloodstream, water was their beverage of choice. Unfortunately, water was not an option for me as it induced uncontrollable choking and coughing, which as I learned from nurses, was the norm for a great many patients suffering from my type of cancer.

In my particular case, all I could taste were the chemicals used to filter the water. I tried Coke which was too painful with the carbonation, tomato juice which tasted like iron filings, orange juice which produced searing heartburn due to citrus acidity, beer, and chocolate milk.

Ahhh, now there's the drink for a radiated throat. Mucous was no match for chocolate milk as they mixed perfectly. And I got the added benefit of the extra calories. Chocolate milk was another entry on my list of lifesavers.

After radiation on Thursday, October 24th, a particularly intense session since they performed an all over Xray which added another 5 to 6 minutes under the mask, I drove down to Dr. Kotz's office to make my appointment for a large bag of fluids. Dehydration wasaffecting my stamina now and the bag of saline solution was such a welcome addition to my wellbeing. I scheduled one of those for each Thursday to augment the fluids I received on Mondays with my chemo therapy.

At the end of the 4th week and with only 3 more weeks to go, I was totally dependent on the pain medicine and cocktails of liquid oxycodone and Tylenol. As I cruised through each day, doing business during the morning and then gluing my eyes and ears to the TV each afternoon and evening, I wanted desperately to see and hear other people who were suffering, and if it was at the hand of an evil villain, so much the better. I craved cruelty toward other human beings and found myself becoming very distant from Joanna and most everyone else that once mattered to me. I couldn't talk more than a whisper so I simply zoned out from any contact with anyone.

I'm positive Joanna was lonely, but also thankful for the relief it gave her from enduring me in the physical and mental state where I resided at that time. It was as if I was in a different life, one with which I was unfamiliar, and yet in a state of mind that I seemed comfortable with.

Day became night and my whole world morphed into darkness. The two warm hoodies Joanna had purchased for me weeks back were worn with the hoods raised up over my head just to personify the darkness. Each day I would awaken in the wee hours, dress and sit quietly waiting for 7:35 to roll around, having thrown down some formula and popped a few pills.

By this time the effect of the painkillers was no longer a perceived high, but more of a dulling sensation that would have landed me a leading role on *The Walking Dead*. In all the 50+ trips, to treatments I do not remember a single episode when I felt inadequate to drive my car through the traffic maze. Radiation overtook chemo as my most demonic adversary. The pain grew so intense that even fighting the mucous became a simple segment of my day, taken for granted that as insidious as it was, I just lived with the damned stuff knowing full well it was going to continue getting much worse. I didn't care. Living in darkness allowed me to blend into the nightmare cancer had become as time became just one minute to the next, one hour after another, amid a blur of semi conciousness.

Now, with the better part of 3 weeks of radiation therapy left, I was swallowing the equivalent of 60-80 mg of hydrocodone (oxy + Tylenol) every day. In the end I would have consumed 350 pills over the course of 45 days just so I could function. I never cared if it would come back to haunt me. Of course, the haunting had already begun.

Friday, October 25 10:12 AM
Good morning Tom. Thank you for your words of encouragement last evening as I was feeling pretty low after lashing out at Joanna once again. I met a family in the waiting area and they convinced me that the last thing I should do is get angry with the person who loves me the most. I know you have told me to be wary of that, but maybe I just needed to hear it from someone else, too. I may have mentioned that I used to take omeprazole for acid reflux but that I could not find a suitable way to take a time release capsule now. The acid sensation in my esophagus feels like it is eating its way through what lining I have left. Joanna is out right now trying to

locate some liquid Maalox which is the only medicine we can find that may help. I just crossed off radiation number 16 (#19 on my wall chart) and am steeling myself for next week's move to left side only radiation.

The test protocol in which I enrolled early on had three main components which involved the cancer patient. Mine was one of 42 studies of this type of cancer, Squamous Cell Carcinoma of the Neck. The study was sanctioned by the New Hanover Regional Med Center and was completely separate from my normal physicians. The vast majority of those involved were men over 50 years of age and in otherwise good health with no other debilitating physical conditions.

The main component centered on the radiation of specific location of the original site of the cancer, in my case on the left side at the base of my tongue, with very little radiation elsewhere. The benefits to the patient included more intense treatment to the site of the primary cell hopefully rendering it devoid of cancer as well as a slightly less period of time under the mask per treatment. This change in the protocol occurred after the 17th radiation treatment and continued until the end. I welcomed this adjustment because of the mask, not really even considering the elimination of cancer. At this point in the radiation therapy, I was totally under the control of the docs and techs, so if they thought this change of course would eradicate my cancer, who was I to question its validity? And for the love of God, even 1 or 2 minutes less under the crushing spell of the mask was nirvana.

Friday, October 25 11:52 AM
So glad to hear that you got a bit more stabilized after the hydration. I can't imagine the acid reflux on top of everything else. And I agree totally with you and Joanna about the pain meds. You are going through enough hell, so you might as well do it with having your pain mitigated to the whatever extent is possible through the wonders of drugs. I did have a little issue with the withdrawal from Fentanyl…but it was minor compared to the benefits during

radiation. Your comment about crossing off the days reminds me of one of the packages I received from a younger sister. It was a chain made of colored paper links. Each one represented a day left of radiation. When I would remove the link, there was a little encouraging saying written on the inside. In the beginning it was daunting to see the pile of links that hung to the floor, but as I became a short-timer, it was a nice feeling to see it shrink each day.

Tom's calendar became the colored links, mine was the chart of days with big black "X's" marking the finished treatments. Sometimes I would wait and let Joanna cross one off or if Tayleigh had travelled from Richmond VA to be with us for a weekend, I would give her the honor of crossing off the Friday before. It was an excuse to get a hug of encouragement even if I did have to move the dreaded tube to the side of my body.

I think we discussed this already, but I found the effects of the chemo subsided right after we stopped administering. Very encouraging. Not so for the radiation. I think it was a week or more that the burn continued to grow after the last treatment. BUT THEN...things did get better. I remember they told me that the trip down the good side of the mountain takes as long as the climb up the treatment side. So 8 weeks after the last treatment you will be well on the way to being the old L-Dog.

I hadn't thought about this before, but during a phone message I had left for Tom I asked about "what happens after radiation treatments are finished?" The significance of his answer was that I now had some sort of bookend to wrap around the whole episode in my life. Mid-January of 2014 was going to be a joyous time for us.

I hope those next 18 treatments go fast for you. How is your weight and overall strength holding up? I'm rootin' for you!
Tom

Sunday, October 27, 2013 3:32 PM
Tom, Tomorrow starts the radiation only on the left side of my neck. Smaller area and shorter time under the mask. Of course, mucous under the mask was very intimidating from a now-swallowing sense during treatment. However, I am cheating now and taking 5mg of Zyrtek every day. The mucous has abated somewhat but it is enough so far to make a huge difference in both daytime and sleeping. It is the one thing I learned from the ER doc that made sense.

Joanna reminded me that people are stoned and drugged out all day everyday all over the country. Therefore I have no worries taking pain meds. They work well and the liquid diet balances out to some degree the constipation threat. So maybe I have found a couple of the silver bullets that you mentioned a while back. At least for the Monday, I return to simply looking forward to Tuesday and crossing off another dreaded day at radiology. The lurking tendency of my oncologist wanting to give me an additional day of chemo "because I am fairing so well with it..." is something I have in the back of my mind as a bummer. I wonder what he would do if I flatly refused to do it. That, my friend, will be dependent on the next two weeks. Kindest and sincere regards, L-Dog

Sunday was always the best day of the week until around 5 in the afternoon when the dread of the next week would creep into my mind and begin to cause the stress which would lead to another sleep-deprived night. On this particular Sunday, heading into the 5th week of my 7- week protocol, the words of encouragement from Tom Haas had once again caused a flicker of light to appear on the horizon. I felt a renewed resolve to fight back harder, even if it was just for Joanna and Tom. My physical self had deteriorated into a cesspool of various ailments, conditions, and fears so far down in my soul that I truly did not care about me. I had three more weeks of radiation, the thought of which simply rendered me helpless in a quest to keep from becoming hopeless. There had been so many "side effects" of both the chemo and the radiation I shuddered just thinking about what may be waiting for me just ahead. I found myself crushing more than one dose of pain killers at a time thereby destroying a simple dosage amount and ingesting God only knows how many at a time. Whether the drugs were helping me cope or feeding the depression I did not know. Nor did I care. In fact, there was very little that I remember caring about. I had become numb to the normal process of living, while fighting intensely through the waves of extremely abnormal events cascading over and ultimately penetrating my body. My daily routine of side effects included ignoring the risks of tooth decay, lying about my bowel habits, slurping mucous out of the depths of my mouth with what resembled a shop vac, taking a shower with a three foot rubber tube hanging from just above my belly button to down between my legs, pouring the foul smelling liquid of life down that same tube and doing so in front of whoever happened to be close at that time. Nope, I didn't care.

I had a rash from my knees to the top of my head, my neck resembled an over cooked waffle, the bottom ring of my hair was falling out, and my tongue was caked with yellow gunk that I had to scrape off multiple times each day. My clothes didn't fit, I was bitterly cold all the time, nausea would come and go at the least favorable times, and what sleep I was getting was, well, a nightmarish collection of bludgeoning murders, sick crimes of passion, and wandering hopelessness. I was increasingly aware that the second prescription of pain killing oxycodone was dwindling rapidly, but that dilemma was solved Friday of the fifth week when there was another prescription waiting for me at checkout. This time it was for 150 tablets, and my first thought was, "How am I ever going to take all of these in just two weeks?" The math worked out to about 10-12 per day!

What I did know, now with absolute certainty, was that the worst was yet to come.

Monday, October 28th, 3:02 PM
Hey Tom. Very scary day at the oncologist today. My blood levels have dipped to dangerously low levels in just one week's time. My weight has dwindled from starting point of 162 down to 144. Dr. Kotz is so worried he has now abandoned ADDING a chemo treatment and suggested that today's chemo treatment would likely be my last. Couple that with the knowledge that my last three weeks of radiation will be more intense each session, and I am hopeful that I can go into that intensity with better blood levels. I have self imposed my own bad self to a life at home without visitors and without going anywhere until my blood levels get back in the normal line. Got my son and grandson coming in from Denver for Thanksgiving. That's my prize for all this BS. Lincoln is 18 months and I"ve only seen him one other time. Going into self-imposed exile may be classic paranoia, but I'm not taking chances any more that I have to. Too close now to catch the flu or some other illness.

Met with the radiology doc today and told him I was running low on oxycodone.

Received a refill of 150 pills. Hopefully that will get me through to the end. When I take 2 of them I also throw down 5-10 mg of liquid Tylenol. The pain is steady but low grade if I do that. I have run through all the Eucerin you sent me and have started on a big-assed bottle Joanna got me from Walgreens. My neck is a dark brown color but so far is staying fairly moist.

Thanks again, Tom. You are the best! L-Dog

Monday, November 04, 2013 6:25 PM (Mass email to all friends and family) Subject: Update to All
Folks, Monday was a banner day. Had a scan before my 23rd radiation session this morning and the scan showed total absence of any tumors. In honor of that, the chemo therapy (session 6 and 7) have been cancelled and I am through with chemo! Radiation will continue until all 35 sessions have been completed. After showing me the scan, the radiation oncologist remarked that it is "most likely that after you are finished here, you will

never have to worry about this disease again! Will schedule the port in my arm to be removed within a couple of weeks. In-office surgery which takes less than half hour.

I asked the radiation doc how long to expect the effects of the radiation to last in the form of mucousitis, sore throat, and lack of normal taste sensation after we are finished on November 20th. I asked "days or weeks or months?" Altho everyone is different, these effects are fairly predictable. So I am pointing toward mid-January to be able to eat normal foods and work into a normal diet within a month after that.

His answer, by the way, was, "Months".

Thanks to all of you for your steadfast support and love. I was overwhelmed from the beginning and still cannot fathom the joy hove have given ma and Joanna each day. November 20th is just around the corner.

Sincerely, L-Dog

Monday, November 4, 9:35 PM
Larry, What great, GREAT news!!! I can't tell you how happy I am to hear those TOTAL ABSENSE words. I will be seeing my oncologist on the 17th of November and am anticipating the same kind of news with my annual follow up scan. I can't believe a year has gone by and im sure you will be able to look back on your ordeal the same way Larry. Now let's get those last radiation treatments finished and let the healing begin. Thanksgiving Day will be a very special day for you and your wonderful family. God Bless you all!!!

With goose bumps and watery eyes... Tom

Tuesday, November 5, 2013, 11:15 AM
I know your news is going to be great, Tom. They covered all the bases and then so I think with your treatments. You emotional response to my news is just another trait that you have that is endearing to all of us who know and love you. Your guidance cannot and will not ever be underestimated...ever. You gave me strength and resolve when I needed them the most. Praying that the 17th brings those words of happiness.

L-Dog

One of the facets of battling cancer details the various echelons of friendships and how the movements from one tier to another, both up and down, were totally affected by that person's interaction during our time of supreme need. Understand, neither Joanna nor I truly understood what we "needed" from one minute to the next. And yet, perhaps because so many people have been affected by someone's cancer, some totally understood exactly what we needed. The upper echelon consisted of Tom Haas and Dr.'s Brinson, Kotz, and Neal. These were the guys who only had to say something to me once, and I would immediately react to it, no questions asked.

They had actual experience with my plight and their four separate avenues on the way to a cure were paved with truth. On the other end of the spectrum were friends and neighbors who never once even called Joanna to see how things were going. One neighbor had actually suffered a minor stroke and heart attack a few months before my diagnosis and I had paid him a visit at the hospital to make sure he would rest easy knowing I was watching out for him, praying for him, and hoping to see him back in the neighborhood soon. Not one time did he try to contact us...and we live right next door. A neighbor lady to the back of us would work in her garden inside an 8-foot wooden fence and Joanna would be working right next to her on the our side. Not one word ever came from that other side of the fence. And yet countless neighbors we didn't even know would stop by, stand on the front porch, and try to bring some cheer with food or flowers, or just a card of encouragement.

I would remember Bob Thieman and the unbelievable sacrifices he made for our friendship, teaching me the value of a trusted and loving relationship between friends. After cancer, none of these interactions were forgotten. What I wanted was to get back to normal and clone myself after those on or close to that upper echelon. I wanted me to be better from cancer, yes. But most of all I wanted to live to be a better friend.

Not long after that momentous and glorious news of the scan coupled with the cancelation of my last two chemo therapies, friendships collided with near-death disaster which struck with a vengeance I had never before experienced. My body, shrouded in a nighttime aura of mind bending pain that sent me to refuge of murder and mayhem on TV and the subsequent (now) addiction to pain killers, ultimately succumbed to another bizarre battle in this war that became unwinnable at seemingly every turn.

The dark shroud of night had fully closed over my face.

CHAPTER 20

FOUR MIRACLES

That CT scan performed on November 4, 2013 had been planned for about a week. Earlier that week, I had been on a daily regimen of Prednisone and Benadryl to combat my allergy to iodine-based contrast dye. During treatment for meningitis 63 years before my cancer, I was routinely injected with this dye which would allow the X-ray technician to see the blood flow though the recesses of my spinal cord. There was a hidden allergy that got worse as years went on until after one such scan in my early 30's for colitis I developed a rash which lasted a few days and itched like crazy. The buildup of Prednisone and Benadryl would fend off any allergy, and the contrast dye would help in discovering the absence of cancer cells.

That's what they told me.

Wednesday, November 6, 2013
Ahhhh...Wednesday after no chemo. What a wonderful feeling this afternoon not having the buildup of nausea. No dry heaves in the morning hours. Hope had crept once again under the black hood of fear and doubt, and I felt warmth instead of a chill on this, a day when the psychological warfare waged by cancer was in

a showdown with a new sheriff in town: Hope. Thursday brought a longer and more powerful day of radiation, and I was able to cross off the big 25 on my chart. After tomorrow, I would be in single digits. What a sight that would be to behold.

The strange warmth inside me was a total turnaround from the chilling metallic feeling caused by chemo therapy. I honestly didn't expect the chill to subside so quickly, but I welcomed the change none the less. And now, my full attention was turned toward radiation.

Although I was still using copious amounts of Eucerin cream on the left side of my neck, it had become a foreboding dark brown with a twinge of spotted charcoal black here and there.

Today, for the first time, itching began, but of course the last thing you want to do to a scabbed area is scratch it and make it bleed. So I resisted that temptation, helped of course by my oxycodone addiction. That's right. I had moved on from "this stuff is habit forming" to a full scale addition to pain killers. I remember my sister, Madalyn, telling me somewhere in week 4 that, "you can take care of that later...just get through it! The thing is I just didn't equate it to addiction with all those negative connotations. In my mind I was following the advice of most everyone and that was to embrace whatever would get you through it.

So it wasn't the physical dependency that had pervaded my body, but the mind games that had erupted and continued 24 hours a day. Sometimes it would be the haunting hollowness which made me feel so alone and adrift; or, other times it would be the face you see on a poison bottle, eerie and evil. Deep down in my soul I knew I was not supposed to be in that state of mind, and yet it was my mind that had overtaken my soul. I was running amuck. My prayers kept me sane and grounded in situations where there was real life interaction with others, especially when Joanna was close. She and I prayed together several times a day just to make sure we both were on the same solid rock of faith that my night-mares were temporary.

The itching would come and go as the days wore on. Radiation was becoming more intense and by Tuesday, the 12th of November the time under the mask had become unbearable. The mucous build up was now in the form of a sticky, immovable boulder sitting at the base of my tongue with more and more feeding it as the min-utes turned to hours. My suction machine was working overtime, and I would take the battery powered apparatus with me in the car so that I could make my throat just before going into the office. Once out of the car I would stop just before passing through the doors and rinse once more with magic mouthwash and then spit it out. Breathing under the mask was a dangerous mix of quick breaths in between gunk flow and very slow, shallow intakes of air so as not to force mucous from my tongue to contribute to the boulder at the top of my throat. There were times I would get light headed from the shallow breathing and would have to succumb to a deep chocking breath just to get past another 30 seconds. Just when I couldn't stand anymore I prayed again for divine interven-tion, "Please God get me out of this mask before I erupt all over the place."

Wednesday, November 13, 5:18 AM

Mornin' Tom,

After this morning, I am down to 5 more radiation treatments. The battle between the mask and the mucous came to a head yes-terday and for the first time, I had to shoot my leg up to the ceiling and signal to stop the radiation. The techs were there unhinging the mask within a minute and sat me up and thrust the kidney shaped puke trough at me. One of them rubbed my back and helped me get my throat cleared. Now I know what waterboarding is like. They asked me if I wanted to continue and by God I was not going to waste even the 2 or 3 minutes I had just endured, knowing that I had maybe 35 to 40 more minutes of radiation left until the end.

I now have a rash on my upper torso and neck that itches like crazy. Nothing seems to abate it no matter what topical ointment I put on it. What the hell will be next?!!!

L-Dog out

Wednesday, November 13, 7:03 AM

You're almost there, Larry. Hard to believe that all of those days/ weeks have passed. You've endured a great deal, and only those that have walked that same path can appreciate what it takes to face each day. Hopefully, some of the effects of the chemo have subsided. I know there are still some rough days ahead, but knowing that you no long have that poison running through you will make it a little easier to bear.

Any indication from the Doc on how long you'll have to keep the feeding tube? Is Thanksgiving a possibility? We're still praying for a speedy recovery.

All the best, Tom

In the blink of an eye, it all fell apart…

An intruder invaded my world on Thursday evening, November 14, after my 31st radiation session, and it changed the course of my protocol for six days. At this point, almost on a daily basis, I was asking, "What next? What are you going to throw at me next?" Of course, I was talking directly to cancer by now. Name-calling was a normal occurrence. Though I made light of it by calling cancer by the names the bastard was, deep under the black hood I shuddered because this one was different. The foreboding was preceded by a look at myself in the mirror and followed by a warning shot of fever.

The itching and rash took on a whole new meaning that afternoon. I had read where the effects of contrast dye could last as long as a week or two, but this episode of a reaction was pushing the outer limits of that estimate. The rash now was down into my lower extremities and onto my face and the top of my head. My hair itched like crazy and I could not stop scratching my scalp. I took a couple of extra pain killers hoping it would make me forget all that was happening, but the oxycodone did not have the numbing effect that they used to.

Thursday night I laid down to sleep about 9 pm and awoke with a start about 10:30 realizing that I had just stopped breathing. When you have suffered from tinnitus for 20 years and all of a sudden you have no more ringing in your ears, it is painfully obvious that the grim reaper is just around the corner. I stayed up all night because I knew I had my usual 8:00 AM radiology appointment and would see a doc then. Dr. Charles Neal was on vacation so I would be seeing an associate doctor in their office. Upon arriving, I told the tech that I was skipping the radiation and informed the receptionist I needed to see the doc immediately. By now, my puffy face, and in particular my lips, had swelled to twice their normal size. Breathing had become laborious which did nothing to calm me down. An hour and a half later, the substitute doc arrived, and I was sitting in front of him. After he had scanned my file for no more than 15 seconds, he looked at me with a smiling face and said, "Now Mr. Davis, what can I do for you and what's this about skipping radiation?"

"I declined radiation this morning because of my swollen face and lips. It would be impossible for me to put the mask on and clamp it down," with undoubtedly a curious look on my face after such a stupid question. I mentioned my swollen tongue and stoppage of breathing the night before.

The doc got out his headgear with the light on it, grabbed a couple of tongue depressors and looked into my mouth. "Well, from what I see your tongue is NOT swollen, and I don't see what all the ruckus is about."

I could see this was going nowhere so cutting to the chase I asked, "What do you think we should do now?"

His reply was, "Stop this nonsense and get your radiation treatment now."

"Ah, no I'm not going to do that, doc.", which unbeknownst to him just saved his corporation millions of dollars. Had they installed the mask on my face and clamped me down onto the table, every blood vessel in both of my lips would have exploded. It was incredulous that this doctor could not see that.

With that, he jumped up, opened the exam room door, tossed my file up onto the counter, and barked, "Mr. Davis has decided he is going to take the day off!"

Then he disappeared. As did I.

Friday radiation was also skipped because, by the time 8 AM rolled around 24 hours later, I was still running a low grade fever. The rash seemed to be getting more red than pink, whatever that may have meant. I went sleepless on Friday and Saturday, maybe catching an hour or two sitting up in the chair and my normal regimen of liquid food has dwindled to almost nothing. As my temperature began to rise to a peak of 100.8 by Sunday morning, the 17th of November, I could no longer swallow anything, even mucous. I was on my way to an Urgent Care facility by 9 AM. All through these 70-80 hours of pure hell Joanna stayed by my side and conveyed an endless stream of cold wash cloths to help combat the heat. Alternately weeping and expressing her concern in any way she could, and yet allowing me to retain my dignity even though I resembled something out of a zombie movie, she embraced the situation with love and tenderness. Here I was in front of now the second physician who studied me for a few moments attempting to come up with some suggestion. He settled for giving me samples of Benadryl.

Perhaps he extended my life, since the pills did seem to slow down the swelling progression, but not for long. In the end the best he could do was to prescribe Fluconazole which I later discovered was primarily used for vaginal infections. My thought was, "OK I haven't had sex since I heard the words "You have cancer!" so long ago. Apparently it did not help my situation. Doc#2 was no help.

By 3 PM on Sunday, while Joanna was well into her gardening, I stuck my head out the front door and waved a piece of paper and left it on the porch. On the journal I had written, "I'm going to the ER." I felt I couldn't wait another second, and off I went. I knew the route as both my chemo therapy and radiation therapy offices were very close to the hospital. When I arrived, the place was teeming with law enforcement personnel from multiple departments and the waiting room was overflowing. I approached the check in desk and was able to muster up a whispered bit of information that she needed to get my admission started. In about half an hour I had finished the massive amount of paperwork and even found a chair to sit and wait for my name to be mercifully called. I felt quite sure that one of two things was going to happen: either I was going to get back into the treatment area and feel immediately better; or, I was going to die right there in a room just off the waiting area and no one would know it until the night crew cleaned up the place. I wouldn't describe my demeanor as calm nor anxious; and the reason for that was that the pain had obtained a threshold so high, coupled with a heinous mixture of itching and swelling from the neck up, and nothing mattered. I was so close to the end of my protocol, and cancer was seizing my body, giving it one more try. One way or the other it was going to be the last battle. Honestly, I had already given thought to losing to cancer's insidious march with a regard only for hostility. Not so fast!

Joanna arrived just after I found my seat and together we witnessed one patient after another dodge a dichotomous mixture of policemen and what appeared to be kinfolk of gang members the police were watching. We learned later that there had been a bloody fight between rival gangs and several of the combatants were in pretty bad shape. Just more chaos to endure. Two hours later I was finally wheeled back into a makeshift cordoned off area and into a cot- sized bed. I remember thinking that I would have been much better off being shot like so many others were at that time, and that would have been fine with me. I was as close to giving up as I had ever been in 67 years.

The obviously frustrated and tired ER nurses got me hooked up with some fluids. The young ER doc was very nice, but when his first question was, "what's going on with you?" I knew Doctor #3 was not the answer. I asked for pain medication which I received immediately and Joanna and I settled in to long periods of silence. To this day, I have the greatest respect for the tender love she expressed during these countless hours of uncertainty, experiencing my pain and frustration, not vicariously, but as real as if the cancer was inside her. If she needed to talk with me she would get up and bend down so her ear was next to my mouth. My voice had become a wheezing whisper and communication was a real problem. Drinking was out of the question and I had been relegated to ice chips. I couldn't even feel the cold water going down my intensely damaged throat.

At around 6 PM Joanna reminded me that she had to drive three hour roundtrip to Lumberton NC to pick up Tayleigh's cat, Haven. Tayleigh had started a new job with NBC 12 in Richmond and was on her way for two weeks of training in Columbia SC. Jojo kissed my hand and was gone. (Later I learned that two Wilmington Police officers had escorted her to her car, weaving their way through dozens of angry people who had overtaken the parking lot.) Though I was alone, I felt the fear subside and calmness pervaded my heart. I knew we had come to the end, one way or the other. My question was, since there are only two finales to a hospital visit: you either go home...or you don't...who would win this last battle?

And in an instant, the answer was conveyed in the form of Four Miracles: The First Miracle: Replacements

Not five minutes later Rich Vena, my friend of ten years walked into my area.

Unbeknownst to me, Joanna had called Rich earlier and asked him to come and sit with me while she went to Lumberton. Rich took one look at me, winced like he had just sucked on a lemon, and turned away from me, obviously overcome by what he had seen. Every part of my head was swollen rendering me unrecognizable. And all I could do for the next couple of hours was sit there and look through the slits that my eyes had become, and think, "Rich is here to keep me alive." True to his friendship, Rich made sure he had me covered until he simply could not stand it any longer. One way conversations with an elephant man was not on his docket, and I knew that. It simply was not in his DNA to try to go on any further. He didn't want to leave but he was spent. Rich had already rescued me. I will never forget what he did for us.

Joanna, in her infinite wisdom, had phoned Bill Hatcher and asked him to spell Rich after a couple of hours. She described Rich to Bill so that he knew it was all right to leave me in Bill's care. Once Bill had mapped his course of action, he collected his best friend, Greg Brown, and they were on their way around 5:30 PM on that Sunday afternoon. With perfect timing, Rich ran into them on his way out and briefed them on what to expect.

The Second Miracle: Speaking in tongues.

As I sat there watching Rich leave, Bill and Greg arrived and sat down next to my bed and started conversation. But there were a few problems. First Bill had forgotten his cell phone which meant that he couldn't communicate via text. Secondly, Greg had forgotten his reading glasses which meant he couldn't see to read any texts. And third, I of course had no voice which meant that I HAD to text. I remember there was an NFL game on the TV next to me and had some hope that we could watch it together to mitigate the communication dilemma but my space was so tiny the TV looked as though it was sitting on Greg's massive shoulders. In the end, this became the most therapeutic part of my stay in the ER as I would send a text to Greg, Bill would grab Greg's phone and read the message aloud to Greg, and then text me back, reading his reply to Greg. Several nurses came in and admonished us to be quiet but it was no use. It was utter hilarity. Man! It was good to laugh. Two hours later, Joanna returned just as the boys were leaving. Breathing had gotten to the point where I just couldn't laugh anymore. Bill and Greg had rescued me. Those two hours of revelry will stay with me forever.

We waited in that little room until midnight when a room became available on the 10th floor, the cancer floor. I was met upstairs by a physician on night duty and he didn't even attempt to figure out what was going on. They wanted to inject a sleep aid into my port but I waved them off, not wanting to get into such a deep sleep, worried that I would never wake up. Exhausted from driving and worry, my sweetie finally went home around 1 AM, now on…

Monday, November 18th.
Four doctors into my condition and still no diagnosis. At this point I knew they were just keeping me alive, working feverishly elsewhere on gunshot wounds, the whole lot of us simply hoping that the sun would rise in the morning. Irrigation tubes, bags of saline solution, and a blood pressure monitor were all hooked up and running. Breathing was shallow and short, but at that point it didn't matter to me. I was in a hospital and no one knew why except there was enough wrong with me to warrant observation.

On this Monday morning, as fate would have it, all of my primary physicians were on vacation. I kid you not. My fever had reached a peak of 103.4 in the early morning and I was given Tylenol intravenously which brought down to a more manageable 102 degrees.

No one had mentioned the word food, nor did I. That was the last thing on my mind. Fittingly I was visited by the chaplain who overstayed his welcome. I was in no mood to pray anymore to be honest with you. I allowed myself to feel forsaken early that morning, insane with fever, uncontrollable itching, and a face which was ready to explode in multiple areas. I had gotten up to go to the bathroom and chanced a glance at myself in the mirror. My lips were bleeding in places with a mucous laden drool dripping onto my hospital gown. My eye sockets looked like small marbles with the eyelids swollen to the point where vision was a chore. I wanted to either run a belt sander all over my itching body or jump into a bath with a mixture of Epsom salts and ice water. The tips of my fingers and toes were ice cold and numb. Is this the answer becoming crystal clear: was I not going home ever again?

The Third Miracle: Dr. Beckett pays a visit.
Around 8 o'clock Dr. Thomas Jay Beckett entered my room and began to ask questions.

He first got me up to put me on a scale to get my weight. I remember seeing 132 pounds and pretty much collapsed back on the bed. With all the liquid calories and nutrients I had poured down my tube, still I had lost 30 pounds in 5 weeks! In my raspy whisper, I mentioned to him the reaction I had to the contrast dye a couple of weeks earlier, wondering if there was a correlation between the allergic reaction and the condition of my face. Dr. Beckett, a man in his mid-40's, very tall, and all starched up in his white smock, was a hospitalist. This I learned later was a visit prompted by my internist, Dr. James Wortman, who had been notified of my admission to the hospital. I answered the best that I could and then asked my own question, "What's wrong with me?" His answer was, "I don't know...but I'm going to find out."

When he then said, "I'll be back in about an hour", I had no confidence that I would ever see Dr. Beckett again. He was now the fifth physician to look at me and he, like those before him did not know what to do. But I was wrong to doubt this man. For within 45 minutes he came back into the room and trailing behind him was Dr. Kenneth Kotz, my esteemed oncologist, having interrupted vacation, and carting his laptop with him. "In looking over your chart, I saw that you had been taking Benazapril for high blood pressure. So I called Dr. Kotz to get the latest readings he had on all your blood work, and most importantly some information on your weight loss," Dr. Beckett explained.

Dr. Kotz went on, "Dr. Beckett told me he had a case where an ace inhibitor (Benazapril) had been used by a patient who was obese and had taken ill. The patient lost a great deal of weight, somewhere in the neighborhood of 20%, and he developed a condition known as Acute Angioedema." "That's what we believe has happened here to you. This condition coupled with your allergic reaction to contrast dye rendered your body helpless, and we need to treat you for this immediately. The fact that you have lost about 20% of your body weight and were still on the same dosage of the ace inhibitor caused this reaction. We have taken Benazapril off your list of meds and put a warning on your chart for any other similar drugs," continued Dr. Beckett. In addition, Dr. Beckett had the nurse start a drip line of my liquid food to start the process of recovery from that standpoint. I lay there in a pool of goo, blending into the hospital bed, trying to make myself understand whether this was all good news... or not.

Dr. Thomas Beckett, having provided the missing link, the diagnosis of Acute Angio Edema, visited my room a third time just around 7 p.m. Though I had not known Dr. Beckett before this event, I had seen Dr. Kotz on a consistent basis each week for 7 weeks. On this day, it was all business. I could tell in Dr. Kotz's voice that this was different. And while I'm at it, I might add that Dr. Beckett saw me for the first time just after 8:00 a.m. and here he was back for a third dose of looking at a zombie some 12 hours later. And Dr. Kotz was "on vacation", yet here he was with his laptop. As broken down as I was, my feeling was, these guys being there at this point in time was "good news/bad news".

The Fourth Miracle: Ghost Rider
The good news was that they were there together, but the bad news was WHY they were there. Quite honestly it scared the crap out of me...again! Because these are the guys you want on your side. But when they were there after hours, both at the same time, I could only think that it was dire. In the hospital, they just appear out of nowhere, and most of the time it's when you would least expect them. There are no more important people in your life when you have cancer than your physicians. And if you are fortunate enough to have a relationship with you doc that goes beyond just doctor/patient, it's a safe bet they think you are going to make it. If you think about it, they get plenty of bad news on a daily basis when dealing with oncology. Dr. Kotz later told me that the burnout rate for oncology physicians is about 20 years and he had set up barriers to try to be aloof on a personal basis, and remain clinical throughout all his cases. As a result, he could tackle every case with the enthusiasm that good endings were always possible.

Maybe it is a bit more difficult to establish a solely professional friendship, one that goes beyond the office and is based on the medical protocol plus a true mutual respect, if the news is going to be bad somewhere along the way. I think it is human nature. But it is up to the patient to bring more to the table than just a race to a cure. You give these guys all you got and then some, just so they know there is a partnership. No one likes a slacker in a partnership. Ad once you both realize you trust each other - the Doc to make the decisions and the patient to carry out the orders- you trust that each of you is making a critical effort to succeed; and, then you become invincible. Not just *feel invincible*...you are invincible.

Of course I could barely whisper so this was not a triangular conversation. The last words I heard Dr. Beckett say were, "We've scheduled a blood transfusion for you first thing tomorrow morning and you are going to be here for a few days." I was somewhat stunned with that news, primarily because I knew for sure at that moment that this situation was more than just a touch of the flu. I had sent Joanna home a few minutes before all that came down, wanting to have some time to myself, and also to afford her a true break and rest. My normal hospital pain medication, I think it was dilaudid, was given around 9 p.m. and I crashed a little after that.

The TV woke me up even though it was tuned to very low volume, and I heard a rustling from the only chair in the room to my right. The fourth miracle...the Ghost Rider...

Slade.

How in the hell he got past everyone, continues to be a mystery. But then again, he *was* the Ghost Rider. Raised in New Bern NC, son of a decorated war hero who had piloted all the big wigs in World War II, Korea, and in early Viet Nam, and a really sweet mother who once pinched me in the ass at her son's wedding, Slade was a short distance sprinter at UNC Chapel Hill turned lawyer. In the first 5 or 6 years of our friendship, Slade was a federal criminal defense attorney based in Wilmington, where let's face it, he defended a lot of drug dealers.

Pardon me. *They were* **alleged** *drug dealers.* 90% of Slade's work was accomplished in or around a jail cell, which truly suited him, but not most of the other attorneys who worked these types of cases for the government. But for Slade, even though his credentials would grant him access anywhere in the jails and past all the security protocol, he normally knew a back way in, or just plain nodded at the guard. I went with him once or twice and on our way out some service entrance I asked him, "Don't we have to check out or something to let them know we're gone?" Flicking my question off like a gnat, He replied, "Nah. They got us on tape. I know where to go so that they see me leave. I don't bother them and they don't bother me. It's a trust thing, L-Dog." In and out like the Ghost Rider.

He had a plan though, hatched in those same jail cells and honed in its infancy to the point where he actually could call it quits and start Jurislink.com, a system somewhere out there in cyberspace that will eventually end the process of attorneys visiting prisoners at the jail. Through Jurislink they now have video conferencing which is secure and does not breach the attorney/client privilege, and the federal government reaps the rewards of savings. He's gonna make it big.

When you are really, really sick there are points in time that happen that are unexplained at the time, but very explainable for the rest of time. I was feeling pretty low. Somewhere along the line I remember hearing the word "transfusion" and could still shudder at the chill of the urgency in Dr. Bennett's voice. The dilaudid finally taking hold, coupled with the oxycodone that was already running though my body, and both of them teaming up with *transfusion* simply put me over the edge and I was ready, if you know what I mean. Let's not kid ourselves, people who are in desperate situations think about their own demise. So, no, I was not immune to those thoughts; in fact, those were the last images I had before dozing off. No longer was I fearing sleep.

I woke up in a cold sweat with no idea where I was. Some sort of mind-numbing program was droning on the TV but it didn't matter because I could barely see the TV let alone what was playing on the screen. There was no clock to help me to get my bearings. I felt lost and quite frankly didn't care. My throat was constricted to the point where breathing had become laborious, mucous felt like it was literally rushing toward that swollen area, my lips were cracked and bleeding as I wiped them on the sleeve of my gown. My eyes were slits they were so swollen. The pain in my neck was so severe I was in and out of consciousness wanting so much just to give up. I was ready to go.

"Wassup, L-Dog?"

Slade was in the chair next to my bed. It was November, so he had some ridiculous stocking hat on his head, and a big wooly sweater which resembled something his grandmother had knitted. I hadn't seen the boy for almost 6 months since he moved out of his house he shared with his wife of four years. For years we called out to each other over our respective fences when we were grilling wings and pork, or if we were just calling out assholes. Slade was 30 years my junior, and the respect he had steadfastly given me befitted the age difference. I love him like a son.

"Slade???"

"They told me I couldn't come up, so I had to fake them out. You know the drill." "How long you been here?

"About an hour" he said. "Been listening to a whole bunch of nonsense coming from over there. Where you been?"

"I been here all day," I replied with some degree of uncertainty.

"I mean where you been since I got here? You sure as hell haven't been here. I'm pretty sure you were someplace else and you were making no sense at all."

The Planet Octron.

Slade stayed all night in that chair. He kept me company, each of us in and out of sleep during the night. He told me I got a shot around 2 o'clock and that nurse said nothing about his being there with me. Hmmm, almost as if he were invisible. The new shift had just come on and I recognized the nurse who normally came in at daybreak. She (nicely) wanted to throw Slade out of the room. I told her (nicely), as I motioned with my thumb toward Slade in the chair, "This man is staying right here..."

"...He just saved my life." And then I cried really hard.

I swear I heard the Ghost Rider, crying too. After my morning pain killer shot, I drifted back into the abyss only to wake up and find that the Ghost Rider had vanished.

But he had rescued me. He got me through that torturous night, conniving to get up to see me as only the Ghost Rider could. His mission was complete. His dad, Jack, would be proud.

I realized once again, as I had all along this treacherous journey into my cancer protocol, what true friendships could accomplish simply through the unspoken love between two human beings. I was humbled and grateful.

I stayed in the hospital until Tuesday afternoon. The swelling had gone down a great deal, my energy level was decidedly higher, and my outlook was brighter. Dr. Bennett had paid me one last visit Tuesday morning, and I was able to hug this man who had saved my life in more than just the medical way. Dr. Kotz also paid me a visit just before I left to go home. He let me read something on his laptop:

"Cases, where angioedema progresses rapidly, should be treated as a medical emergency, as airway obstruction and suffocation can occur. Epinephrine may be life-saving when the cause of angioedema is allergic. There are as many as 80,000 to 112,000 emergency department (ED) visits for angioedema annually, and it ranks as the top allergic disorder resulting in hospitalization in the U.S."

Most physicians will tell you that the most valuable resource in finding a cure to any disease is the patient and their history. It is why, at every office and for every visit, nurses and physicians alike ask you questions that seem redundant (birth date, allergies, medicines, family history, your history, etc.). Over the course of my treatments these issues were asked dozens and maybe hundreds of times and I would sometimes laugh with the care giver about answering them over and over. Never again will I make light of any doctor's office visit knowing the question, "What is your date of birth?" will be followed with "And what medications are you taking?"

Dr. Kotz informed me that my radiation oncologist, Dr. Neal, had returned from vacation and was waiting for me at his office just across the street. He told me it was imperative that I resume my radiation treatment and finish the last four sessions. Tomorrow would be a morning and afternoon double header and so would Thursday. And there I had it: the end of radiation.

They would have finished everything they could do.

A short while later the lead nurse came in with some papers to sign. She asked me if I was ready to leave. As Joanna and I walked to the elevator that Tuesday afternoon, I looked up and down the floor, knowing I was one of the lucky ones. I had won my battle with cancer's greatest challenge. Had we won the war? I didn't know the answer to that and certainly wasn't going to take anything for granted after this last indignity which had been dumped on us over the past 7 weeks. I did know one thing though. I knew the answer to what my hospital finaale' would be…

We were going home.

CHAPTER 21
FULL CIRCLE

Wednesday, November 20, 2013 9:59 AM

*G*ood morning, Tom. I have been remiss from any one-on-one communication over the past week or so. As it grew close to the end of the
protocol, it seems as though I had more inquiries than normal. Then the
thing with the doc having his head up his ass sort of catapulted communication to new heights. Over now.

*Last evening Joanna and I had some champagne, mine of course
through the tube.*

*Interesting concept. It wasn't a normal celebration but it'll do. I
hearken back to an earlier email you sent describing the 7 week ordeal as
something that would go by fairly quickly, which now seems as though
it truly did. I tried some of your ice cream and chocolate milk at room
temp on Sunday and the results were dismal as I knew they would be,
but it's a start. It certainly must be a combo of swollen throat/tongue
and non-use that is impeding the swallowing motions. I really want to
fast track that segue from tube to normalcy, so if you have any sugges-
tions please let me know. I realize you never did the tube, but still, you
may have some tips.*

Wednesday November 20, 10:45 AM
Larry, So happy for your celebration. I got my great news on Monday with my 1-year anniversary visit with my chemo oncologist. No sign of any cancer left on the PET scan!!!

Yahoo!!! Today Linda and I celebrate 44 years with each other and really know the meaning of our vows..."in sickness and in health". During my visit with the Doc my biggest complaint was the sticky, mucous that lingers in my throat and the continued difficulty of food going down as ti once did when I swallow. He said that the two were linked and the main cause is the lack of saliva production. The glands go fried on both sides. He said sometimes that come back in 6 months...sometimes in a year...sometimes in 2 years...and unfortunately sometimes never! I know mine are starting to come back but still have a way to go. I find that the Biotene tooth paste does help...but only temporarily. My throat was still swollen 3 months after the end of the radiation. I went in for a procedure where they put a flex tube down your throat and inflate it to stretch the opening. The put me to sleep... attempted the procedure, but the Doc said that there was so much selling that it was just pushing it from one side to the other so he stopped and said that we would have to just let time heal some of those things. I do remember getting discouraged from time to time dui=ring the healing process. One of the things that really helped was remembering some of =my darkest days (you had more that I did!) and comparing how far I had come. I remember looking in the mirror one morning and noticing that I no longer had an red or burned skin on my face and neck and realized that no that long ago I was ready to "throw the towel in" on living. And even now...when one of my pills is stuck to the gunk on the back of my throat and won't go down...I still say...that's a whole lot better than things were a year ago.

Now with all this being said, you could have your recovery a lot faster. And let's hope that is the case.

Wednesday, November 20 11:16 AM
Congratulations, Tom! Wow whatta relief to know that after one year you have no signs.

As for the 44 years, ain't it grand that us old coots can still say we are in love with the same babe who stole our hearts years ago? I am very happy for you and Miss Linda. Discouraging words about the mucous lingering on, though. I was in this study where the first 17 radiation treatments were on both sides and the last 18 were only on the left side where the cancer was. I'm not quite sure what to make of that vis a vis the salivary glands. I have my first follow up next Wednesday and I will try to get him to drill down on that. I did ask him several weeks ago whether or not the mucous abatement was days, weeks, or months after the completion of the protocol and he immediately said, "Months!", so I am doing what Jack Reacher does, "hope for the best but prepare for the worst".

Thanks Tom L-Dog

There is so much good information to remember from this last hospital episode if ever you or someone you know has an unexplained illness whether tied to another disease or not. Not all doctors are prepared to go to such lengths as Dr. Kotz and Dr. Bennett were. They actually did some extensive research in a short period of time. I fully understand the constraints physicians have on a daily basis. But saving lives is what it should be about, shouldn't it? In the case of my harrowing trip to the emergency room and then to admittance into the hospital itself, the entire ER staff was hamstrung by gang violence and the ramifications thereof. They were busy saving lives that very well were teetering on extinction. But to miss a diagnosis for a malady that happens 120,000 times a year in hospital ER's is troubling under any circumstance. The urgent care facility should have been able to draw on that 120K statistic also. To shrug your shoulders and just say, "I don't know", and given the history of drugs that a patient is taking, acute angioedema should be somewhere on the list.

Indeed, medicines effecting a positive result in one body for any length of time, can be lethal if your environment changes, which is what happened here. Who would have thought weight loss would team up with blood pressure medicine in combination with an allergic reaction to contrast die to cause such an adverse reaction? That may be the point: with the internet at our fingertips, perhaps a mere moment of search could yield a perfect answer to a problem. You just have to take that "moment".

Here are some examples of miscommunication that happened just while I was in the hospital:

- The charge nurse received a call from the radiation oncologist's office wanting to know
- why the hospital was not sending me over for my daily radiation treatment. That happened both on Monday and Tuesday. In fact, on Tuesday I was wheeled down to the radiation oncology department at the hospital so that I could be preached to by a friend of the substitute doc who wanted to jeopardize his career by badgering me into taking radiation. Obviously, by throwing my chart up onto the counter and proclaiming that I was a malingerer for not wanting my treatment, no notes were made regarding his examination of me, such as it was. That physician not only jeopardized his career, he neglected his partner, Dr. Neal, and the entire practice. And of course he placed his patient in extreme danger.

I related the entire incident to Dr. Neal when he returned from vacation and saw the bewildered look of astonishment on his face. The following week, during a treatment session which did not include a visit with Dr. Neal, I was placed in an examination room and in walked the substitute doctor. He said he "wanted to make sure I no longer misunderstood the method of treatment" he used in our previous meeting. And incredibly, his last words to me were,

"Of course having never met you before that time, I didn't realize that's not how you looked normally." Wow.

If you were to look up *Acute Angio Edema* and its list of side effects, number two on the list is "can be fatal".

While reading *The End of Night* you have learned that a diagnosis of any type of cancer is a recipe for a multitude of diseases, maladies, sicknesses, and side effects. Your physicians are not superhuman and therefore cannot predict those "extra's" that may happen along the way to your cure. They may know most of them that exist, but to lay all those out for you in the beginning of your long ordeal would be a cruel way to start treatment. Why burden you with information you may never need? However, you and your caregivers need to be on a daily hunt for what is happening to you. If anything looks out of order react to it immediately. And, if your docs don't respond to your questions, or if you have to see someone other than your regular doctor, it is up to you and your team to speak up. Had I consulted Dr. Ken Kotz earlier in my life threatening ordeal, even though he had been uninvolved for over a week after dismissing me from chemo therapy, I could have been spared us a great deal of anguish.

Cancer has a complete agenda and that is to kill you. Cancer loves confusion and indecision. Cancer loves people who don't fight. Cancer loves unintended mistakes.

Cancer delights in and is bolstered by people who don't care. Don't make it easy for cancer to win.

I subsequently finished my 35 days of radiation by participating in a fun-filled double header with two treatments each of the last two days. The techs had always told me that since I could not yell out, if I ever needed them to stop the radiation immediately that I was to just raise my hand or a foot to get their attention. On the 34th treatment it happened. The mucous was so prolific that my normal routine of using the magic mouthwash in the car and them spitting in the bushes just outside the office entrance simply did not work that time. I kicked up with a vengeance so that I could sit up and conjure up a really fine "hocker" and spit into the waste basket that Pete was holing for me. Whatta guy! But it didn't matter to me. I had doubled up on my pain meds too, so everything else was the same as it always was.

That afternoon I was finally finished with all my treatment, radiation and chemo. As I walked out the door I raised my arms with fists on the end of them in a Rocky-like pose, and at 130 pounds, thinned out hair, pale skin, tube in my belly, surgically scarred, cracked lips, tinnitus levels at an all time high, no working salivary glands, neck as crisp as well done bacon, virgin tissue throughout the inside of me neck, mucous thick enough to gag a sword swallower, taste buds no longer providing their namesake, body temperature seemingly south of 80 degrees, dehydrated, 4 inches less of a waistline, disappearing muscle mass, hollowed out eye sockets, ill- fitting clothes, voice reminiscent of Marlon Brando in The Godfather, strung out on pain meds, and a future as unknown as a new born baby, this cancer was history.

We had won the war. We had beaten cancer into submission with a body that could no longer function properly and with a mind that ran on the fumes of exhaustion. But I had one part in that beat up 67-year old body that never gave up...and that was my soul. The outpouring of affection, the cheerleading by my friends and family, and the astonishing support and love from people I hardly knew, had kept my soul intact, mostly insulated from becoming as dark as many of the nights Joanna and I had endured.

Surely, the surgeons and physicians cured my cancer, defeating that physical presence of a very cunning adversary which had visions of taking me deep. With absolute certainty I would not have survived without Tom Haas, my mentor who had no peer, my friend for life. My prayers had been answered even though for brief moments in time I had lost my way. And some warmth began to creep back, as I thankfully realized how I would love Joanna for the rest of my life with everything I could muster every day I would wake up next to her.

7:13 PM
Went in for a procedure where they put a flex tube down your throat and inflate it to stretch the opening. They put me to sleep...attempted the procedure, but the Doc said that there was so much selling that it was just pushing it from one side to the other so he stopped and said that we would have to just let time heal some of these things. I remember getting discouraged from time to time during the healing process. One of the things that really helped was remembering some of my darkest days (you had more than me!) and comparing how far I had come. I remember looking in the mirror one morning and noticing that I no longer had any red or burned skin on my face and neck and realized that not that long ago I was ready to throw in the towel on living at all. Even now, when one of my pills is stuck to the gunk on the back of my throat and won't go down, I still say that's a whole lot better than things were a year ago. With all this being said, you could have your recovery a lot faster. And let's hope that's the ase.

There it was, a subtle shift in responsibilities in the friendship on November 20, 2013, the date I finally finished my radiation and had one day of freedom from torture under my belt. My mentor who had guided me throughout the weeks of the unknown began to need me in much the same manner as I had needed him. Tom was one YEAR out from ending his protocol and was experiencing many of the same roadblocks as I was. I could feel his exasperation. It was as if, now that his job was completed, he fell back into his own post-treatment rut. My new life, the one after cancer, immediately charged me with a responsibility to make good on the promise I had made to myself months ago: to be a better friend to all.

At this point I truly did not understand this role reversal, but knew it was a position that I would carry forward for as long as was alive.

CHAPTER 22

CHRISTMAS 2013

Heavy snow blanketed the I-95 corridor with winds up to 30 mph making for a slippery, wind chilling Christmas night in 2013. Driving was especially treacherous from the DC area into suburban Richmond, Virginia due to an early sheeting of icy mix which formed the layer beneath ever-accumulating snow. It was a time for most families to gather around the fireplace, perhaps tear open the remaining gifts, and savor the pumpkin pie complete with eggnog or a glass of cold milk.

A week earlier Joanna and I were making our final plans for travelling from Wilmington to Richmond for what would be our 23rd Chirstmas with Tayleigh. When any of the 3 to 4 yearly planned visits to our daughter arose, we always made sure we contacted Susan and Temple, hoping to get together with them for dinner at one of the fine restaurants Richmond had to offer.

These kind and wonderful people, descendants of two of the city's oldest families, had been Tayleigh's surrogate parents ever since their chance meeting at Stella's restaurant soon after she moved from Albany Georgia to Virginia's capitol city in September of 2011. Stella's is a family owned Greek establishment with clusters of tables around one long family-style table with 12-14 chairs.

Joanna was in Richmond helping Tayleigh organize her new digs when they decided to go somewhere for supper.

It was a weekend night so the restaurant was bustling and the only two chairs were at the big table. There amongst the others having dinner, were Susan and Temple. Having raised three children themselves, all close to Tayleigh's age of 29, was certainly a plus and a building block for trust. Within days of meeting my two girls, Susan had even found a basement apartment with one of their cousins (there seemed to be many) that was only a couple blocks from their home and the neighborhood was deemed safe enough for Tayleigh to go on her morning runs, which many times were in the dark. We felt she was safe, mentored in the same common sense way that we would, and minutes away from any help she may need. But there was even more. I can only describe the intrinsic qualities exhibited by Temple and Susan as having the ability to calm Joanna's fear of the unknown for her daughter landing in a city where she knew no one. She instantly became part of their family…and so did we.

It came as no surprise when Susan called Joanna to tell her that they would be away on Christmas Day, 2013 visiting their son in Maryland and insisted that the three of us celebrate our gift exchange and dinner in the warmth of their home. Susan said Temple had stacked the wood for the massive stone fireplace in anticipation that we would want everything to be just like home. Normally I would have declined, not really wanting to put anyone out of their own home on such a special day. And who knows, I did not want to make such plans and then have to adjust for the eventuality of the predicted snow storm cancelling either of our trips to see our family members. According to Susan that was nonsense and if such things happened to effect a change in plans, we were all family and that's what Christmas was all about. She said with finality, "That's a win-win for all of us…and you will be at our house for Christmas dinner." And so it was settled.

The real reason for trying to decline such a warm invitation was that I simply did not want to be around anyone else. I had a rash over 60% of my body. The last time they had seen me I weighed in at my normal 160 pounds and resembled someone they had come to know as a good friend. Now I weighed less than 130 pounds and looked as though I was one step from the grave. Talking was still an effort even now 4 weeks after the last radiation treatment and I was exhausted by the time evening came around. My days' end normally was around eight o'clock as my body attempted to rebound from the onslaught of trauma my cancer treatments had wrought, and by the early evening I was toast. I had given up the oxycodone without any tapering three weeks before and still had the intermittent wretching and coughing spells that surely would upset everyone. I was a mess. But the most intimidating possibility would have been if Temple and Susan could not make the trip to see their son and there we would be sitting at their table, and me with my feeding tube making everyone uneasy.

Nope, I told myself over and over that I did not want that for these kind folks to have to endure watching me pour my foul smelling Christmas dinner down that two-foot apparatus That's what I told myself. In truth, I had secretly planned for this to be the first time I attempted to eat solid food and the worry of what would happen simply intimidated the hell out of me. I didn't know if choking would occur, or worse. My mind wandered toward accepting the possibility that I would "fall off the wagon" and reach for some pills to get me through any tight spots that might be presented. Once again it was all about food. The fact that I felt like crap was always secondary because I had felt that way for an eternity and it had become a way of life for me. The last thing I wanted was for my paranoia and physical limitations to ruin any joy for Susan and Temple and of course for Tayleigh and Joanna. Susan gave us no choice. She said she would be hurt if we did not accept their offer. It came to pass that I buried that paranoia, and Christmas Day of

2013, at Susan and Temple's beautiful old stone home bathed in ivy, presented me with the greatest gift I could have imagined.

The feast was a traditional favorite with roasted turkey, mashed potatoes, both stuffing and dressing, Joanna's cranberry/orange fruit dish, cinnamon sweet potatoes, rolls, green bean casserole, both pumpkin and cherry pies, and champagne. Normally, I would have been at the center of the kitchen activity as I was not only on holidays but every day. My penchant for cooking had grown over the years to borderline obsession about how to prepare (non) well balanced meals. But I was woefully out of practice and now our plans had changed. Our decision to allow Mr. and Mrs. Kroger prepare our dinner was easily agreed upon and our order was placed. There was still some cooking to do but mostly our task was simply to get everything warmed up to be presented on the table at the same time.

Susan and Temple had embarked years earlier on a massive renovation of their century old home and many rooms had been completed and were magnificent. The kitchen however, was to be their last landing place in that endeavor and was something out of Saturday Evening Post. The huge gas burner stove was tucked over in a corner underneath hand carved wooden cabinets housing a plethora of spices, dry goods, canned jellies, and various and sundry other concoctions that I'm sure were not on any recent inventory list. On the immediate left was a refrigerator that even a second hand appliance store might reject and the door opened into an awkward position toward the oven door. The porcelain sink was all the way across the floor so that anything that might drip on the wood planked floor would simply disappear into history just as the thousands of drips before them had. A huge window with leaded glass panes looked out over the front yard of snow covered bushes and trees, limbs hanging in the balance hoping a thaw would save them from bending so far down that they would break.

Dozens of drawers creaked and slid open and shut in dozens of different combinations from stuck and difficult to open to opening just short of falling to the floor. Every kitchen utensil known to man was available for us to misuse because we honestly didn't know what the vast majority of them were used for. The only modern kitchen convenience was a refrigerated wine rack sitting on top of a counter with an ice machine complete with scoop underneath which reflected the priorities Temple had as far as his contribution to the kitchen was concerned.

In other words, their kitchen was magnificent.

As we prepped the various dishes my fears of eating food for the first time began to subside. Susan and Temple had indeed made it to Maryland and it was just Joanna and Tayleigh and me bumping into one another, each of us with our own personally designed tasks taking precedent over anything else. The champagne was chilling on ice and the bird was in the oven. Aromas of past Christmas's filled the old kitchen as they had for over a century. The rash that had plagued me for over a month, the soreness in my throat, the monster poking out of my stomach, and the crunching feeling lodged in the pit of my soul caused by the lack of pain meds (that was the "cold" turkey on that day) became secondary and almost forgotten. Through some electronic wizardry, Tayleigh had hooked up some festive music fit for the occasion and singing ensued. Normalcy was almost amongst us and I knew that on this day, the date of the birth of our Savior, the soul inside me which had endured the unimaginable, was being touched by Jesus Himself.

At one point, shortly after we had everything on its way to being warmed to perfection, Joanna came into the kitchen from somewhere in the house, and said with tears flowing down her face, "You guys have got to come in here to see this." The three of us passed through a brick and tiled enclosed portico which was dotted with antique tables and lamps. There was even a floral three cushion old style glider which faced long high windows where our wandering eyes took in the back yard of this old mansion. Snow was falling in the dim light of dusk as we made our way through another arched doorway into the dining room. In and of itself, this was the crown jewel of the home, complete with a table which could seat a small army and several glassed hutches full of heirloom dishes and glassware. Portraits and original prints hung here and there in perfect harmony with the chandelier which brought everything to light in all its majesty. And there, in the midst of family history was our own personal Christmas setting, which Susan had hidden from us until the most perfect of times.

The massive table had been covered with an embroidered cloth which intimidated the hell out of me because it did not have a stain on it. Joanna would tell you that her husband was the biggest hazard to clean textiles that ever lived. If she hadn't been crying out of joy I'm positive she would have sat me down and made me promise that I wouldn't spill, tip over, or drip anything on that tablecloth. On the end of the table closest to the door and on both sides of that end were three settings of simple yet elegant china, stemmed crystal glassware, sterling silver flatware complete with all the forks and spoons which would have made Emily Post extremely proud. At first I thought perhaps Susan maybe thought this could very well be my last Christmas dinner, but that thought was fleeting. I quickly came to realize that she would have done this for anyone she loved and I would have given anything at that moment to push aside the tube protruding from my belly and reach out to give her an intense hug. To say that I was momentarily stunned would have not done justice to how I felt. Joanna, Tayleigh, and I were now all crying. And God was whispering to me, "Eat, L-Dog. Eat."

The time had arrived to pop the cork on the champagne. We opened the door leading out to the front yard and decided that the cork should end up somewhere that months later could be found and lead Temple and Susan to wonder how it got there. We each had our long stemmed champagne flute at the ready and I poured.

Too cold outside to linger, we went into the kitchen to say a prayer and toast to the One who loved us most. As Joanna and Tayleigh began to sip, I raised my four layers of clothing, pulled out my feeding tube and poured a few ounces into my stomach. I had made my mind up to take this easy path since my entire digestive system starting with the tip of my tongue and rolling down my raw, radiated throat was just not ready for alcohol and fizz in any combination. The sensation of alcohol in my stomach was an indescribable feeling of instant heat which reversed the process of swallowing and made its way up my esophagus and into my mouth. What a rush!

On that day, Christmas Day 2013, with my two girls, and in the inviting warm and loving surroundings of that old home punctuated by the musical sounds and the wafting aromas of the season, we sat at the King's table and I taught myself once again to eat like a human being.

As Joanna and Tayleigh cleaned up everything after our feast, I went into the living room to prepare a fire, around which we would open our gifts for each other. Of course, the fireplace had already been prepared for us. The newspaper was crumpled up and the logs were perfectly arranged on the grate. Long handled matches lay on the hearth. Temple had written directions on how to open the flue. Even I couldn't have screwed that up. As the first match brought the fireplace alive, I heard Joanna's phone ring in the distance. I thought Steve, Kristi, and our grand kids, Lincoln and Brynn were calling again. When Joanna didn't bring the phone into the living room I wondered who it could have been.

"You're not going to believe this," she said with a big smile. "Susan and Temple are on I-95 and are going to be here in an hour or so depending on the roads. They wanted to be here with us tonight." In that unspoken moment, we knew that Temple and Susan had left their own family to be with ours. Friendships don't have a season, and yet this was the most beloved season. Friendships are normally the strongest when you are the closest. This one was from afar. Friendships rely many times on love, sometimes faith, and sometimes fate. But the truest of friendships rely upon trust. You trust to open your heart and soul to someone of some difference: distance, gender, history, race, status, religion, philosophy, language, or any type of difference. If the trust is there, friendship can grab any or all of those differences and glue them into a bond that will last a lifetime. And if you have cancer, your heart is so broken it is easy for kindness to flow into that abyss. Trust seals that break and cancer has become a catalyst for healing instead of destruction. That's what happened here.

Temple burst in the back door with hugs all around and Susan followed right behind him.

We all sat around the fireplace after a round of heartfelt hugs and some more tears. We had gifts for them that certainly did not measure up to the magnificence of their Christmas gesture to us, but no one cared. They looked at me and lied about how good I looked back at them.

Though I couldn't participate in a lot of the conversation, I found myself looking off into the distance and thinking about Bob Thieman, Rich Vena, Greg Brown, Bill Hatcher, Big Dog and Paul, and all the friends who had rescued me over the past five months. I thought of Dr.'s Ken Kotz, Charles Neal, George Brinson, James Harris, and Jay Beckett. I heard Dr. Jim Wortman's voice say, "You have cancer!" I remembered Pete the radiation tech, Crystal, Bridget, Molly, and Nurse Betty. Thankfully I recalled those unknown souls who had lifted me up in their prayers many times over. I smiled as I remembered Steve and Lincoln walking into my heart at Thanksgiving. I shuddered remembering three days at New Hanover Regional Medical Center when my life hung in the balance. I remembered the common threads running through the past five months. Tom Haas, the man I would never forget... Joanna, the one who taught me that love was based on trust and if you had both, one made the other stronger...and the dozens of people who had showered us with the type of kindness that only comes when you truly mean it. It was like a kaleidoscope of events flashing through my brain as the conversation dimmed and the crackling of the wood in the fireplace ceased. I closed my eyes and thanked my Lord for giving me the strength to push through the horrific days and nights of the month between Thanksgiving and Christmas of 2013 as I stomped on the demons of pain and drugs and despair.

Cancer was gone from my worn out body. My mind was cleared of pain killers and the backlash of quitting cold turkey was almost history. I had tasted food for the first time in many weeks, and was able to keep it right where it belonged. I set my sights on January 19, 2014 (and the appointment I made the very next day) to have the feeding tube removed, 91 days after it was installed.

I knew then at that instant that I was going to live.

And when I opened my eyes, all I saw was my sweet Joanna smiling back at me. She knew where I had just been for those few moments of reflection. All I saw was love. And, oh yes, relief. For it was at that second when time stood still, the words that Dido had sung once again sang in my soul and I finally responded to cancer and all that cancer had wrought,

"I can stand over there,
And you can watch me walk away, And celebrate
The End of Night."

FAITH AND FEMININITY

A s I sit here today, my body void of cancer, my soul rescued from the dark shroud of addiction, the life I once had behind me and the new one bursting with promise of love and hope, I desperately want to spin this epilogue from a web of fear and pain to an ending shining with happiness and joy. Oddly, if I am unable to totally finish writing this story about my friend, my fervent goal will have been achieved. Her life of wonderment has been filled with promises made and kept, to be sure. However, the concurrent life of wondering and long-time lingering uncertainty has followed Kathy step for step for over sixty years.

And now, as she sits in the back seat of the car, outwardly calm but inwardly scared once more, waiting for yet another trip to a hospital surgical operating room, I approach the rear car door to wish her well. With husband Mike sitting in front smiling at all of their neighbors in a fitting display of loving friendship, I saw the fear etched on her sweet face. It wasn't that she was shaking; it simply was a coping hopefulness that she would see us all soon in a triumphant return to her home.

"You know what my mama used to tell us kids", I asked? She looked in my eyes and paused, waiting for me to answer my own question. "She told us that she always put the orneriest kid in the back seat". And there it appeared, just for an instant, a remnant to be sure, gleaming eyes lighting up a smile nonetheless. Kathy let go of my hand, reached up as she had done once before, and placed both hands, warm and soft, against my cheeks, and we brushed a kiss on each other's lips. As I blended back into the group which had gathered in a send-off to our friends, I was left standing, wondering if I would ever again see my sweet friend.

Kathy's Story

I had no idea how I was going to make it through my first New Year's Eve that night in 2013. Once again, I was in that cancer victim's mode of believing everything after cancer treatment was "the first time". It was obvious that I was going to be in the midst of revelers eating and drinking, and raising hell, although this group looked to be as low key as I had seen in some time. Quite frankly, partying was the LAST thing on my mind, so the milder the better.

Still having intermittent bouts with choking on most solid food, still relying to some degree on liquid nourishment through my feeding tube, and still having no taste buds functioning at more than 5-10 percent, I asked myself, "so why was I there?"

The answer was clear: I went to Tom and Marie Douglas' home that night to make sure Joanna was with her buddies. She craved the camaraderie that could only be forged with her girlfriends. For sure, she had earned this night out to blow off some steam. As I lay on our bed watching her "get ready", I marveled at the great measure of patience she displayed as she changed from one outfit to another, the jewelry needing to perfectly match the outfit, and the shoes...of course the shoes had to blend in just right. Once the task of the adorning threads, leathers, and bling had been decided upon, then came the makeup which transformed her

alluring face into a soft radiance which surely had a switch somewhere that she turned to the perfect spot on a dimmer. Picasso
could not have done any more justice. I noticed as the ticking
clock personified the signs of stress just 30 short minutes prior to
the time we needed to leave. And right before she stepped into
her outfit, the finishing touches were placed on her blonde hair,
using a plethora of intensely heated utensils, and blow dryers powered by Boeing itself. From the tips of her toenails to the wispy
curls she was a knockout.

In describing how I got ready, you need only know that I was
clothed in a shirt and pants each three sizes too big, sporting absolutely no beard to shave, remnants of a brown spotted radiated
neck, and a cowlick that only a steamroller could tame. I was pretty
sure I resembled Alfalfa in Our Gang. It didn't matter. I was going
to the ball with the most gorgeous woman on the planet; and, as
a bonus, I knew Tom Douglas had a big ole brown stuffed leather
couch in his upstairs TV room adorned with a blanket hanging
over the back. I was destined to "celebrate" New Year's Eve asleep,
right there.

That night was the first time I met Mike and Kathy. They were
part of the group of a dozen or so revelers who would celebrate
with hugs and kisses after the ball dropped. When all of them
had finished dinner, we sat at the table, and though I would fade
in and out of conversation, I learned vicariously of Kathy's fight
with cancer (the type of which was unknown to me). In my eyes,
Kathy was easily the second most beautiful person in the room.
Her angelic gaze across the table belied the grief and trauma she
and Mike had endured for what I guessed, and later learned, was
8 long years. At that time none of us knew the extent of the physiological atrocities cancer had forced upon her. Surely, I thought,
this warm and poised woman had eased her way through her cancer experience. Nothing, and I mean absolutely nothing, could
have been further from the truth.

She looked like an angel. Beautiful at 71, just as she must have been at 21, Kathy was happy to be "well", albeit guarded in her optimism. At the time she was in apparent remission from her latest bout with cancer while I was still a gaunt, radiated zombie. Looking into her eyes across the table I saw kindness, sweetness, and the joy of being with friends. Her love affair with Mike was clearly evident as she told stories of where they had lived over the years, stories about their two boys and their grand kids, and in particular, musing about how happy she was to be alive. At that moment, on a night that I usually would want to kick 2013's ass out of the house, what I truly and desperately wanted, was to feel as good as Kathy did. As time went on, I was to learn my self-centered approach to cancer was a pitiful substitute for what I should have been doing. I should have been caring.

Having made it all the way to 9 o'clock I disappeared to the confines of the TV room and blended my ravaged body into the couch. I had lost so much weight, now down below 130 pounds, that I barely made a dent in the leather of the couch. But that wool blanket was just the ticket I needed to get where I wanted to be. I fell asleep listening to the voices below, hearing Joanna's every now and then, happy and confident that she was having the good time she deserved. I don't know if she forgot about cancer for those 3 hours, but I fervently hope she did.

I awoke in time to kiss Joanna for the first time in 2014.

Earlier in this book you read about mentoring and how Tom Haas rescued me literally dozens of times from the fear of the unknown. How bad was the pain going to be? How long before "this" or "that" would "start" or "end". What are my chances of getting through this week? Is there any detour around that moment in time which defied goodness? Can you help me? Hundreds of questions must be carefully answered by the mentor so that the cancer patient has hope, but not false hope. Cancer victims want the truth and we pretty much know when the truth is not being spoken. Only in the darkest of times do we want to be alone with our thoughts, which in reality are fears. After suffering for so long with the actual cancer and then all its siblings of horrific maladies that accompany the main event, there are moments when we want to give up and just let it take us away. The human spirit yearns to be optimistic. The human body tells the truth.

Mentors to me are acquaintances who become caregivers and then, if you are lucky, friends for life. Two years after we had met at the party, when I walked through our neighborhood to visit Kathy for our first interview, I thought perhaps this was an opportunity for me to give of myself as a mentor. As I approached the front door I whispered a prayer for strength and support. It was at that moment that I realized this path I had chosen was much more than simply helping someone get over a tough spot. Kathy was already my friend; and so, the prayer was altered to one of thanks. Thank you Lord for giving me the opportunity to hear Kathy tell me what courage really meant, while at the same time never acknowledging her strength. I was already humbled when I reached the front door. We had seen each other several times since that evening in 2013 and Mike and I were serving on the Board of Directors of our community Home Owners Association. Mike and I are a perfect match for that body of governing. Mike was ever the pragmatist, and I was the loose cannon. But that day at their front door, my heart was at peace knowing that my friendship with Kathy would become one that would last a lifetime. It was, as they say, meant to be.

The door opened as I stepped up to the porch and there she was, a radiant smile belying a battered and besieged body, but validating an unflappable will to conquer and survive. Kathy pushed the door open, placed her two warm hands on my cheeks, and sweetly kissed my lips.

From that instant on, no longer did I wonder if she would allow me to write her story in a way that would heal some of her wounds and bring some light to anyone who would read these words. These would be her words; tales of a life well spent with reflections of a champion. As the two of us sat in her living room, serenity fell over me and allowed me to open my heart, just as I began to ask Kathy to open her heart right back.

As fate would have it, Kathy at age 10, had lost her mother to breast cancer. It was 1953, back in the *dark ages* of cancer research, so when the docs found a lemon-sized lump, they knew with certainty that there was no hope. Her mom lived out another fractured year and was 43 when she passed away after fighting her cancer back in those days when there was a stigma associated with the "C-word". It was a topic to be avoided due to the soaring statistics of doom. There is no doubt that cancer patients, still after all these decades, have a button somewhere deep inside that is always "on" when it comes to doom. Kathy didn't even know what disease her mother had, or what actually had caused her demise, because for that whole year, no one mentioned the word cancer in her presence. The doctors said, "We'll have a cure for this in ten years." But not then; not in the 1950's...

It was shortly after the neighbors finally took Kathy up to her mother's bedside and pulled back the sheet which lay over her face, that the word cancer hit her ears like a gun blast. At that time doctors and researchers postulated that breast cancer was caused by an imbalance of the hormone estrogen. In this case though, this was an "aggressive" cancer, one with no origin that they could find. Her mom was sick for a year and then suddenly she was gone. Kathy was left, at the young age of 10, where wonder became worry... what was this cancer disease that took her mother so fast, and what would it mean for her future? She vividly remembers the cold shivers stemming from the unknown which, as a child, could only be described as scary. It was the type of fear that had her figuratively looking back over her shoulder to see if the shroud of darkness was descending upon her. As time went on and Kathy forged her own life with her own family the fear faded away to a flickering, lingering thought of "what if?" Thinking of it another way, Kathy has lived 63 years of her life without being able to wake up in the early sunlight and love on her mom, neither physically nor mentally. And now, in the twilight, six decades later, cancer has robbed her of the most vivid recollection of her mother: It has stolen her femininity.

When Kathy turned 43, the age when her mom passed away, the darkness reappeared, spiking her awareness once more, creating anguish for her two boys and for Mike as she once again was a scared young girl trying to cope. Twenty-four years later her lifelong fears exploded into reality when in 2010 she was diagnosed with endometrial (uterine) cancer. And for the first time, her Duke Doc said those three horrible, searing words, "You have cancer". Sitting there in the physician's office, all of her dreams were at once relegated to distant memories, as cancer lit up the marquee, just as it always does.

Born January 30, 1943 in Cincinnati (we laughed realizing we were born the same place only three years apart) and growing up in the greater Cincinnati area with three sisters and a brother, her goal of attending University of Cincinnati culminated with a degree in retail merchandising. She and Mike married when she was 21 in 1964. It seemed that Kathy's degree was perfect for not only her current location, but almost anywhere. After all, department stores were numerous in every decent sized city. Mike was beginning his career with United Way, a career that would span almost 4 decades and take them to nearly a dozen locations in the United States including the beginning in rural Elkhart Indiana, through a tour at their Washington headquarters, and to New Mexico where Kathy learned to love Mike's resident family even more. In between all of those moves, they had two stints in Wilmington, and knew for sure that this was where they wanted to retire. At one point while we were talking, Kathy mentioned that she eventually rose to Area Manager for Federated Department Stores. Her specialty was "Ladies Ready-to-Wear". With that, I started to laugh. Ladies ready-to-wear? According to my resident expert, Miss Joanna, there is no such thing. I have been taught that women's clothing is conspiratorial as far reaching as the shops in China. Designers of women's clothing make sizes which are supposed to be static but they are a frustrating maze of unpublished half-sizes and incorrect measurements.

During these early years Mike and Kathy had son, David, and a few years later wanted to add another child to their family, hopefully a girl. It didn't culminate fast enough, so they sought the advice of a fertility counselor. Together, they gave it one year of "hopping to it" when Kathy would summon Mike during prime time ovulation but it just wasn't happening. Concurrently they were searching for a daughter through legal adoption and became very close to finalizing that process. Even the bedroom was papered pink. Lo and behold, Kathy became pregnant...months later the delivery nurses brought the baby out in a pink blanket... and Kathy told Mike to not be fooled by the color of the blanket... it was a boy...and they were thrilled beyond belief. Baby Greg was escorted home to his new pink bedroom.

Promotions for Mike with United Way, from Cincinnati to Elkhart to Louisville Kentucky to Wilmington to Alexandria (DC) Virginia to Albuquerque New Mexico, to the Twin Cities in Minnesota, and back to Wilmington to retire strengthened their lives together. They learned how to sail, and then took up golf together in New Mexico where there was no water.

They cheered on their two boys, David excelling in football and baseball, Greg starring in wrestling and swimming. Kathy had earned a masters degree in social work and had fulfilled her life-long dream of positioning herself into the child guidance profession.

Early in 2005 Kathy had undergone a double hip replacement to correct a congenital condition which was slowly rendering her immobile. The first surgical replacement was a complete success and three weeks later the second operation was performed. Evidence of a problem became reality when she was asked to flex her left foot, only to discover that she could not. Analysis proved that during the surgical procedure, the sciatic nerve had been profoundly damaged. The orthopedic surgeon remarked that it would take some time to "come back".

Kathy is as feminine a woman as I have ever met, eclipsed perhaps only by Joanna. She enjoyed "dress up" occasions, of which there were many in Mike's line of work. Gowns and shoes to match adorned her closet only to come alive with her perfection of blending colors and fabrics.

If short skirts were in style, Kathy had those, too. After that failed surgery, try as she might there was no pair of shoes that she could wear to match her outfits. The two-foot brace she had to wear on her left leg, even after two additional major surgeries to correct the mistake, had to be fitted down into a shoe that was as bland and dull as her dresses were spectacular. Her self-image was challenged and conscious of what she was facing. All she could do was live with it, alone with her thoughts of fleeting femininity. Though she lives with this condition to this day, no one would have ever known it.

By all other accounts they were firing on all cylinders until March of 2009 when signs of trouble began. There were some bleeding issues and a hysterectomy was planned. The old fear slowly crept out from deep inside her soul, the dark foreboding hood of doom began to cover her up, and soon she knew it was more than just a hysterectomy. Kathy remembers as instantaneous and ultimately on-going, how she confided in her primary physician with pleas of "something is not right". The hysterectomy was put on hold and her physician in Wilmington decided that Kathy should go to Duke Hospital in Durham for tests. However, a biopsy was required for the referral and subsequent acceptance of Kathy's case before Duke would admit her. The biopsy was performed in

Wilmington, but a devastating error occurred when the physician's nurse failed to report the finding immediately. Ten days later, the doctor called Kathy and Mike apologizing for their failure to divulge what their initial tests showed, which was a thickening of the lining of the uterus. If something of this magnitude were KNOWN to be aggressive, wouldn't a physician be more thorough? Precious time had been lost.

In January of 2010 a full hysterectomy was performed at Duke University Hospital and brought the devastating news of endometrial uterine cancer. At the same time, the harvesting of over 20 lymph nodes meant that the physicians were "going for the cure".

Aggressive. She had heard that term mentioned 58 years ago. They might as well have described it as cancer on steroids, "just like my mother".

When Kathy related this error of delayed notification to me, I remembered the original CATscan I had, and how the radiologist had missed the cancer at the base of my tongue. Like an apparition, Dr. George Brinson appeared just then and reminded me that he indeed discovered what others had missed. As I shifted back to reality I realized Kathy's story was different, much different. Her version of Dr. Brinson saw the scope of the cancer but chose to not divulge it for whatever reason. What if that had been me? What if after a needle biopsy said "no cancer" and the radiologist said "no cancer", we had just simply proceeded down some other path to some different and false diagnosis? At what stage would the correct diagnosis have been confirmed?

Once again, my heart broke for this soft and fragile woman whose great heart and determination were so clearly evident. Though the definition of femininity may mean what a woman is wearing or her mannerisms or even her stance on various social issues, for Kathy, feminism came from deep inside her soul and she loved it dearly. She loved all the dress up and makeup and hairstyles more than any other facet of the mortal world. She had been left only with memories of her mother, the most vivid of which were the "dress up" times. For as long as I have known Kathy, I would have never guessed that part of her inner self was under siege.

That's how beautiful she IS. Once again, her womanhood was being chipped away.

When we are close to those who have any cancer, we rely on what the victim wants in the way of credibility; ie. Our appearance...our mannerisms...our pain...our despair...our love...our hate...our speech or our gait, or perhaps simply our vapid gaze of resignation. All of that was etched on my face for six months in 2013. Kathy had managed to hide that from all of us...for 60 months.

The treatments had worked, Mike and Kathy were told, and her endometrialcancer was history. Most cancer victims have a battery of yearly follow up tests which monitor their findings after treatment. For Kathy it was a PetScan which looks at the entire body from neck to groin. All the thousands of lymph glands proudly show what they are made of, good or bad.

Organs such as the liver, kidney, pancreas, colon, and lungs are brought to light.

Prior to Kathy's one-year PetScan she developed a persistent cough which perpetuated for days on end, constantly interrupting daily routines with the hacking, ever-strengthening in its power and regularity, robbing her of normal conversations. Her breathing had become laborious and unsteady to a point where she knew once again something just was not right inside her. At night, falling asleep became scary each time the thought of conveying governance of breathing to a Higher Power. Her primary care physician treated for allergies on several different fronts, and Kathy found the results lacking in any credibility.

Kathy insisted once again that her body was warning her of inconsistencies. She tired of the "wait and see" posture, and her pleas were finally heard in mid-summer of 2011. The scheduled PetScan was moved up to confirm or deny whatever it was that was causing the respiratory maladies.

Before she even left the scanning facility, the nurses said, "You need to immediately head for the emergency room. We have alerted them that you are on your way."

As fate would have it, the physician in the emergency room was a pulmonologist who sadly conveyed two notices of bad news: the PETscan showed a lesion in the upper right quadrant of her left lung and led to a search for the primary cancer cell. Was it lung cancer or was it endometrial cancer of the lung? The result of the needle biopsy of her lung confirmed that it was indeed endometrial cancer. The significance of this outcome meant that this particular cancer event was related to the endometrial cancer of the uterus. And there was no way to know if this was the last they would see of endometrial cancer in Kathy's body. Even more urgent, the mass was blocking her bronchial tube and inhibiting her breathing. He immediately scheduled a next-day operation to insert a stent into that area to open up the breathing passage and cautioned the hospital nurses to watch her closely. The doc spoke to Mike in the hallway outside their hospital room, acknowledging that he was "...worried she may not make it through the night".

Life itself hung in the balance that bleak night with that old nemesis, the dark shroud of cancer, hovered just off in the distance waiting to advance its destruction once again. Neither Mike nor Kathy slept a wink, holding on to each other as if they were mired in a downward spiral that they could not stop. The bond they had shared for those creeping minutes and hours seemingly blended each individual human being into one person, each heart beating as one, and with every labored breath, a silent victory was claimed. It was a quiet night. It was a long night. Would they make it until tomorrow?

Kathy remembered thinking back to the original diagnosis of endometrial cancer and the word "aggressive". In fact, that was ALL she was thinking about as she was wheeled into surgery the next morning to receive her stent, which was to be inside her for a full four months to ensure no breathing problems would recur while she endured the pummeling of radiation and the appetite killing aftermaths of chemo therapy. The eventual diagnosis was NOT lung cancer.

This was endometrial cancer of the lung. And it was... "Aggressive."

Mike wondered what the odds were that Kathy would have endometrial cancer in two areas, because that's what Mike does. He is a problem solver. His research provided some information that was both specific to Kathy's current condition as well as foreboding. "Aggressive."

He discovered the facts that virtually all cancers, including cancers of the blood and the lymphatic system (leukemia, multiple myeloma, and lymphoma), can form metastatic tumors. Although rare, the metastasis of blood and lymphatic system cancers to the lung, heart, central nervous system and other tissues have been reported. A metastatic tumor is always caused by cancer cells from another part of the body. In most cases, when a metastatic tumor is found first, the primary cancer can also be found. The search for the primary cancer may involve lab tests, x- rays, computed tomography (CT) scans, magnetic resonance imaging (MRI) scans, positron emission tomography (PET) scans, and other procedures. However, in some patients, a metastatic tumor is diagnosed but the primary tumor cannot be found, despite extensive tests, because it either is too small or has completely regressed. The pathologist knows that the diagnosed tumor is a metastasis because the cells do not look like those of the organ or tissue in which the tumor was found. Doctors refer to the primary cancer as unknown or occult (hidden), and the patient is said to have cancer of unknown primary origin.

I gasped when I read the word "occult" from an article Mike had discovered. I knew what that meant to me: fear of the unknown. It meant the primary cell of the endometrial cancer had not been found. The memory of the undisclosed complications from the thickening of the uterine wall became a catalyst for uncertainty and incomplete trust of those medical professionals now in charge of her well-being.

Over those next four monthss, Kathy became wary of the speed with which the cancer had spread. She was well aware of the percentages of survival with lung cancer, but not endometrial cancer of the lung. The docs assured her that they could isolate the cancerous mass and destroy it with radiation while the chemo therapy would once again treat the entire body, seeking to destroy any and all other cells that carried her specific type of the disease. The 31 massive doses of radiation, where no pain was involved in its actual physical assault, began to flank her fears of further cancers and caused Kathy to channel her energies into regaining strength. Mike and Kathy concentrated on declaring all out war on the epic after-effects of her recent therapies, unable to move from an hour-to-hour series of battles toward any longer-term worries. And once again Kathy lost her hair, her eyebrows, her eyelashes, her curvy figure...

...her femininity. This time, this second time she fought against cancer, the after effects were catastrophic. As she spoke of loss of appetite, scuffles with friends and family about "you gotta EAT!", and fear of needing a feeding tube, I reeled in the revelation of the common ground of our respective cancers. Mike would go on daily hunts, sometimes multiple times, looking for some type of food Kathy might attempt to get down. As Kathy's weight loss approached double digits they discovered a couple of shakes that she could drink and digest.

The difference of our experiences with food was that Kathy was able to swallow any type of food, she just didn't desire it. Each had the same effect on the caregivers and family, hastening them to sound a never ending chorus of calls for eating something to shore up stamina. Not only did this fall on deaf ears, it would prompt the only harsh words spoken. Eating became almost impossible.

And so Thanksgiving came and went, and Kathy now wanted to set her sights on the Christmas feast and her goal to sit down to food that she once loved. The chemo therapy had ended in early autumn with the hope that once again this cancer villain had been vanquished; and indeed, another routinely scheduled PETscan confirmed that the area in her lung was now void of endometrial cancer. The exuberating rush from good news lasted only a fleeting moment, for tragically, it was also discovered that Kathy had a spot in her right breast which looked familiarly suspicious. An immediate biopsy was performed and there was no doubt that this was NOT breast cancer. It was endometrial cancer of the breast...and it was,

"Aggressive".

There would be no radiation this third go around. Chemo therapy once again ensued in spring of 2012 and Mike and Kathy, having just returned to some sort of normalcy, began the long climb to therapy completion. Kathy, having just noticed hair re-growth and some slight weight gain, once again served up those familiar womanhood traits, God-given each one of them, to the demonic cancer."...her femininity." And once again, somehow Kathy summoned the strength to endure everything that was, by now, relatively speaking, "old news". Her life as she knew it had been a series of 6-month blurs, from one cancer diagnosis and treatment to a brief attempt to return to a life worth living. She relived the atrocities of fighting cancer, to the relief of hearing it was exterminated, and then to the next cancer sighting. Anticipating the end of treatments forever, to the reality of their return engagement, was now her life.

Months later, the chemo therapy once again was completed and a ray of hope shone brightly as Kathy received the word that both of her breasts would remain intact. The only challenge that remained was to conquer the after effects of hideous nausea and get back to normal. New Year's Eve of 2013 brought us to the same place at the same time. My recovery efforts clearly mired in fighting mode, Kathy's expertly disguised, each of us dealing with our own demons on our own terms. In 2015, a couple of incidents involving intermittent dizziness and immobility were catalogued in the back of her mind almost as if bringing them to anyone's attention would give them more credibility than they deserved. Mike had helped her navigate from the couch to the bathroom one of those times where disorientation grabbed hold of her and threatened to not let go. There was a persistent numbness to her upper extremities, especially on the left side.

Along the way to recovery in spring of 2015, Kathy began to have intermittent UTI's, urinary tract infections. Discovery of this malady, somewhat normal resulting from chemicals having passed through her veins, began as a simple diagnosis and a simple cure. Antibiotics, prescribed by her primary care physician, would run their course, symptoms would all but disappear, but then they would return. Her routine PETscan on the horizon, Kathy simply wanted to get this infection under control and then pray that her scan was for once in her life, normal. But it was not to be. And this time it was a double whammy. The PETscan revealed that the endometrial cancer had returned to her lung, and her docs at Duke had begun a treatment of new cancer drugs which now could only provide maintenance of what cancer she currently had. The drugs had a lot of promise and so Kathy began to take those powerful, but relatively untested new pills. Her doc at Duke calmly but truthfully told Mike and Kathy that the medical community was no longer on a path to curing this aggressive villain, they were now focused on "maintenance" of her cancer. "Had all of this been for naught?! I fight all these months and years for this?! Is this all I get to hold onto: Maintenance! ", she thought, with utter disdain and surrender. Eventually, when calmness prevailed, Kathy resolved to "take what I can get and make the best of it."

It came time for her regular physical routine tests for Kathy to have a colonoscopy.

During that procedure the urologist found the perpetrator of all of the "urinary tract infections" which as it turned out weren't the problem at all. Kathy had a raging case of diverticulitis. The primary care physician had missed the diagnosis of the problem relating to the UTI's.

Once again, the physician having not searched for all potential diagnose proved to severely damage her ability to remedy her new cancer in her lung. Not only was surgery needed for the colon, but the administration of the new cancer drugs had to be halted. It was revealed that taking those drugs while attempting to heal from an operation removing the diverticulitis- damaged part of her colon, would inhibit the body's healing from the surgery. She had to immediately stop taking the drugs and could not resume that protocol until after the total healing had taken place. Her cancer would have to go untreated for months, and the primary care doc's lack of thoroughness would cost Kathy 4 months of "maintenance" of her cancer. And she knew, her cancer was…

"Aggressive".

As I sat with Kathy on this my final visit prior to her surgery, I heard this now frail and emotionally demolished innocent friend that I loved say, "Cancer in not my top priority now". I've got to get through this surgery and I'm not sure I am up to it."

"Could anyone blame her for that defeatist attitude?", I thought to myself. Though I was writing the last few sentences of a book that I hoped made it into the hands of cancer victims past, present, and future, cancer caregivers, and all those who vicariously became entrenched in the dark world of cancer suffering, I summoned all the pathos and composure I could muster and asked, "Have you given thoughts to what the future holds for you, given these latest developments? If your doctors tell you that the future is cloudy, what would you want to do with the rest of your days?"

"What would I do if I was told to 'get your affairs in order?'", she asked. True to her quest for normalcy, for a life unencumbered by cancer and the seemingly one hundred complications it wrought, Kathy spoke these words of hope, "I want to be able to be strong enough to get on a plane and see my grandchildren. Along the way, if I could squeeze in a trip to the Baja to see the birth of the whales, that would be enough."

I laid down my pen and pad and crawled over to the other side of the couch where this angel sat wondering if there were more miracles in God's bag of tricks. I wrapped my arms around her, and felt hers around me. They were strong and intensely warm. We held that embrace for a while and as I moved back I looked into her eyes and asked, "Will you dance with me on my 70th birthday on September 24, 2016?" Kathy's face was beaming with pink cheeks, gleaming eyes, and a smile that would break a hundred suitors' hearts, and she said,

"I enjoyed our interview today. I hope I gave you enough information. I am going to beat this damn cancer and dance with you on Sept.24th. I feel blessed to have you and Joanna as my friend."

Kathy's surgery is tomorrow, January 26, 2016. January 30, 2016 The surgery to excise an area of her colon was pronounced a "success" and there were no complications arising from the operation. She was to receive two whole units of blood which would go a long way to bringing Kathy back to normal blood balance. The physical therapist described how it was best to get up immediately and walk about, but not to a point of overdoing it. And there it was again, that feeling of disorientation, and some nagging numbness to her left hand. The gastroenterologist surgeon noticed and immediately called in a neurologist to examine Kathy and he ordered an MRI to be completed "stat". Now in its sixth year of steadily marching toward the conquest of Kathy's body, an original work of feminine art like no other, cancer struck for a sixth time. The MRI discovered the cancerous tumor in her most secret of places, her brain. A protocol of inject able radiation ensued to try to reduce the swelling around the tumor. David and Greg had been called in from San Diego and Minneapolis respectively. Mike, as he had been for over 51 years, was by her side every second.

February 22, 2016
Walking up the alley on my way to Mike and Kathy's home, I tried to remember her beckoning smile. I tried to hear her voice lifted in laughter. I felt her tears on my cheek as we last embraced. Kathy's younger sister had travelled in to Wilmington, along with oldest son, David. Mike was home. A grin slowly edged its way toward my lips as I anticipated the joy which would come with entering their home for the first time since Kathy's diagnosis. Today I would get to see my friend again. As I strode through the front door into the living room, I saw Mike, David, and Sis sitting at the far end of the house eating lunch. A soft little voice from my immediate left called out to me from the couch, "Hi, Larry". And there she was all wrapped up in the coziest blanket I ever saw, a bandana around her head, and her piercing blue eyes just as bright as they could be. Though I knew Kathy's story would be the epilogue, the last words I would write about my cancer experience, I was certain that this would not be the end of Kathy's Story. Frail and beaten up, Kathy displayed the most courage of anyone I had ever seen. I knelt down to her and hugged her close. And I told her that I loved her.

The three others gathered around the sofa and began talking "family". Their mood was upbeat and positive. It was not like they hadn't been down this road before. I had realized on the walk down to the house that I never asked Kathy about her first date with Mike. Sis and David's ears immediately perked up to hear that story just to make sure what they had heard before was true. This was no time to fib...truth is all we needed to know now. Mike was a senior in high school and Kathy a junior at the same school when the story unfolded. When Mike prodded Kathy by saying, "I had a 1941 Mercury convertible", Kathy finished by saying, "...and we went to a movie". Things got real interesting as you might imagine in front of a little sis and a son. I had stumbled upon the right question hoping to get the right answer in front of the right people.

Sis asked, "was it a drive-in movie or in a theatre?" What a great question! To which both Mike and Kathy replied in unison, "It was a drive-in movie."

"Mike, did you actually tell Dad that you were going to a drive-in movie?!", Sis asked in feigned disbelief.

"Well, not exactly." And Kathy tilted her head back and laughed until it hurt. David, pouncing on the very core of the story, queried, "Was the top up or down?"

Mike, blushing for the first time that I had ever seen, responded with, "The top was up and no, I did not tell him we were going to a drive-in movie."

We never know what the future holds for us. However, memories of days past can either haunt you or humor you. Today, after all radiation, all surgeries, cancer throughout her entire frail body, and the assault on her femininity, Kathy relived that night cuddled up next to the man who has loved her every second since. Today, love was in the air once again.

February 25, 2016

All the family has been called to come to Kathy's side, most of them arriving the day after tomorrow. Joanna had been itching to see Kathy for a couple days and finally the window was open for a brief visit this morning. She seems to be holding her own...is cognizant of everything around her...remembers things (probably better than I do!)...and continues to laugh, albeit quietly. Hospice continues the thrice weekly visits to bathe her and administer meds.

Kathy appears to be resting comfortably, wrapped in her green fluffy blanket when awake and calmly breathing effortlessly when taking one of her numerous daily naps. She jumps at the chance to order a pizza, or gulp down some ice cream, but that is only a dream. Food intake is almost non-existent now...

March 4, 2016
Hospice of the Lower Cape Fear is now the last home Kathy will have. Joanna and I visited her today and saw just a shell of this remarkable woman who just a few short weeks ago allowed me to write her story. While at her bedside, Joanna beckoned to me to realize that Kathy kept looking up as if she could see the angels hovering above her...waiting to take her Home where she never again would be sick or in pain. She has only hours to live, knows it, and embraces it as best she can. I leaned down and kissed her forehead and then moved my lips close to her ear and said, "Baby, I have a favor to ask of you." Kathy replied, "OK."

"When you land on your cloud, will you watch over Joanna for me?"

This sweet woman, now simply spent after her long fight with the demon cancer which had plagued her for so many years, shifted her head toward me so that I could look at her beautiful face and smiled, "I already have her on my list."

Though she will not be with us on that day in September, I swear her eyes were dancing with me at that, our last moment together.

Kathy Thompson
1/31//1943 – 3/11//2016

53300813R00143

Made in the USA
Lexington, KY
29 June 2016